JONATHAN M

'That Bloody Band'

Mixed Feelings, Music and Mayhem
50 years a Bandleader

with a Foreword by
BRADLEY WALSH

CONTENTS

For

All Musicians and their Partners
'Things can only get better'

By

Jonathan Nicholls
'CHEERFUL SACRIFICE'
The Battle of Arras 1917
(Pen & Sword Books 1990)
Available on Amazon

FOREWORD

I have known Jon Nicholls for many years and I well remember his band Mixed Feelings when they backed me in cabaret when I was a stand-up comedian at several venues in the London and Herts area back in the seventies. They are a fantastic live band and I still love appearing with them at the 'Make a Wish' Ball, held at the Dorchester Hotel, every November. We always have a laugh.

I recently booked them to perform at my son Barney's 21st Birthday Party and it was without doubt, the best party I have ever been to! It couldn't have gone any better and the commitment shown by Mixed Feelings was unbelievable! I am so glad and thrilled that they were part of it.

Reading this book takes me down memory lane to those days when bands were really 'live' and not just playing along to backing tracks. From smoky, Working Men's clubs and pubs when we hardly earned any money, to posh weddings and parties at The Dorchester and Grosvenor House hotels. It's all here and loaded with funny anecdotes and more.

It's a remarkable and hilarious transition from Jon, who was a London copper, to a top London Bandleader and it has all the laughter and tears of life on the road, which I remember so well. They were good days and this book certainly fills a niche in music history and should be read by anyone who might be interested in finding out what it was really like to form a band and perform in the '60s to the modern day. More so, anyone connected with the entertainment business or show business should read it, for entertaining it is. I love this band and was proud to be part of all that.

Bradley Walsh, July 2020

INTRODUCTION

The inspiration to finally sit down and finish this book came from a song, 'When I Was A Boy' by Jeff Lynne of ELO. I had that same dream too. It later developed into an obsession and eventually concerned a popular band called 'Mixed Feelings'. It led to my long-suffering wife declaring, 'All he thinks about is that bloody band!'

She was right of course. Although Mixed Feelings never made any records or appeared on *Top of the Pops* we were one hell of a band. We played everyone else's music and mainly played what the audience wanted.

We wanted to perform and *perform* we did, becoming one of the most sought after and fashionable modern party bands of the time. Everyone wanted us, in spite of copious amounts of alcohol consumed and consistent rumours of mayhem and misbehaviour, whenever we performed. We kept dance floors packed at home and abroad, performing to over two million people.

I aggravated more than one bandleader and agent. How could a bloke who was a London Police Officer and who couldn't read music, create this hugely successful band? As one London agent commented;

> The London band scene was all very cosy. The traditional
> dance bands, like The Ray McVay Orchestra, The Joe Loss
> Orchestra, Ken Mackintosh and Johnny Howard and His Band,
> all had London's West End stitched up until Mixed Feelings
> arrived on the scene and changed all that. They were without
> doubt, the best in the business. It signalled the death knell of
> the big bands. Mixed Feelings set a yardstick but were often
> accused of miming, or playing along to backing tracks. Many

bands copied them but none were as good. I used them on all
my top jobs. 'You can't book better than the best.'
Howard T'Loosty. 2019

Some years ago I wrote a book about the First World War, called
'Cheerful Sacrifice' which deals with the bloody battle at Arras in April
1917. It was Military History and moderately successful. It is still in
print.

This book could not be more different. My publishers, *Pen & Sword*
wanted nothing to do with it. It is certainly no rosy advert for Mixed
Feelings. It is the story of my personal journey, bumps and all, through
the best part of a lifetime, of making music and having one hell of a lot
of fun in doing so. Growing up in the sixties and forming my first band
before joining the Metropolitan Police, is essential to the story, which
led me to Mixed Feelings, a band which performed at over 6,000 major
events, from the West End to the Middle East. During the nineties,
we were the busiest professional function band in the UK, performing
at corporate events, weddings and music festivals, working with many
celebrities at home and abroad. We were described by more that one
agent as 'simply the best'. I have kept diaries from when I first picked
up the guitar in the early sixties to when I finally turned it in in 2015.
This was on the advice of my son, 'Dad you *are* too old to rock n' roll'.
I certainly felt it.

Running a busy function band is no easy task. It can easily drive you
to drink and in some cases, drugs. It will certainly give you grey hairs.
I have gleaned personal stories from my diaries, many of which were
written down at the time, often in the first tense, the day after they
happened.

Mixed Feelings was created as the 'small show band with a big sound'.
incorporating three or four dynamic singers and first-class musicians. I
have since been personally blamed for terminating the reign of the Big
Bands, which had dominated the London West End since the Second
World War, with their formation quicksteps, foxtrots and waltzes. They
also bored the pants off the majority of my generation. Nothing sounded
more 'naff' than 'She Loves You' played by an orchestra. It was time for
a change. The Beatles led the way.

I have covered my early village life in Deanshanger in the 1960s and
the rise of my fascination with music and the burning desire to form a

band. Much of the book describes the characters that shaped the band(s) and the humorous small incidents that arose on many gigs. It has given me a platform to discuss the sometimes dodgy, merits of musicians, singers, roadies, agents and more.

It is neither politically correct or for children and some readers may be offended or even repelled by my use of extremely obscene language and sexual innuendos. I hope it does not degrade the book too much but that's how it was. Musicians swear as horribly as plasterers and policemen. (With apologies to plasterers).

It is also purposely written for anyone remotely interested or curious about bands and the entertainment industry from the '60s onwards. It is also written for musicians. Life is short, so it is for them to remember and perchance, smile. You will have been there.

As long time saxophonist, Jez Guest said,

> I have played in many bands during my musical career but there was nothing ordinary about this band. It was a British version of 'Spinal Tap'. Mixed Feelings was a real soap opera – I'll never be in a band like that again.

Finally, it is also a tribute to the talented musicians, singers and people that I have had the privilege to personally know for over 50 years. Many of them have encouraged me to write this book and some have contributed personal memories. I am sorry that I have had to leave so much out. However, I hope you enjoy reading it as much as I have enjoyed writing it. Some may even deny it ever happened.

So did Bill Clinton.

Jonathan Nicholls. Hemel Hempstead. October 2020

PART I

1

DEANBEATS

There were three musical instruments in our little council house in Deanshanger. A battered Spanish guitar, which I think Dad had brought back from the war, a beautifully polished upright piano and a curious thing called a 'zither'. No one in our family could play any of them. Although the cat could get a Siamese tune out of the piano when made to dance on the keys.

The piano was religiously kept in tune, by my church-choir, singing mother, Dora, who doubtlessly hoped that one day, I would play it like Russ Conway or least, become the organist at the village church.

I would eventually be sent for piano lessons at the age of 12. The teacher was a Mr Laurie Eales, who lived in one of the posh houses opposite the church. He was a white-haired old man who chain-smoked Consulate menthol-tipped cigarettes and would blow clouds of smoke over the keys as I struggled to find middle C.

I certainly hated it and was determined to play the guitar. So I skilfully dodged out of his dreary lessons after just one month of forced nicotine intake. There was very little skill employed in the dodging. I just didn't turn up. I hid on the grassy bank of the playing field next to the tennis courts, in the evening sunshine, with the other village lads. Hands in trouser pockets, we watched some of the older village girls in their pleated white slips play tennis. To lewd comments as they bent over to pick up balls, we were given delightful glimpses of knickers. Meanwhile, 'Meaty' the butcher's son, passed his purloined Woodbines around and we lit up. We all carried Swan Vesta matches because lighting fires in the countryside was fun. I listened intently to the boys' inane sexual chatter and thus expanded my vocabulary of profanity.

I regret dodging those piano lessons now. One of the most important assets to any band is a good keyboard player. I admire people who can play the piano and read music. I failed miserably to make it as a piano player. Mistake *number one* in being a bandleader.

Mother, by then the village Avon Cosmetics lady, was undeterred. She was determined that I would one day make the church choir. She had previously heard me singing in bed when I was around eight years old and said, 'I sounded like a little angel.' This was all down to singing at primary school, those unforgettable songs from The New English Songbook. I knew every rousing verse of, 'Hearts of Oak' and 'The British Grenadiers'.

Sunday was a special day of the week, although for me not the happiest. It was as Mother said, 'The Lord's Day' and it was also the day we had the best meal of the week. Roast pork and crackling, with homemade, apple sauce with huge slabs of Yorkshire pudding and fresh vegetables picked off Dad's garden. So fresh, I would find a cooked caterpillar in the florets of cauliflower.

Sundays saw the majority of the village boys down the playing field, with their footballs, kites and cricket bats. However, 'The Lord's Day' became a dismal reality for me, as I had to attend church no less than three bloody times. My mother was determined that I would progress in the Christian church by becoming a vicar or at least a missionary to darkest Africa.

Morning service was at 10.30 am, which lasted for an hour or so, then I would go to the men-only, Duke's Head lunchtime session with Dad and sit outside in the Pig and Whistle with other bored kids, while he supped ale and yarned with the other Dads.

I was limited to a small bottle of Taylors' lemonade and a packet of Smith's crisps, complete with that little blue, waxed bag of salt. Dinner was at 2pm and woe betide Dad if he had one pint too many and was five minutes late. After dinner I had to walk to Sunday school, which commenced at 3pm. About ten other unfortunate kids were there too.

My friend, Keith Chapman and myself were expelled from the church vestry by the virginal Miss Capel, for being, 'rude boys.' I had burst into uncontrollable laughter at 'Chorus' time, when singing 'H-A-P-P-Y.' Keith had elbowed me in the ribs and commented that he could see Jill Henson's knickers, gleefully pointing them out as she sat with legs akimbo. Now that's 'H-A-P-P-Y', and a free 'flash' was one benefit of making us boys sit opposite the girls.

I would get home about 5pm for tea of lemon curd sandwiches and Madeira cake and then be told to get my collar and tie on as it was church at 7pm. I would have to do my school homework as well. If I were fortunate, I would be left at Nan Nick's house, where there was always a sumptuous tea of pig's brawn and pickles. Cousin Sonia would be there too but to get out of church, I had to feign some sort of illness and eventually ran out of ideas. Toothache was the best excuse because it meant Dad dipping a wad of cotton wool in neat Haig whisky and sticking it on the gum. It actually worked and numbed the tooth. It was then I acquired the taste for whisky.

If no illness was feigned or believed, I was consigned to listening to the tedious tones of the Rev. John Benson. His sermons were horrendous and seemed to go on for hours. The only thing I remotely enjoyed about church, was singing the stirring hymns of 'Jerusalem' and 'For All The Saints' which I also sang in bed. However, I was determined to get out of this depressing Sunday church situation, as soon as I grew up.

Although I was a fresh teenager at 13, I was not really interested in girls and had not reached masturbatory level two, which according to Roger Price involved both hands. The eagerly awaited arrival of the *Grattan Catalogue* was a font of curious fantasy into the mature female body. I thumbed through the heavy book with my left hand, in order to get an eyeful of the ladies lingerie section. I also remember being introduced to the 'post-horn gallop' of *Parade* magazine at Scout Camp. It was also at this time that my Christian name of 'Jonathan,' was shortened to 'Jonah' by my fellow pals of Swan Patrol.

I only once saw Dad pick up that old guitar and strum it. That was after a heavy Saturday night session at the Fox and Hounds, when he came home as pissed as a mattress. He couldn't play a note but thought he was Tommy Steele. The guitar was dreadfully out of tune but all six strings somehow remained intact. Dad made such a racket trying to belt out, 'Singing the Blues' that Mother came down and blamed him for waking up little brother Mark, who appeared in his pyjamas to see what the row was about.

Mark lightened the mood by spectacular feats of noisy flatulence, which would send him purple in the face. In fact, his trombone voluntaries were more tuneful than Dad's guitar efforts. 'Stop it!' Mother would yell with a remark she would never use in front of the Parson, 'If he is not careful, he will shit himself.' Mark was never careful.

Dad, in the meantime and totally oblivious to her grousing had dropped the guitar and got stuck into a tumbler of whisky and a plate of corned beef and mustard door-steps that Mum had left out for him. He would then knock the jar of pickled onions over and demonstrate his incredible skill at football by kicking them at the cat.

Next morning brought the atmosphere of the tomb, as he attempted to fawn a dismal apology for the pickle juice on the carpet. The whole room stank of vinegar and stale fag smoke. 'My darling I am so sorry about last night.' Mother took a lot of appeasing but a box of Black Magic would usually do the trick but not before she had issued chilling threats of, 'There will be no Sunday lunch,' or even more intimidating, 'I shall run off with a black man.'

For my part in currying her favour, I had to take a basket and pick the pea pods off the allotment and shell them for dinner. I would get a clip round the ear for eating them. I soon realised that I lived in a madhouse but it was a happy one that gave me time to nurture my great interest in books and reading. The days of computers had not yet arrived

Looking back, growing up in the Northamptonshire forest village of Deanshanger gave me an idyllic childhood. We kids learned to swim in the nearby, crystal clear waters of gravel-pits. Gigantic holes dug in the ground to provide gravel for nearby RAF Silverstone runways in World War II. Our Dads taught us to fish and we would eat the fish we caught. The most delicious of which, was the 'Royal' Pike.

We carried fearsome, razor-sharp knives and some of the boys wore huge 'Bowie' knives around the waist. (No one got stabbed) Wearing our Davy Crocket hats, we played games of 'splits' with our knives thrown dangerously close to our toes and tackle.

We collected all species of bird's eggs and ate the tasty eggs of moorhens and coots, which were taken by swimming over deep water to their nests. We would disappear into the woods and fields for days on end. Sometimes we took our pellet guns and fired them recklessly. (No one got shot) We played games of war and swore dreadfully, like our Dads.

My maternal grandmother was Lizzie Bazeley and she was largely responsible for my early interest in History. When I misbehaved, (which was as often as possible) she told me that 'Old Bony would come and get me,' a dire threat exacted on her as a child by her mother. She also told me that my long-deceased grandfather had been 'gassed on the Somme' and 'He was at Third Wipers.' What was that all about?

That old guitar had caught woodworm, so I decided to revive it by stripping it down, sandpapering it and filling the holes with plastic wood before applying a coat of clear varnish. It was my first guitar and was nameless but I was proud of it. I fitted a set of Cathedral strings and learned to play 'Apache'.

In the days before electronic tuners, 'Apache' was a great way to tune the guitar if you kept the tune in your head. 'FBI' was the first bass line I learned. Bert Weedon was right, anyone can 'play in a day'. That old guitar was also great to pose with in front of my dressing table mirror, after applying a dollop of Dad's Brylcreem to my Tony Curtis 'quiff'. A splash of Old Spice and a *Parade* centrefold under the pillow made me a man.

I mimed to that stinging guitar solo on, 'You Really Got Me.' It had me dropping to my knees and rolling theatrically, onto my back in the throes of a Dave Davies impression. It was the most extraordinary guitar riff of the day. I reckoned I could well impress the girls if they saw me playing that. If only I *could* play.

The useless zither was unloved and lived in a dusty black case under my bed. It was acquired from my ancient Aunt Lily. It was a strange instrument, with about 40 strings and funny little push down buttons, which pressed felt pads onto the strings to change the key. My brother swapped it for pair of flippers.

Sitting on the freezing school bus, which left from outside the church at 8am every morning, conveying half a dozen of us kids to Towcester Grammar School, I heard David Phillips say, 'The Beatles are on

Crackerjack tonight!' I turned to my best pal, Nick Gould and invited him to watch it at our house. Furthermore, he could stay for his tea.

Now Dad had always been a gadget man and was one of the first in the village to acquire a Bakelite Bush television with a nine-inch screen. This strange looking box was set up on our almost permanently empty drinks cabinet in the front room. Whereby Dad swore and cursed as he fiddled with knobs trying to improve the grainy picture. He purchased an outside aerial and placed a huge magnifying glass in front of the tiny screen. This powerful magnifying glass, I soon discovered, could be employed to start fires by angling it at the sun.

Cup-final day was a boisterous, men-only event at our house, which occasionally fell on Church Jumble Sale day and so Mother was happily out of grousing range. Several of Dad's village mates would cram into the front room, armed with crates of India Pale Ale.

The room was a blue fog and the inhalation of cigarette smoke irritated my chest. All his pals were heavy smokers, Dad being no exception, who was never without a Players Navy Cut in his mouth. I guess this was the legacy of war years and a token of their generation. Dad would often quote, especially after half a dozen pints, 'Press on regardless', the motto of RAF Bomber Command. He had been decorated for his bravery as an air-gunner during the war, although always too modest to talk about it. He never wore his medals on Remembrance Sunday. He never spoke about it. Mother told me it was because 'Remembrance Day made him sad,' as he grieved the loss of some of his young aircrew mates. One of whom had been the best man at their wedding.

The other family 'gadget' was a vintage valve-radio, which sat in the chimneybreast recess. Its sinister face terrified me when I was little and I would not venture near it. On a Saturday evening, with the usual fag on, Dad would sit in the armchair next to the beast and listen to Sports Report. He would wait for the valves to warm up and then tune the huge clock-dial on the face, until he picked up the irritating tune which always accompanied the day's football results. He would carefully tick off the scores of peculiar sounding teams, such as 'Queen of the South' and 'Forfar' in his *Daily Mail*, no doubt nursing the forlorn hope that he might win the pools.

As I reached my teens, I realised that the old radio was not a monster but a real friend and it provided a new source of musical entertainment for me. I noticed strange names on the dial such as 'Hilversum' 'Stavanger' and 'Luxembourg.' I believed Luxembourg to be an insignificant little province of France. I still do.

I quickly discovered that I could turn this dial to 'Luxembourg' and through the maddening whistling of frequency loss, make out the silky vocal tones of Cliff Richard singing, 'A Voice In The Wilderness,' backed by Hank Marvin's subtle guitar tones. This was fabulous, until interrupted by some old fart telling me how to win the pools, 'My name is Horace Bachelor'. Nevertheless, it truly was 'The Station of the Stars on 208 medium wave'. To an adolescent boy, it was a musical goldmine.

This was all very well but the Top Twenty chart programme was not broadcast until late Sunday night and furthermore I was not allowed to listen to Luxembourg in the front room, as mother wanted the TV on. As a result, and after genuine promises to stop swearing, acting up at school and bashing the bishop, I was gifted a lovely Bush portable radio for my 13th birthday.

It was a wonderful present for a new teenager. The problem was, this small valve radio needed two huge batteries, which cost a small fortune to replace. So when the batteries expired, which they quickly did, I was bereft of sound. The aerial on the thing, was in the lid and so the radio only worked with the lid up, which meant making a substantial tent under the bedclothes on a Sunday night, complete with bicycle lamp, a packet of Smith's crisps, a Jaffa cake, and a mug of Tizer, to settle down to the best Pop-show of the week.

In spite of the constant fading and phasing, my favourite tunes, were Cliff's, 'Bachelor Boy' and Mike Berry's 'Don't You Think It's Time'. But how can you listen to 'Shakin' All Over' quietly? The volume just had to be whacked up. This ran the risk of the radio being confiscated by an irate Dad, just back from the Duke's Head and off to bed. He had to be up early for work in the morning.

'Crackerjack night' and Nick arrived early and stayed for his tea, after a stressed Mother had checked to see that she had another tin of spam, which would be sliced and served with Branston pickle and mash. Prior to The Beatles appearance, we had a spectacular trouser-cough recital from chubby-arsed brother, Mark, who was wearing his favourite green cotton shorts.

'What a rasper! Can you do another one?' asked Nick. Mark was duly encouraged and, in his efforts to impress, let go with an air biscuit that sounded like a drowning motorbike. 'And another?' This time, in spite of his red-faced contortions, there was a mere disappointing, '*splatter*' and Mark hobbled guiltily into the kitchen. There then followed, much to our amusement, a loud 'slap' and a deathly scream from Mark. Mother came fuming into the front room, 'Now you have made him shit himself!'

Undeterred, we watched The Beatles perform, 'Love Me Do.' It was a revelation. Even better was 4 November 1963 and The Beatles were appearing on the Royal Variety performance. It was the occasion when John Lennon made history. I have never forgotten it. Before closing with a raucous version of 'Twist and Shout,' Lennon delivers one of the most memorable bits of stage banter:

'For our last number, I'd like to ask your help. Will the people in the cheaper seats clap your hands? And for the rest of you, if you'll just rattle your jewellery!'

After that fantastic performance from The Beatles, I was probably not the only teenager determined to form a band. I wanted to do just that. Show off and play the guitar! I never slept that night, even though it was school in the morning. With music going through my head, I had formed a band! I didn't want to miss that school bus. Now, who were my best mates?

There was obviously Nick Gould. He would be on lead guitar, although he had never picked up a guitar in his life. He was a shy but stimulating companion, with whom I had walked miles into the Northamptonshire countryside, in our endless search for kestrel's eggs and invaders from Mars.

Then there was Malcolm Taylor. He was a village boy and fellow Towcester Grammar School pupil who, when out of school, always had a fag in his mouth. A blonde-haired, inveterate, 'big-head' with an Elvis quiff. 'Tates' as he was generally known, was always combing his hair. I believe he even carried a comb in the pocket of his rugby shorts so he could comb his hair at half time. He was just the 'right stuff,' for a band front man.

I clearly remember one afternoon, Jim Fiddy, the village Constable, wobbling alongside us on his bike, as we deliberately walked slowly, hoping he would fall off. He ordered the underage Tates, to 'put that cigarette out,' which he had lit up as soon as we had got off the school bus. Tates, with utter disdain flicked his fag into the road. Within seconds of our ancient constable pedalling off, he lit up another Park Drive, muttering 'Bollocks to Mr Plod.' Tates thought himself special and he wasn't wrong. He owned a real electric guitar and could actually play it. He had a decent voice and could 'croon' like Cliff Richard. He also fancied himself with the girls. He was in.

I noticed that my cousin, David Nicholls, would finger-tap on the back of the bus seat to the rhythmic sounds of the radio. He was an avid bird's egg-collector too. He *must* be able to play drums. The school bus driver was the popular Ivan Smith of Smith's Coaches and he would turn up the radio when 'Glad All Over' came on and we would all bash along to it.

So my first band was formed on that school bus. My three pals wanted to be in on the action. I was determined to be the bass-player. I had never played a bass guitar but it was so *macho* an instrument and I assumed it would be easy to play. Plus, I loved the look of bass guitars and have never lost that love. I desperately wanted a Hofner Violin Bass, of the type played by Paul McCartney.

The word went around 'Shanger' that 'Jonah has formed a Beat Group.'

On a freezing Saturday morning in January 1964, Dad, who had recently passed his driving test, took me in his little Austin A35 to the Midland Music Centre in Northampton. It was one of the most thrilling days of my young life. Northampton was a vibrant music town and there were numerous sexy bass guitars in the shop, including a gorgeous white Fender Precision bass, which was totally out of Dad's price range. I was 15 years old and needed money to embark on this rocky road to stardom. I knew little about bass playing, or the science of bass amplification. I profess that I still don't.

I needed money to finance this expensive hobby. I had done a bit of work at Jack Smith's village farm, my first winter job there, being on freezing Saturday mornings, when I had to dig the rock-hard, six inch thick slabs of foul-smelling chicken shit out of the wooden huts. I hated that job and got flea covered, causing me to scratch for days as we only had a bath on Friday nights. Nevertheless, I got half a crown a time.

I was also doing a daily delivery around the village for the Co-op corner store, which entailed delivering groceries by cycle. Big soap powder boxes of household items, were carried in the huge basket on the front of the cumbersome bike, which I managed to regularly fall off, as per one day when the boxes were stacked so high, I could not see over the top.

I pedalled on laboriously, as I knew the street of Ridgmont, where we lived, like the back of my hand. Or so I thought, until I crashed head-on into Barry Reynold's gleaming black Vauxhall saloon, which was parked outside his house. As expected, he came running out and furiously imploded in an outpouring of expletives when he saw the bonnet of his pride and joy, covered in Persil. He called me a word, which refers to that concealed part of the female anatomy as, 'not in decent use' according to the Oxford Dictionary at Towcester Grammar School library, where certain bored kids, having nothing better to do at lunchtime, researched English profanities.

I would often take my eight-year old brother in the Co-op bike basket, for a bumpy ride down the 'back fields' and would deliberately crash the heavy machine into stinging nettles. Mark flying arse over head out of the basket! Anybody would think he was being murdered and housewives, Olive Goldney and Joyce Chaytor would come running out to see what the horrendous screaming and dancing was about. His fat thighs were stung to blazes and I had to collect dock leaves to cool his tingling legs. For delivering groceries to the village and performing such clever stunts on the bike, a miserly George Crouch, the Co-op manager, paid me the sum of £1 per week.

To raise more funds to pay for the new bass guitar I was also doing part time work, at nearby Wicken Rectory. A country vicarage later turned hotel, run by an unconventional, country parson, the Reverend Paul Hoskin. The Rectory was essentially a home for wealthy old people and eccentric mad-caps, including the Vicar himself.

I turned up one Saturday morning and asked the corpulent rector for a job. He said, 'Are you Cyril Nicholls' boy?' I replied in the affirmative. 'Dear little Cyril was one of my Scouts!' he retorted. I got the job. Paul Hoskin commonly known as 'Old Hocker', had formed the 1st Deanshanger Boy Scouts in the '30s. He was also horse racing mad and a close friend of Dorian Williams, the famous BBC Show-jumping commentator. Other village boys and girls were employed at this house of fun too, namely Stan Matthews, Colin Farmer, Nick Gould and his sister Marilyn.

Stan Matthews would become the first proper drummer in the band. This was purely because he owned a brand-new drum kit. He simply turned up at the Memorial Hall for our first rehearsal with a lovely blue marble Premiere kit. Stan Matthews was in, Dave Nicholls was out. So David was my first sacking as a bandleader and he had never even lifted a drumstick. He never made a fuss. He just did a lot better than me at school.

I have always loved guitars and that first experience at the Midland Music Store I shall never forget. Local budding musicians were beginning to gather in the shop as was par for the course on a Saturday morning. It was my first taste of musician 'chat'. Guitars have a unique smell and the smell of leather, plastic and varnish is arousing. This feeling would always grip me whenever I enter a music store.

Most of the basses were out of my price range, so I fixed my attention on a Rosetti bass 7, hanging in the window. It was the cheapest bass in the shop but looked dazzlingly beautiful. It cost £27 and was a dark plum red colour with white Egmond pickups. I wanted to try it out and plugged it into a red Lucky Seven Bass combo, which sported two 10" speakers and was a massive 7 watts in power. It felt cool, as my hands ran up and down the slim neck. It sounded great in the shop. I tentatively twanged the A string with a thick 'bass' plectrum and refrained from playing the corny FBI riff, as I was self-conscious in front of other watching musicians.

It also sounded good in our front room, where I had learned the easy bass riff to 'You Really Got Me', which turned me into a perverse, Peter Quaife. All this beautiful noise was accompanied by shouts of, 'tone it down a bit or the neighbours will complain' from Dad.

Little did I know, after investing my hard-earned cash in this nice-looking bass set up, that it would sound *absolute shit* on stage. The combo was simply not up to projecting the smooth bass tones I needed. I wanted some punch too but the speakers would simply 'fart' when bottom 'E' was plucked, causing the baffle cloth to flap like Nan's drawers on the washing line. It was not up to the job when competing with any guitar amp.

However, we were up and running! There now grew a permanent competition between Nick and Tates, as to who could play the loudest, which led to Dad, in his official capacity as 'manager', striding over to the stage and also telling us to 'Tone it down a bit'. Consequently, I was extremely disappointed with that shit amp, especially as I would still have three years to pay on it. That guitar looked sexy in the mirror but it would be many years before I found a decent bass amp.

So, in that music shop, Dad puffing and grousing, reluctantly signed the hire purchase agreement for my acquisition of the bass guitar and amp, at a grand total of £49. He insisted, 'You must earn enough money to pay back the loan or the police will come and seize it.' Thereby commenced my love affair with bass guitars.

Whilst in the music shop, I was thrilled to see Nick Gould arrive with his dinosaur of a father, who the village boys disrespectfully called, 'Jackophus Tack'. He had a fountain pen at the ready to sign for the HP. He glared at me scornfully as if it was all my fault! Nick remembered:

> I made a friend of Jonah since I moved to the village when my Dad got the job as Primary School headmaster. We were also chums in the Scouts and would go brook-jumping and bird's nesting together. But when the 'Beat Boom' started, Jonah was the inspiration behind me acquiring a guitar and joining the band. Consequently, the Midland Music centre was our meeting place one Saturday morning. My first guitar was a second hand, Voss Les Paul Copy. A cheap, German guitar at £14.00 on tick. I also bought the Lucky Seven Guitar amp. I really had stars in my eyes and Jonah certainly ruined my academic career. I lay in bed night after night, dreaming of stardom, instead of doing schoolwork. I spent homework time practising on the guitar. Jonah made me learn 'Wipeout', an instrumental number by The Surfaris and the first 'tune' we learned. It was the introduction song to *Ready Steady Go* and soon became our opening number, even though Stan could never get that fucking drum beat right.

Malcolm Taylor recollected:

> We were just village boys. I had taught myself how to play guitar and knew the chords for many easy pop tunes. We

were all in the Scouts too and three of us went to Towcester Grammar School. They were exciting days and it was a real joy to play and perform. It was Dad who paid for my first guitar. It was a VOX and was advertised in *Practical Wireless* magazine. It cost £11 and had to be assembled. The neck bolted on and the electrics put in place behind the pick guard. I had that guitar for several months before I got the Hofner Club 60, of the sort used by John McNally of The Searchers. That was a cracking guitar.

Our first rehearsal was planned, but where? Fortunately, Uncle George Lee held the keys to the Village Memorial Hall, a dusty tin roofed shed, dedicated to the memory of village boys that had made the ultimate sacrifice in the two world wars. He offered the hall for our rehearsals, providing it was not being used for Bingo sessions. Sundays became favourite days for rehearsal as it would finally get me out of the hated church attendance, much to my mother's disappointment.

In your first band, rehearsing is exciting fun and you simply live for it. We would rehearse every night if we could. Saturday was also possible, Rugby football permitting. There was nothing like being on stage and making your own music, no matter how dire it sounded.

The rehearsals for our 'Beat Group' became a social occasion for the Deanshanger village youth. That old memorial hall became a popular Sunday meeting point with kids coming from as far afield as Potterspury and Roade. We even had an impromptu doorman in a somewhat vacant, 'Rocky' Hollis, who would collect tuppence admission from each kid before he let them in. The money raised would go to Uncle George for 'hall maintenance' or more likely, a packet of Woodbines. On some Sundays, there were upwards of sixty teenagers on the premises. I now realise that it was a perfect gift to their Mums and Dads. Sunday was the only day of rest and a wonderful opportunity, in the absence of the kids, for 'hiding the sausage.' No wonder I was popular.

Malcolm Taylor recollects;

> Mick Russell built our first PA system. It was amazing how so many village boys wanted to be part of it. 'Bilko' Marshall was our 'roadie'. The first mikes & PA consisted of Ex-Army earphones with the earpieces converted to microphones. I think the polarity was reversed or something. Mick made primitive, microphone stands and adapted a big valve amp retrieved from

a radio gram or wireless. The speakers placed at the front of the stage were two wooden fruit crates with pink and white polka dot covering. His Mum's curtains I think! A small 8" speaker, extracted from an old wireless screwed to the baffle, would distort like hell when I hit the top notes in, 'Make Believe' but we were happy!

Tates occasionally sounded like a Dalek but Mick Russell's primitive public address system worked. Every time I hear 'Video Killed the Radio Star' by *Buggles,* that initial 'nasally' vocal reminds me of Mick Russell's PA. I guess he was our first sound engineer but he was as mad as a hatter.

As far as PA systems went, in those infant days of band amplification, the era of the giant PA stacks either side of the stage had not yet arrived. I went to see a touring show with girlfriend Linda, featuring The Dave Clark Five, at the Bedford ABC. Either side of the stage was a single Vox column, which contained 4 x 10" speakers. I believe that is the same PA used by the Beatles when they toured the UK. I left the ABC at Bedford with my ears ringing! A Vox PA was in our dreams.

We had still not settled on a name for the band. The word had got around, however, that Deanshanger had a 'beat group' and on the same day as our very first rehearsal, we did our first gig, when we were invited to perform in the Conservative room for the Cricket Club Dinner that night. Were we ready? No! Did we want do it? Yes!

We did a 15-minute version of 'Da Do Ron Ron' in the key of C, twice. It was an easy song, as there were only three chords in it and Tates knew the words. We then attempted the gorgeous song, 'Will You Still Love Me Tomorrow,' although I just played the notes of C, A, F & G all the way through it. Learn those four magic chords and you can play most songs. I could play them on guitar too. A week later we were asked to play at Passenham Fete in the great barn of the old Manor House, which was the family home of Commander Lawson RN. We were given free lemonade and homemade cakes. Once again, 'Da Do Ron Ron' was most popular.

The following Friday the local rag, *The Wolverton Express,* described the fete as a 'great success' with music provided by beat group, 'Jonathan Nicholls and the Moonrakers'. It was much to the utter disgust of Tates, who dragging on his fag, said 'We not fucking well having that!' ('Moonrakers' was a name given to Deanshanger folk, after a village drunk on his way home from The Beehive on a Saturday night, had tried to rake the reflection of the moon out of the 'cut' the slang term for the Grand Junction Canal).

The name of 'Jonah and the Wailers' was suggested by Dad. Tates, star of the band and sporting a new Teddy Boy hair cut - courtesy of Bill Boots the village barber - took another long drag on his fag and said, 'We not fucking well having that either!' It was eventually suggested by Stan that we call ourselves simply, 'The Deanbeats' and the name stuck.

It was about this time, that I found myself my first 'proper' girlfriend who had recently moved to the village from Preston in July 1963. Her Dad, Jack Singleton, was a millwright and had found work at the local Deanshanger Oxide Works where the Lancashire boilers needed maintaining.

It was love at first sight for both of us and I considered myself a lucky but unworthy boy. I was the envy of my village pals. Although my Mother griped that I was 'far too young' to have a girlfriend and 'You just be careful you don't put her in the family way!'

Little did I know then, that Linda would be my partner for life and would have to undergo the difficulties of being married to a Police officer *and* a musician, two professions that were top of the 'divorce charts'. Plus, she would endure the torments of shift work, gigging and me staying out all night. It would happen to her *twice*. No wonder she said many times, 'You think more of that bloody band than you do of me.'

Nick, often a difficult bugger, remembers,

> We were doing a gig in the village hall one Saturday night with a Northampton band called The Rebels. I watched them perform and thought we could never be as good as that and I simply bottled out. I fucked off and went home. It was stupid thing to do, as we were on stage at 10pm. Jonah came and got me and told me I had to do the gig. He gave me fresh confidence, (enforced by threats of extreme violence) so I went back and did the gig, which went OK. I was a proper twat in those days!

The date of that actual gig was Friday 23 October 1964. The following day, I had recorded in my diary that 'I went to the Empire Cinema at

Wolverton with Stan, to see the brilliant film, *Zulu* (and not for the last time). We had 'gig money' in our pockets for Mars Bars, Kia ora and shared a packet of Woodbines too. We were musicians. We had bonded.

Northampton was our local big town. Famous for shoe-making, it had some great music venues. It also possessed a top-class rugby football team, 'The Saints' and a lower tier football team, 'The Cobblers'. It also had another good produce: Bands.

Our Memorial Hall at Deanshanger regularly held events put on by the Cricket club, Football club, Buffalos and more. These happenings would take the form of a Friday or Saturday night village dance, with a good band, usually from Northampton. It was the era of the fledgling 'beat boom' which put Doug Dytham's Rhythm Aces out of favour with the kids.

I remember besides The Rebels, seeing great bands such as The Homelanders and The Tornados, led by Alan Robinson but the band which influenced me most, with their forceful style of music, which I quickly emulated in The Deanbeats, was The Quick and the Dead. I saw this 4-piece outfit twice at the Memorial Hall and made a mental note of the music they belted out with such energy. 'Jack's Girl' was their opening instrumental number, followed by, 'In The Hall Of The Mountain King'. Then came 'Egypt' and 'Reelin' and a Rockin''.

The guitarist who gave them this unique sound was the talented Dick Botwood, who I believe, came from Roade. I think he played a Red Hofner Verithin and that injected into a Vox AC 30, gave him a stinging sound. The bass player was Tony Pinner. He used a small Elpico amp, which sat on a huge, homemade double 12-inch speaker, bass cabinet which did the rounds with other bands in Northampton. You could feel it half a mile away.

There were only three of them on instruments; guitar, bass and drums, plus a male vocalist. They were loud and good. I liked the songs they did, which consisted of a lot of Chuck Berry. They were very much like Johnny Kidd and the Pirates, a great British band, which would also influence me greatly, especially guitarist, Mick Green, of whom it was said that he was the first guitarist to play lead and rhythm at the same time. His dynamic style, later copied by Wilko Johnson, was the sound of the Fender Telecaster. That was the guitar sound I wanted in my band. Little did I know then, that Mick Green and the legendary Pirates would perform at my son's wedding in 2003.

I think all bands, at some time or another, have banged out the timeless, 'Johnny B Goode' in the key of 'A.' That extraordinary Chuck Berry riff and the introduction to 'Move It' were the essential guitarist's 'licks' of the sixties and showed a guitarist could play. With a bit of arse kicking, Nick would get there.

Working as a waiter at Wicken Rectory, enabled me to pay the HP on my bass but the work was very tiring. I loved rugby football and would play for Towcester Grammar School on a Saturday morning, then play for Wolverton RFC first team, in the afternoon, then go out on a gig that night. I would be at the Rectory at 5am the next morning to prepare trays of early morning teas and assist with breakfast. I was also still at school, so somewhere over that weekend, I managed to cram in homework and see Linda, who would often come and watch me play rugby.

I have to say at this point in the narrative, that Towcester Grammar School was a fine old English Grammar School with excellent teachers and set in pleasant, rural surroundings. The old school, founded by Archdeacon Sponne in 1538 stood on the Brackley Road and I have very fond memories of it. One of my big regrets is that I did not take school seriously. I was privileged to go there but abused the opportunity in the early years, by simply, 'being a twat' and I wish now, that I had taken music class seriously and learned the notes on the recorder. French lessons at which I caused regular disruption, would have helped me in later life too.

My main interests were Art, History and English Literature. I loved Rugby Football and made the first team at the age of 15. At that precise age, I pulled my socks up and began to take school more seriously. Maybe it was because I had found a regular girlfriend and needed qualifications for a career but I didn't have a clue what I wanted to do, other than be on stage. I remember in lessons, writing out song lists and designing guitars. I eventually left that splendid school, age 17 with a meagre 5 'O' levels.

Old 'Hocker' suddenly decided to get married. Everyone was in shock. Was he not the archetypal, bachelor gay? 'Silly old bugger,' was how cook Mary Carter, saw it. However, he was running short of funds.

He read *The Racing Post* and gambled daily on the horses. He smoked heavily and drank pints of Gin and Martini. In short, he could no longer afford his hedonistic lifestyle on the wages of a country parson. Even the income from his elderly residents was insufficient to pay for the racehorse he so desperately wanted. In his sights, was the rich target of a Miss Helen Falconer, a wealthy but crabby, single lady of Scottish descent. She was a senior resident at the Rectory.

As the Vicar himself, said to me, 'I have offered my hand in marriage to prevent her giving all her money to bloody animal and bird charities.' In all seriousness, he wanted to get his hands on her money and buy the Rectory outright. He popped the question when drunk and she, as pissed as he was, accepted. Consequently, on Monday 28th September 1964 they tied the knot and the thoroughbred racehorse, Silk Cut, was purchased, much to Hocker's delight. Although the name was soon changed to 'Half Cut.' He immediately asked for The Deanbeats to perform at his wedding.

A marquee had been erected on the Rectory lawn and at 8pm The Deanbeats were due to start. The caterer was the impossible Derek Taylor, another mad local character. Stan and his old Dad, Jim 'Spinner' Matthews, had got there in the early afternoon and set up the gear before the crowds had arrived. We had a single Watkins dominator amp, which the generous, 'Hocker' had bought us, thanks to Stan, some weeks earlier. It was now our main PA system. As 'Tates' remembers;

> Our benefactor was of course, the Rev. Paul Hoskins of
> Wicken Parish. Stan was the son he never had, so he was very
> fond of him and through Stan, extremely generous towards
> our band. A word from Stan and a new amp was purchased.
> We duly performed at his wedding, which was the talk of
> Deanshanger and Wicken.

The Watkins Dominator Amplifier was a superb workhorse for any budding band or musician. The best guitar amp at the time was the Vox AC 30 and although both amps were British made, Charlie Watkin's Dominator was more versatile and much cheaper than the AC30. It was an impressive looking, pale blue and white, triangular shaped combo and housed a 17-watt amplifier. That mighty 17 watts sounded more like 100. Plus, it had four inputs so we poked lead guitar and two mikes through it. We stood it sentinel like, at the front of the stage. It cost just under 40 quid. Nick takes up the story;

> As for the Watkins Dominator Amp, we knew how good
> these amps were but could not afford one. 'Hocker,' the
> eccentric Vicar of Wicken, bought it for us, along with a new
> Premiere drum kit for Stan or 'My little Bunny', as old Hocker,
> affectionately called him.

The opening song for the Bride and Groom's first dance, was left to us to decide and in my youthful wisdom I chose, 'Do Ya Wanna Dance' by Cliff & The Shadows. The moment came for the first dance and as the Bride and Groom waddled onto the dance floor the band started. I had told the band the opening number but not all had listened and Stan, with three Brandy and Babychams inside him, went into 'Wipeout' and it sounded like an Indian war dance. Fortunately, the Bride and Groom were too pissed to notice as we stopped and started again, much to the amusement and 'Haw-hawing' of Best Man, Dorian Williams and his horsey chums, the complete masters of onanism.

We got it right at the second attempt and bounced through this relatively easy Cliff number. Nick had even mastered Hank's guitar solos. For his part, in the first dance together as man and wife, the tall, pear-shaped Hocker simply stood on the dance floor waving his arms in the air. He seemed unable to move his feet, while his wobbly bride, who had downed far too much Dry Sack Amontillado, fell straight on her arse. It was bloody funny but not half as comical as watching him trying to pick her up.

We only played for a one-hour set and a few drunks eventually staggered onto the dance floor. All had consumed an immense amount of Moet & Chandon champagne. We did the gig for free, which was a shrewd move, as Hocker had already bought us the amp. He told us to 'Help yourselves to the bar,' which I learned then is one of the finest things that any client could ever say to a bandleader. 'You have a wonderful band,' said a delighted Hocker. 'You made my silly bloody wife fall over!'

We hit the bar and literally helped ourselves. We all got terribly pissed. I stupidly, drank red Martini neat. A disgusting Italian sweet wine, that tasted of pine trees. Stupidly, I guzzled the whole bottle. Old Spinner took me home with my head hanging out of the van window and Dad found me on the back garden lawn, where I lay gurgling on my back and throwing my guts up. He helped me up the stairs to my bed, in which I spewed up again. Dad turned me on my side into the 'recovery position'. I never made school next day. I never drank red Martini again. My diary entry simply records, 'Hocker's wedding last night. Got drunk.'

We rehearsed and rehearsed whenever we could. Tates's version of 'It's Only Make Believe' would bring loved-up girls to tears. We got better and more adventurous. 'Stand By Me' was a great ballad, plus 'Sweet Little Sixteen' and 'Route 66' were belted out.

Some of the songs we did were;

Wipeout

Apache

Walk Don't Run

Money

Shakin' All Over

Sweets For My Sweet

Not Fade Away

I Wanna Be Your Man

Needles And Pins

Walking The Dog

You Better Move On

Sugar And Spice

Da Do Ron Ron

Walk In The Room

Will You Still Love Me Tomorrow?

Don't Throw Your Love Away

Johnny B Good

Save The Last Dance For Me

I had persuaded my friend, Alan Holloway, to ask his electrician Dad, if he would build me a decent bass amp. He worked at Dewicks Electrical Store in Stony Stratford and one of his specialities was repairing old valve-driven radios. The Club 7 amp was practically useless and sounded like a wet fart when I hit bottom 'E'. I was really pissed off with it, as it was totally useless for stage use. Not the first time I would be ripped off.

Tates and Nick were playing louder and louder and having rows about who should be the loudest and there was me struggling to be heard.

Trouble was, I was still paying for the unwanted amp. So 'Uncle Ken' Holloway said he would build me an amp. It took him about a month. I waited impatiently for delivery.

Soon the great day arrived. It was an open-back, gold painted cabinet, with one 12" Goodmans speaker, with those infamous screw-in coffee table legs. Its heavy valve amp was rated at 15 watts and it weighed about a hundredweight in total and was the start of many problems for my young back – even though a suitcase strap handle had been screwed to the top. Back trouble is an affliction encountered by all bass players at some time in their careers. There would be heavier combos to come but the amp was certainly better than the Club 7, which I lent to Tates, as it was perfect for rhythm guitar. Dad lent me the 15 guineas to pay for it.

Mother hoped we would play at the church and maybe progress to a Billy Graham convention. Dad, who continued to manage us, insisted that we do his favourite Jim Reeves number, 'I Love You Because'. We did it to please him and Tates sang it splendidly. It went down surprisingly well at most venues. There were only three or four chords in it. Which made it easy for me.

Spinner drove the equipment to our gigs in his little black van. Nick recalls,

> Our first road manager of course was 'Spinner' Matthews, Stan's old Dad, bless him. He was probably about 70 years old. He would drive our kit around in a little black Austin van. Later a green Commer van was purchased purely for our use. He was known as 'spinner' because when he threw a dart it always spun and rarely hit the dartboard! He was a very generous old guy, as were all the Matthews boys. He bought me my first beer, a pint of Double Diamond. I well remember him sitting in the bar with a dewdrop dripping off the end of his nose into his pint! He wore an old cloth cap. If it was a posh gig, he donned a Trilby. He was a Steptoe senior look alike.

It was handy to have a real telephone in our house, (*Wicken 255*) courtesy of the Deanshanger Oxide Works, where Dad had been promoted to Personnel Manager. The number was printed on our primitive business cards. We were performing every weekend at social events at surrounding villages, usually for football & cricket clubs. We loved it but needed to step up on the gigs. As Tates remembers;

Our first major venue was the Palace Ballroom at Wolverton. An old converted cinema and it would be open most nights of the weeks. Mondays was a good night and we would perform on the top stage at the venue, the bottom stage being used by the main act. We performed with Screaming Lord Sutch, Pinkerton's Assorted Colours, Peter Jay and the Jaywalkers, Billy J Kramer & The Dakotas, Manfred Mann and The Small Faces who were really little people. Paul Jones of Manfred Mann was really nice to us and gave us some good advice. Like 'Don't give up!'

I loved playing at the Palace where we could use the good house PA system which consisted of two VOX columns. I remembered going to the Palace when it was a cinema as a little boy, when Mum took me to see *Rin-tin-tin*. When the Palace finally closed as a cinema, a guy called Eddie Green who owned the famous California Ballroom in Dunstable purchased it. He managed to obtain a music and dancing licence and many famous acts and bands of the 60s performed at The Palace.

It was situated on the main Wolverton-Stratford road and right next door to the Craufurd Arms Hotel. Alcohol was freely available at both venues, which would often lead to massive punch-ups, both inside and outside the venue. As always, the Deanshanger boys reigned supreme.

The main source of revenue at this venue, especially on week-nights, was Zetter's Bingo. In the summer of 1964, I was taking my GCE 'O' levels and Dad would rarely let me stay behind to see the main act, as I had to be in bed at a 'sensible' time. So he would pick me up and cart me off home as soon as we had finished our performance. Not to mention the fact that I had revision to do.

We usually got paid in cash for these appearances. Our job was to warm up the crowd, then leave the stage to generous applause, following our predictable finale of 'Save The Last Dance for Me'. Five shillings each was paid to us, straight out of the till by the Palace boss. I was rapidly learning about life and absorbing it like a sponge. Mum thought I was growing up too fast.

We were billed with one well known band, which had a bit of a novelty act and it was the first time I witnessed what was called, 'Love-Making'. The dressing room was on the upper floor next to the top stage and we had just finished our performance when I went straight into the dressing room to get changed, as Dad was waiting at the stage door for me. Nick, Stan and Tates had gone straight to the bar.

There was a low counter and sink in the dressing room and I went in only to find the headlining singer stuck between an open pair of thick white thighs, belonging to some hefty blond lass, who was sitting on the counter and making 'groaning' noises. I only looked for a second before turning away in shock but my eyes captured forever, an image of red-suspender clad white thighs and flimsy red knickers, hanging off one ankle. The guy's trousers and underpants were around his ankles and his white arse was pumping like a Fiddler's elbow. I never did see his face, just the mane of long greasy black hair down his back. He was due on stage but he didn't stop his demonic knee trembling just because I was in the dressing room. He must have been on something that Tates said were 'Vinegar strokes'.

I hurriedly packed away my guitar in its plastic zip-up bag and legged it out of there just as she was getting really noisy. It sounded like she was in pain with all that fearful wailing. So that's what Doris Day was singing about. Or maybe she was his backing singer and they were merely rehearsing for part of the act?

It was my first experience of backstage sex 'capers', so common in the sixties. I was quite shocked, as most 15 year olds in those days, would be. On reflection, there were *always* young girls queuing up at the dressing room doors for stars' autographs – or so I thought. I afterwards realised it was to get themselves a quick dressing room table ender or knee trembler with a star.

Nowadays, it seems the popular trend is to make an easy buck by allegations of sexual assault against 'ageing male stars of yesteryear'. Misguided and gullible police forces have wasted millions of taxpayers' money to investigate what was merely a harmless 'goosing'. It happened all the time. Any female who willingly set foot in the smoke-filled and whisky-sodden dressing rooms had to be at least game for a 'titting up'. Ugly girls were usually considered safe and passed over to the roadies – unless Stevie Wonder was about.

2

FENTON WEILS.

The winter of 1964 was a busy time for The Deanbeats. I loved performing and was trying hard to master the characteristics of the bass guitar. I practiced at home whenever I could and eventually became efficient but never proficient. At first, I had sore finger-tips but these slowly hardened up with constant playing. I would have given anything to possess a real Fender and I remember around this time, Eric Haydock of The Hollies playing a six-string Fender bass. I loved his unique bass sound on the early Hollies hits. The prospect of a six-string bass terrified me. I had enough trouble with four strings. I set my sights on saving up for a Beatle bass of the Hofner Violin type, played so masterfully by Paul McCartney. They cost 55 guineas. It would probably take around five years to save that amount, unless Dad would sign more HP documents. So, I would Dream On.

On Friday 20th November 1964 we performed at a gig at Old Bradwell Village Hall from 8-9pm. We were on with 'Braddle' band, The Fenton Weils and it was there I first met guitarist Dave Crooks and singer Alan Leeson. Dave Crooks had made the national press, by making his own electric guitar including every component.

Dave was an apprentice sheet metal worker in Wolverton Railway Works. He was a couple of years older than me. I watched the band warm up with, 'Smokestack Lightning' with 'Ringo' Leeson playing a wailing harmonica. Most of all, I liked Dave's guitar playing. He made that scruffy home-made guitar sing. A sound made even more delicious by its injection into a Vox AC 15, which was the earlier version of the AC30. It was incredibly loud.

We started dead on 8pm, as required and the hall was almost empty, nevertheless, we were not deterred and soon it began to fill up. We belted out numbers like, 'Walking The Dog,' 'I Wanna Be Your Man,' and 'You Better Move On,' all 'early and easy' Rolling Stones stuff. I wanted to watch the Fenton Weil's set but we had another gig that night.

We quickly broke down our gear and loaded up the new Commer Van that Spinner had bought for us. From there, we drove to Wicken Village Hall where we were performing at the Cricket Club Dance. We all piled into the van and Spinner adjusted his hat and glasses and was cajoled into driving faster than a milk float to get us there.

We arrived by 10pm and by 10.30pm, were ready to go. The hall was quite packed and the air fogged with cigarette smoke. We played a stonking gig and soon the floor was jammed full of cavorting dancers, some trying to waltz to our fast beat music!

So continued our warm association with the little neighbouring village of Wicken. We even started rehearsing at the village pub, The White Lion, where we could have the annex room for free, as long as people could watch us and we purchased a beer or two.

The successful Cricket Club Dance had not escaped the ears of the Reverend Hoskins and the following morning, I reported for work at the rectory and 'Hocker' called me to his study and booked the band for a private party to be held in the reception area of the Rectory.

This event was on Wednesday 9th December and was for twenty-five special guests. These were friends of the Parson, including Peter Baines, an airline pilot, who would eventually purchase Wicken Country Hotel, as it was later called. We played for free and the promise of a good dinner. It was the first time I ever ate fillet steak. This time, I avoided the deadly Martini 'Tinto'. At the end of the event around 11pm, I was called by Hocker, together with Stan to his bedroom and study which was on the ground floor. He was pissed and 'wanted the boys to put him to bed.' Although he was newly married, his wife lived upstairs in her own quarters.

He had drunk far too many Gin Martinis and could not get his trousers off. He was a big man over six feet tall, who weighed over twenty-five stone. He sat on the edge of his bed. Stan and I managed to get his jacket off, then his shirt. Stan undid his belt and flies and we whipped his enormous grey-striped trousers off. Leaving his vest and pants on, we lifted his heavy white legs into the bed. The request to, 'Pull my socks off' was obliged by Stan, as he pulled the covers over him. 'Wonderful band!' Hocker garbled, 'Bloody wonderful band, lovely boys.' Then came the question, 'How much money do you want?'

I replied quickly, 'Nothing Sir, we did the gig for free.' He said, 'No no, I want to sponsor you. You must go to London and buy the best equipment.' I looked at Stan he looked at me with wide eyes, 'One thousand pounds?' said Stan meekly. The vicar's reply was short and sharp. 'Bugger off.'

I remember his sad eyes with huge bloodhound bags as he stared at me. 'I'll give you five hundred quid. Take it or leave it.' I replied instantly 'We'll take it!' My heart leapt with joy as I thought, 'Beatle bass here I come!' That was a hell of a lot of money. 'Pass my cheque book and my glasses.' He wrote out a cheque, payable to Stan, for five hundred pounds. 'Now bugger off and let me sleep.' So we left, leaving the kindest man on the planet to his dreams.

Stan Matthews remembered;

> It was all very well but he gave us that money when he was
> pissed. The next day he wanted the money back! Then he said
> we could have it but would have to pay him back! When he
> was in a good mood, usually when pissed, he told me to forget
> about it and we could keep the money. This bickering about
> the money not being paid back went on for months. Then he
> found out that his wife was planning to leave more money to
> 'the birds'. So he purchased two BSA air-rifles, for you and
> me to shoot up the coconuts she had put out for the birds on
> her bedroom window sill. Every day she would put out fresh
> nuts and we would creep out into the garden and shoot them
> up, until we smashed a window. Then there was trouble as he

denied buying the guns, telling her he knew nothing about it. Later when he found that she had included him in her will, he encouraged her to learn to fly and paid for flying lessons for her. She was soon banned from flying because she was always too pissed. But there was a method in his madness. Anyway, he soon forgot about the money, when she bought him a racehorse.

Friday 11th December 1964 was my 16th birthday. I was at school that day and very excited. Nick and Stan, together with Nick's Dad and Spinner, who drove the van, went to Denmark Street's Sound City Music Store in London's West End. I was not allowed to go to London with them, as I was taking exams.

We had a gig that night, at Towcester Grammar School and were appearing with the Northampton Band, The Missing Links. We really needed a PA system and a couple of guitar amps too. I hoped the money would be enough. I also told Nick to get me a Hofner violin bass if he could.

They turned up in the village at 4pm, and delivered a brand new Hofner Violin Bass to my door. Oh! The smell when I opened that beige hard case! I could hardly eat my tea for excitement. I lifted it from its case and kissed it. Then I tuned it up and played the bass riff to 'Shakin' All Over'.

I was picked up for the gig an hour later, which was in the school canteen. It was the senior school Christmas party and about eighty young people attended as we exhibited our newly acquired gear. What a backline! The lads had bought a brand-new Harmony semi-acoustic guitar for Nick and two Selmer 50 watt combos with the green winking tremolo eye for Tates and Nick plus a massive Selmer 'Goliath' 1 x 18" bass 100 watt speaker cabinet with a Selmer 50 watt Treble 'n' Bass valve head for me. It was a fantastic birthday present and I now had a decent bass set-up.

We had hit the gear jackpot and out of that five hundred quid had enough money over for a couple of Reslo microphones and chrome stands. Our PA was the guitar combos. The gig went well but I stupidly set the amp to full bass and full volume! I also took off the treble. Result was a massive 'boom!' which caused crockery to slide off the lemonade counter. Nothing so low in frequency had ever been heard in the old school before.

The Head Boy, Alan Folwell, said to me, 'Jonah your bass made me feel sick!' I was delighted! I thought I was really making an impression with my sexy Beatle bass and huge cabinet. However the problem was the sheer size of it. It was almost as tall as me. It would never fit in the boot of an A35. It had to live in the van, winter and summer. I later chopped it in, at the music shop in Northampton, for a Selmer 'David' cab 1x15, which sounded tighter and was half the size of the Goliath.

I also recorded that on Monday 14th December we had performed at the Palace in Wolverton with The Small Faces. They were brilliant. We did several more gigs at the Palace. We had a good following of fans in the village, which travelled with us and boosted the crowd wherever we played. That's why the Palace gave us so much work.

We performed at the Memorial Hall on New Year's Eve and Eric Matthews, Stan's eldest brother, took us to Wicken Pub at half-time. I now felt really important as I drank a Bitter Shandy, which Eric had bought me, and admired myself in the bar mirror. I was now dressing as a 'Mod,' wearing my mother's short fur coat, butcher-striped trousers and back-combing my hair. I wanted to look a rock-star. Tates said I looked a twat.

Eric Matthews was now on the scene full time and it was proposed we should sack Dad as manager. He was not 'trendy' enough and was a pipe-smoking, Jim Reeves fan. Stan and Eric turned up at the house one Saturday morning and simply said, 'Cyril you are sacked.' Dad took it well, although he warned me that Eric Matthews was a 'wide boy' and a 'crumpeteer.'

Nick remembered the colourful, Matthews family again;

> Eric was Stan's eldest brother, who also helped out with driving us around and sorting out our clothes to wear on stage. He was what you would call a 'road manager'. He was a bit of a 'shagger' too and could pull the birds. He became our full-time manager. He was no Brian Epstein but he did buy us all shiny grey, Beatle jackets and red ties to wear with our black school trousers and white shirts. We all looked very smart and professional. The band also had an unofficial mascot, which was the Matthew's family pet dog, 'Jacko' but his name was soon changed to 'Jumbo' because he got so fat as the result of giving him Penguin biscuits and bars of Cadburys' Milk Tray.

He also used to be fed a Chocolate Digestive biscuit, dipped in Advocaat liquor. In fact he got so fucking fat, he couldn't get on the sofa, let alone in the van. We did the Rufus Thomas number, 'Walking The Dog' and dedicated it to 'Jumbo Matthews.' He was killed by kindness.

Eric Matthews officially became our manager on 10th January 1965 and promptly got us a shed load of bookings. We held a band meeting at Stan's House and decided on a new name for the band; The Restless Knights. Although that name never materialized in reality. Amongst other silly suggestions were The Spinners, after Stan's Dad. That name had already been taken by some boring Liverpool folk group.

At this time, I noticed that Nick was getting increasingly sullen with the direction the band was going. He wanted to play more Soul and Motown music. He had brought Blues singer and TGS boy, Keith Baud, temporarily into the band, who had influenced him. On Tuesday 26th January 1965 he announced that he was leaving. It was a bombshell, but not unexpected. As he said himself, 'I left the band to join Keef Bord's Big 'T' Roll Band. I felt it more 'hip' than The Deanbeats and they played lots of Soul music.' But they never had The Deanbeats 'date sheet'.

It was my first major 'blow' as a bandleader, to find that my best friend wanted to leave for pastures new. I certainly loved Nick as a brother. My diary recorded, 'Nick left the band today, plus that fat-basket, 'Baudy'. He is like a little kid.' Nick also left school later that year, taking an apprenticeship in graphic design but he eventually joined the Royal Navy. He said himself, 'It made me a man.'

We now urgently needed a lead guitarist. Tates was competent with chords and a solid 'rhythm guitarist,' with his new Hofner President. He constantly stuck his smoldering fag on the guitar head, perched on a cut string-end, as was the fashion with many 'smoking' guitar players in the '60s. We continued to rehearse and perform, with just the three of us and even auditioned a couple of keyboard players, but I was not mentally ready for keyboards, even though The Animals' 'House of the Rising Sun' was a breath-taking hit, with Alan Price's distinct Hammond organ so dominant on the track. Tates quickly learned the chords for 'House of the Rising Sun' and we featured that popular number at every gig but we still needed a good guitarist.

Linda had recorded in her diary on 30th January, 'Jonah is worried about the group.' Yes, I was worried. It would not be the last time that I would spend a sleepless night, looking to replace a wayward musician or singer.

My fears were soon allayed when on Thursday 4th February, myself, Tates and Stan were rehearsing at Wicken Pub when out of the blue, Dave Crooks turned up with his guitar! He had heard we were looking for a new guitarist and The Fenton Weils did not have any gigs. He brought with him his friend Malcolm 'Chalky' White, another apprentice sheet-metal worker at Wolverton Works.

It was great to watch Dave play. At last a skilled guitarist who could play note for note, the stinging guitar solo in 'You've Really Got Me'. He was a loud and forceful guitarist and note perfect. He liked a beer too and for me, ticked all the boxes, so I invited him to join the band there and then. He said he would, 'let us know.' I bit off my fingernails that night.

Much to my joy, he turned up for the following Sunday rehearsal, at the Memorial Hall. Not only was he a brilliant guitarist he was also a clever 'inventor.' Apart from making his own guitar, he had invented a 'fuzz box,' doubtless employing his metal work skills, which was a huge metal dustbin-lid of a plate, with a foot pedal on the top, which he plugged into his VOX AC15. The Spencer Davis group's 'Keep on Running' sounded better than the original! If only we had a Steve Winwood to sing it! Tates did a reasonable job on vocals and also belted out the chords, with that distinct, 'on beat' rhythm.

Dave Crooks comments;

> Brian May was not the first to play a home-made electric
> guitar! I had a long connection with electric guitars when,
> at the tender age of 4, Dad gave a mandolin to my brother,
> which I subsequently pinched and taught myself three chords.
> My public debut in my first 'band' was playing 'South of
> the Border' on my electric mandolin, with a war surplus,
> tank commander's strap-on throat mic, acting as a pick-up!
> However, listening to Hank, I just wanted to play guitar!
> I couldn't afford a guitar so I made one. Dad was a French
> polisher and advised me to use 'Sapele' mahogany. He gave it a
> lovely finish but it was not 'cool', so I painted it red like Hank's

Fender Stratocaster. The fret wire came in a tight copper coil, which I pulled straight and hammered the frets in. What a mess, but it did the job and looked the part. Learning to play that difficult guitar prepared me for better things. I later made and fitted a 'tremolo' unit, which was surprisingly good.

At Wolverton Youth Club, we formed our first real band, The Fenton Weils. Alan Leeson was on vocals – because he knew all the words - George Lipinsky - because he had a bass guitar and 'Basher' Bates, because his dad had a drum kit. Plus of course myself, who by this time, knew the chords to most of the songs. I bought a Morris Minor and a Vox AC 15. I quickly learned how to use controlled feedback and loved experimenting with different sounds.

Dave also played the lingering, Shadows instrumental, 'Sleepwalk' brilliantly, with masterful use of his home-made tremolo arm. We played that tune over and over again. It was always a winner at any gig, to start or finish a set. After that Sunday rehearsal, we all went to my Nan Nick's house, for Sunday tea. It became a regular meeting place for food and family gatherings.

Nan was wonderful grandmother and a fantastic cook. She had laid out the usual weekly feast of cold meats, including homemade pig's brawn and cold roast potatoes, vegetables and pickles of all types. Pickled cauliflower, onions, and 'Jerkins.' There were also, jugs of sweet parsnip and elderberry wine. She could make wine out of anything, including dandelions, blackberries and peapods. It would be made on a Monday morning and left to ferment in an old bathtub. Consequently, the house stank like a brewery. By Friday morning she was drinking it. She would sit in her chair by the fire everyday, drinking the fizzy and cloudy concoction with her sister Gert and brother Bert, talking absolute bollocks.

I think that Sunday feast and homemade wine, finally persuaded Dave Crooks that he should join the band. Also, my cousin Sonia, one of our biggest fans, giving him seductive smiles, was further encouragement. Linda commented in her diary: 'Sonia is mad on him.' I was still hoping that he would give me some good news as he had not yet said he would join. He was playing his cards close to his chest. It was Grandmother

Gladys who finally convinced him, 'You are welcome to come for your tea anytime, my duck.'

We practiced again on the Tuesday night at Wicken Pub and on Sunday at the Memorial Hall. We were sounding good and soon had 'Fortune Teller' and 'Tobacco Road' under our belts. We traded Nick Gould's redundant guitar and amp in at the Midland Music Centre, together with my Rosetti bass, for a Selmer PA and a Watkins Copicat Echo Chamber.

We were sounding better every rehearsal. I loved my Hofner bass guitar. The neck was narrow with an easy action, which was helpful if you had small hands. Unfortunately the flat wound strings did not give much tone variation, but I was happy. 'Shakin' All Over' in the key of 'E' was sounding just like the record, once Stan had mastered that tricky, Clem Cattini two-bar drum link before the lead break. It took half a day's practice for him to get it right. Consequently, Stan was 'thrown a lot of fucks.' Most bands have played 'Shakin' All Over' although few drummers get the drum link right at first attempt. After practice we all went to Nan Nick's for tea. It was Sunday 14th February and Dave announced over a glass of cloudy rhubarb wine, the fabulous news that he was 'definitely' joining the band.

The next day, Eric had got us booked at the famous Maple Ballroom in Northampton. This was to be on Thursday 18th February just four days later, as one of the bands had let them down. The word was spreading that The Deanbeats were a good band! We still had a long way to go to match the excellent, Homelanders who were top of the bill that night.

The Maple Ballroom was so called, because it had a unique, sprung maple dance floor. It was an old Billiard Hall in Bridge Street and money was invested in it by local businessman, Harry Charles who opened the doors in October 1964 and adverts in the *Northampton Chronicle & Echo* showed top acts of the time, such as the Four Pennies, The Baron Knights, Manfred Mann, Johnny Kidd & The Pirates, The Who and The Hollies. We were booked to play at the Maple Ballroom for three consecutive weeks. Primarily because Harry knew that The Deanbeats would bring a coach load of fans from our village.

Consequently, our devoted fan and mad village boy, Mick Russell, booked Smith's coaches of Potterspury, with Ivan Smith behind the wheel. We thought we got these gigs at the Maple because we were a good band! But sadly, it was not necessarily the case. I was disappointed to learn that it was because we brought forty supporters with us, all paying the 6 shillings admission fee, with girls admitted for 3/6d before 8pm.

The second week was with Tony Jackson and the Vibrations. He had recently left chart-topping band, The Searchers, and I was a massive fan of the man, who had the distinctive lead voice on 'Sweets For My Sweet' and 'Sugar & Spice', plus he also played a Hofner Violin bass.

Our band did quite a few Searchers' hits but I took them all off the song list for this particular gig, as I knew Tony would cover them all. I arrived at the stage-side dressing room with Dave Crooks and our now 'regular' girlfriends, Linda and Marion, were also with us. To Dave's astonishment,

> We had set up our gear on stage, tuned up and gone to the
> dressing room where the party was in full swing. This was
> *before* the gig. The Vibrations were nice guys and we were given
> a warm welcome, the girls being especially popular. The party
> was red hot and the booze flowing and I was astonished to find
> that Tony had drunk the best part of a bottle of whisky before
> he went on stage and the rest when he came off.

The Deanbeats did their usual warm up act, to an enthusiastic crowd who were screaming, 'We want Tony!' Making the most noise were the Deanshanger girls, marshaled by 'Hattie' Pateman, who were lining the front of the stage. Tony went through the main Searchers' hits, despite the screams and what looked like knickers thrown at him. Then to my amazement, he put his bass down and lay on the front of the stage, snogging with several girls for the rest of the show! The other three Vibrations, to their credit, played on. The dressing room after the band came off was a boozy riot. I was not surprised to see one of the Deanshanger girls, with her tongue down Tony's throat. She later jumped the coach and went back to his hotel in Northampton for a 'glass of wine and a snack.' I think that's what she said.

The following week saw us in support to the Nashville Teens, who had a top-ten hit with 'Tobacco Road'. As usual, we went to the dressing room and the Nashville Teens - all six of them - were already there with the booze flowing. Linda walked in first, followed by Marion. As soon as Linda entered, with both hands full, carrying her coat, handbag and my bag, she was grabbed by the short-arse of the two singers of the Teens and subjected to an over-amorous hug, accompanied by the customary, 'Whey hey hey!'

I was none too happy with the dirty little sod and was about to smack him in the chops but noticed we were heavily outnumbered. He quickly realized that Linda was not the usual dressing room bimbo and apologized. Fortunately, Linda saw the funny side of it. It was rock n' roll! However their act was rubbish.

As Dave Crooks remembered,

> The Teens went on stage and you couldn't hear much above the screaming, they were not that good and you could hardly hear the vocals. We did two sets and, in our second set, did our own version of 'Tobacco Road' which was not necessarily, their own song and our version was far better than theirs and set them off screaming again. As it happened, we all got on well and eventually enjoyed a beer with them, but we soon got out of there as it was invaded by predatory females. The Nashville Teens were in town!

The last gig we were booked on at the Maple ballroom was as support to The Kinks and we were all excited about it. Posters were printed and posted in the village from which there was a full coach load going and many of my Towcester Grammar School classmates had bought tickets. To my personal disappointment and to everyone's dismay, the bloody Kinks never turned up. 'Snowed in, in Birmingham,' was the lame excuse and 'Ray Davies has the flu' was another. Dave Crooks commented that, 'Ray Davies was suffering from wanker's cramp.'

There was just The Deanbeats to appease a crowd of 500 people who had paid to see The Kinks, so we gave the best performance so far, with raucous renditions of The Kinks' current hits, 'You Really Got Me', 'All Day and All of the Night' and 'Tired of Waiting for You', to the huge delight of the Deanshanger mob which *owned* the Maple ballroom that night. Further entertainment was provided by means of a spectacular fight between the losing locals and the 'Shanger' lads, led by 'Bomber' Bartlett.

We never played the Maple again. Maybe it was because there was always a massive fight if the Deanshanger boys were in support of the band. In any case, crowds at the Maple were dwindling and it changed its name to the farcical, 'White Bicycle'. It became a 'disco' before fading into Northampton 60's folklore.

Tates was now becoming restless. He had excelled himself with his great vocal performance at the Maple but soon after told me he was thinking of packing up performing altogether, as his voice was beginning to give way. He had also found a regular girlfriend and made us smile, when he described giving her a right 'seeing to' on his Mum's best cushion. I suspected she had managed to persuade him that he was missing out on life and missing out on her as he was always out with the band at weekends. He had also started a full time job with a Wolverton Printing Company.

On Friday 26th April, 1965, Tates announced his departure from The Deanbeats. Dave had been bringing over Alan Leeson, vocalist from the now defunct Fenton Weils band, to rehearsals and as soon as Tates had left, we had a new vocalist, backed by a 'power trio' of guitar, bass and drums. Tates had left his Hofner guitar with Dave, as technically it was purchased with funding from 'Hocker'. In 2019, Dave told me he still had that guitar!

As always, I was sad at the departure of a good friend from the band, but I was excited too, as the arrival of the harmonica playing, Alan 'Ringo' Leeson gave us another string to our bow. Alan Leeson was an interesting character. He dressed very 'Mod' and had the hairstyle of Ringo Starr. He actually looked the part of a band front man and would go on to 'sell' the band. Singers sell bands. His voice was not strong, but he sang in pitch and his performance was very laid back.

'Leek' as we preferred to call him, brought to the band, a good opening song, 'Papa's Got a Brand New Bag'. We also played some popular rock and blues 'standards,' such as, 'Too Much Monkey Business', 'Smokestack Lightning' and 'Reelin' and Rockin'', Also a great finishing number – not entirely in character with 'Leeks' appearance on stage – but he sang it well, was 'Unchained Melody'. This was long before The Righteous Brothers had a monster hit with it. It was a uniquely, beautiful song and we rehearsed it continuously. As Dave comments, 'The rehearsing paid off and we soon got plenty of gigs.'

We had long stopped wearing stage suits, as Dave Crooks with his powerful personality, was a rebel about clothing and wanted to wear denims and T- shirts. He emphasized his point by wearing a white T-shirt, freshly laundered, pale blue jeans and Winklepickers. He proved we could look trendy without uniforms.

At this time, we gained a new manager. Eric Matthews had lost interest in the band with WT *aka* 'Woman Trouble' (the main reason why musicians leave bands). Brother Stan hilariously commented, he was busy, 'Banging Betty in Buckingham', 'Poking Pam in Potterspury' and 'Stoking Stella in Stony'. So Dave's best pal, Chalky White, took over.

Malcolm White came from another planet and was always 'spaced out'. He popped pills and introduced young Stan to 'ganja' and other forbidden substances. Dave and I avoided his offers of a 'smoke' or a 'purple heart' and stuck to beer. Nevertheless, smoking dope did not seem to affect Stan's drumming or his happy demeanor and he rapidly became a friend of Chalky White - much to Dave's annoyance - as at the time, Dave considered Chalky his best friend and Chalky had simply 'dropped him' for Stan, who was by now, the proud owner (courtesy of Hocker) of a beautiful brand new Rover 90.

Chalky knew dodgy nightclub owners and other dubious characters of the day and night. Neither Chalky or Dave were keen on the name, The Deanbeats. So, we adopted the curious name, Fenton Weils, similar to the name of a second-rate bass amplifier. We were no longer a 'beat group' but a 'band'.

Dave turned up at our new rehearsal venue, the very grubby and spider-infested, Old Stratford Memorial Hall with a lovely brand new, apple green Gretsch Anniversary guitar, which he promptly dropped face down on the floor, when his home-made, guitar strap failed. There was fortunately, not a scratch on it.

This beautiful instrument had cost more than his car. Talking of his car, Dave had written off his old Morris Minor totally, after rolling it spectacularly into a field, after misjudging a sharp corner in the aptly named, 'Folly Road'. He had then bought a flashy, Mark 1 Cortina, in glorious British Racing Green.

Soon our intrepid inventor had adapted his car to fool the Fuzz with drop-down 'L' plates and different registration plates. He also had a nifty box of tricks to deter tailgaters, such as a rear-firing water cannon.

To my horror, he also 'adapted' his brand new Anniversary guitar by drilling holes in it and fitting a cut-off switch to the body under a Bigsby tremolo arm, which acted as a manual tremolo effect, like a decaying echo. No echo chamber was required. It sounded beautiful, especially on 'The Hall of the Mountain King.'

The next band item for Dave to 'improve' was the sound of his humble Vox AC15 amp. He promptly fitted louder 'Fane' speakers and increased the valve voltage to raise the output. The Vox was certainly maxed out but it never failed. Our new Selmer PA system and the 100watt amp, which continually blew when overloaded, was next on the list for improvement. Soon 'Doctor' Dave had sorted that out by replacing the valves with solid-state diodes, kindly 'donated' by British Rail, Dave's daytime employer.

Looking back over the years, I now realize that the tall, apprentice sheet-metal worker Dave Crooks, was ahead of his time. He was a brilliant inventor, guitarist and singer. He would one day, make a small fortune by inventing a safety lift for the miners at a South African Diamond mine. He also armed the Commer van with a powerful .22 'Original' air pistol doctored above the legal limit, thereby promoting it to a firearm. Needless to say, a few crows were shot on the way to gigs and a few streetlights extinguished, on the way back. He did however, meet real calamity in the 'Fenton Weils' with his fascination for explosives.

Dave himself takes up the story about a gig that went awry,

> My past catching up with me! The date was Saturday 13th
> August, 1966. Bletchley had an annual fête arranged by the
> Rugby Club, which included a piano smashing contest. We
> were due to play at The Wilton Hall that very night, so the
> band entered the competition. The problem was that the local
> police had also entered a team and a large barrel of beer was the
> prize. Our turn came in the roped-off arena. Instead of getting
> stuck in and smashing the piano with sledge-hammers, I started
> playing the haunting, piano intro to Ketty Lester's 'Love
> Letters' which unfortunately drew the crowd inside the cordon
> as they thought we were playing a gig. Our trick was that I had
> rigged an explosive charge at each end and a huge smoke bomb
> in the middle. The plan was to blow the ends of the piano off,

then emit lots of smoke when I hit a certain piano key, which I had wired to the charges. We then intended to sledge hammer the debris through the 12" hoop.

So I played 'Love Letters' and hit the note. Bang! One end off! I looked round to find people dropping. Shrapnel had hit the crowd. Oops! I had used too much explosive. I also got a large wood splinter in my thigh. Several onlookers had been hit by flying debris. The local Territorial Army unit was also there and the Police asked them to defuse the bomb at the other end of the piano, connected to another note. Private 'Nipper' Downing took one look at the smoking remains of the piano and said 'No fucking way!' and quickly marched the platoon away. Somebody eventually cut the wires. The contest was immediately cancelled and ambulances called. Thankfully, there was no real serious injury to anyone. The cops didn't get their beer and we were chased away by the livid police officers who wanted to kill us, as they had no chance of winning and guzzling the beer. We were also prosecuted and banned from the Wilton Hall.

The incident also made the *Daily Mirror* and headlined the *Wolverton Express*. Dave was later arrested and charged with being a 'public nuisance' and he put his hands up at the local Magistrate's Court a few days later. He says he was 'threatened with imprisonment, fifty lashes, castration and worse.' He escaped with an 'almighty bollocking from the Beak and a five pound fine.' Dave became a local hero and our fan club membership increased. Everyone wanted to book, The 'explosive' Fenton Weils, providing we didn't play the dreaded, 'Love Letters'. Every time I hear that song, I laugh.

One date that will stay in my mind was Saturday 30th July 1966, when we performed at the Bedford Corn Exchange and were on with a band called The Surfsiders. The square outside the Corn Exchange was packed with circulating motor cars blaring their horns. This was the day that England won the football World Cup and I had watched it with Dad that afternoon. We had a bigger telly by then and stood up for the whole of extra time. Dad shed tears when Bobby Moore picked up the Jules Rimet Trophy. Looking back over my shoulder, I have seen my country win the Football World Cup, The Rugby World Cup and the

Cricket World Cup. We must be the only country in the world to win all three trophies. I am a proud and lucky man by birthright.

I managed to get myself sacked from my job at Wicken Rectory, after moving Hocker's wife Helen's, antique 17th century 'pillar and claw' breakfast table in the dining room, when one of the legs fell off. It was riddled with woodworm. Consequently the cumbersome table would not stand up and kept falling over.

I duly reported the matter to the Vicar, who promptly called me a 'bloody clumsy bugger' and told me to get a 'bloody hammer and nails and fix the bugger before his bloody wife found out.' I went to the toolbox in the scullery and took a heavy club hammer and some six-inch nails to the dining room.

There was no one about, so I tried to nail the loose 'claw' to the 'pillar.' That didn't work, as the thick nail split the claw in half. Needless to say, I had failed 'O' level woodwork at school. With an army officer's ingenuity, I resolved the problem of the wobbly table, by nailing the other two claws attached to the pillar, *to the floor*, with the six-inch nails, being driven with great force directly through the claw, carpet and floor boards. The table then stood of its own accord!

All hell broke loose at dinner that night, when the 'Dry Sacked' Lady Helen tried to move her table nearer the wall and almost ruptured herself in the process and fell off her chair. It didn't help matters by my screaming with laughter. I was promptly fired by the pissed vicar, who told me in true Biblical fashion, that I was, 'A bloody stupid bugger' and I was to 'Bugger off and never, ever buggering well, come back.'

I went home and told Dad that I had been sacked and he seemed quite happy, as he never really liked me working there. Even though 'Hocker' was a generous benefactor of the band, Dad thought Wicken Rectory was a den of iniquity but it was through working in the Rectory kitchen that I had learned how to cook. One of life's essential skills. The following day, a sober Hocker phoned and wanted to give me my job back but Dad took the call. 'Paul, he will not be coming back as he is now working for me.'

Dad, as Personnel Manager of the prosperous Deanshanger Oxide Works, gave secure employment to many men in the village. Nepotism, reluctantly on his part took over and I never entered Wicken Rectory again. The following day, I was sweeping the factory yard and loading sacks of powdered iron-oxide on to lorries.

The Fenton Weils were busy playing at quality gigs at bigger dance hall venues and were now hacking up and down the newly opened M1 to Birmingham, Coventry and Nuneaton. These long hours on the road proved too much for Alan Leeson, who was suffering from WT and he left the band under amicable circumstances. Therefore, Dave, Stan and myself, became a 'power trio' and it was a most enjoyable but short-lived music period.

We had a very slick 'Mod' act covering several hits of The Small Faces, The Kinks and The Who. We were top-drawer and loud. Dave carried the mantle of lead vocals with his great voice. He was a real 'Stevie Winwood', with Stan and me offering vocal support. We were soon spotted by a top Southern agency and offered a lucrative summer season in Jersey.

Dave still had six months to serve with his apprenticeship at Wolverton Works and couldn't do it. Neither could I. I was now 18 years old and no longer a schoolboy. I was the proud owner of a new Austin mini-van and still loving gigging, although I suspected Linda was getting fed up with it. After considering a career as an Army Officer, a Quantity Surveyor or member of the Fire Brigade, I had finally set my sights on joining the Metropolitan Police in the new year of 1968. This was instrumental in my plan to marry Linda. The Met Police would give us a place to live.

So, I reluctantly sold the lovely Hofner bass, which I had stupidly painted white, for £25. I also sold the Selmer 'David' speaker and treble & bass fifty head. We sold the supercharged PA system and split the money. Stan continued working as hotel manager at Wicken Rectory. Thanks to Hocker, he made enough money to be able to pursue his dream as a successful racing driver, eventually going to live in South Africa and Spain. We had kept in touch but he sadly died in 2015 and Nick, Tates and I attended his funeral in Milton Keynes. Dave Crooks went on to prosper in South Africa with his clever mining industry inventions. He now lives in rural France. We are still in touch, as I am with Nick and Tates.

My brief, but glorious experience of the exciting sixties band scene was over. I was proud to have been part of it, but it was time to grow up.

I promised Linda it was, 'goodbye to all that' and I would never pick up the guitar again.

PART II

3

LONDON BEAT

It was 6am, Monday 1st January 1968 when Dad drove me to a freezing Wolverton Station, then solemnly shook my hand as he wished me luck. I was just 19 years old and had flown the nest. I was off to the 'Smoke'. I had been accepted for the world's finest police force, the Metropolitan Police.

I was proud that I was going to be a part of the legendary 'Force' – never a 'Service' – which had smashed the criminal gangs of London and, with the theme of *Z Cars* ringing in my ears, I set off to start the next chapter of my life, that of a London 'Bobby'.

I pensively arrived at Peel House in Regency Street, Westminster, after lugging my new suitcase about a mile from Victoria Station. There, in a Dickensian classroom along with sixty other new recruits, I was 'sworn in' by Assistant Commissioner, Sir Robert Mark. From there, I was 'bussed' to Golders Green Police Section house, to sleep overnight, before being further bussed to the famous Hendon Police Training School. I had only been to London a dozen times before, when being taken to watch Arsenal by Dad, or to the Imperial War Museum. So life in this great city was about to begin for me.

To my horror, on the first day after being 'sworn in', I discovered that it also meant being 'sworn at'. In my boyish naivety, I didn't believe that policemen swore. Mum had told me they were all good Christians. 'Get your fucking hair cut' were the first words of welcome, addressed to me by Sergeant Charlie Fogg. 'Who do you think you are? A fucking musician?'

I was also referred to as 'country cunt', for no reason, other than my broad Deanshanger accent, by the unpleasant, SPS (Station Police Sergeant) Wilson. I became homesick on the very first day. I missed Linda. I missed my Mum, Dad and even missed my brother.

My new billet was a brick hut on the old RAF Hendon Aerodrome and it was bloody cold. There was an electric fire around which everyone sat smoking and coughing and 'bulling' their boots for parade next morning. The ex-army recruits found this an easy chore before disappearing to The Greyhound pub for a few jars. 'Bulling' boots however, took me some weeks to master. In the end, I simply cheated with clear nail varnish, painted over the toecaps.

There was heavy snow falling that first night on the aerodrome and I wondered what the hell I was doing there. I phoned Dad. 'Dad, I want to come home.' His calm voice reassured me. 'Stick it Mate. It will all be OK. We will see you at the weekend. We'll go to the pub, Mum will make a nice roast dinner and you can tell me all about it then!' I phoned Linda and told her that I missed her. She told me that she loved me and looked forward to seeing me at the weekend. I felt better and so stuck it.

Life at Hendon Training school soon became fast and interesting, once I had got used to sharing sinks, freezing toilets, carbolic soap and 'Izal' toilet paper. We were woken at 6am. Army drill was imposed upon us, made more bearable by the hilarious comments of formidable drill instructors such as Sid Butcher, who could put Windsor Davies to shame.

Yes, Sergeant Sid, we *were* all wankers. We got up at the crack of dawn and shivered in the shithouse and shower. We listened to BBC Radio One and that bloody Tony Blackburn, who actually cheered us up with his shite jokes and choice of songs. One of which, 'Daydream Believer', takes me back there now.

This 'country cunt', soon learned about Stop, Search and Detain (not a Supremes' song) Aggravated Assault and 'the intentional application of force', Criminal Damage and the more interesting, Sexual Offences act of 1956 where I learned about Bawdy Houses, Brothels and Bordellos. The daily instruction was witty, sharp and precise. Done with real humour, one of the *essential* requirements of a police officer.

I soon discovered that I must never volunteer for anything, even when SPS Wilson enquired if anyone had an 'O' Level in English language, to which I keenly raised my arm only to be ordered to 'go fetch' an old bicycle laying 200 yards away, for the purpose of a 'personal injury accident'. Whereby, a cadet 'stooge' in civvies appeared and was ordered to lay in the wet road with the bike on top of him. We recruits gathered around and set about reporting 'a failing to stop, personal injury road traffic accident'.

This entailed the recruit being taught to shout out, 'Did anyone see what happened?' and when I asked, 'Is there anyone injured?' SPS Wilson said, 'Well of course there is you daft fucker. Unless he's having a sleep in the road!' The twattish expression, 'political correctness' had not yet been invented.

We were issued with a heavy black book, which was also useful as a doorstop. This was the 'Instruction Book', large sections of which we had to learn by heart. We were tested every day, which was an ordeal but I managed to pickle through. The week was brightened by the fact that every Wednesday afternoon was used for playing sport and in my case, rugby football. I quickly made the Training School team and had my first experience of the extreme violence of Police rugby at the new Bushey Police Club, near Watford. We were playing the local Hertfordshire Police team, which quickly developed into a colossal brawl. The Herts Police objecting to being referred to in the lineout as 'Toy Town Twats'. I escaped with just a black eye.

This is not a story about my life in the Metropolitan Police but it would be impossible to talk music, without reference to it. I owe a lot to 'The Met'. It was good to me and was a great job. It paid generous rent allowance, which covered my mortgage. We got paid for playing rugby in the days before professionalism. It paid my wages when I had broken my leg twice and dislocated a shoulder playing the game. It gave my family security. I was proud to be part of the Police 'family'.

After 13 weeks at Hendon Training school, I became a 'real' cop and was posted to Paddington Green Police Station 'DP' which was then part of 'D' Division. The area covered was from Maida Vale to Marble Arch, Bayswater Road to Gloucester Place. 'The Nick' was a gaunt looking old building where they had filmed, *The Blue Lamp* with Jack Warner as Dixon of Dock Green.

There was a wartime atmosphere about The Nick and Paddington was an exciting and busy 'manor'. I was welcomed to the Station by a smiling Duty Sergeant, George 'useless' Eustace and duly posted to 'B' relief, which was about forty police officers strong and led by an Inspector and four or five sergeants. We worked shifts and night duty was 10pm – 6am and three weeks long, with one weekend off a month. We regularly paraded thirty constables for 'Beats'. Sometimes we were allowed to 'pair up' if a pal was on an adjoining beat.

Many legendary detectives were active at 'DP' when I was there, including John 'Ginger' O'Connor and Malcolm Campbell. Dick West, who was a Detective Constable befriended me and assisted me to write my first entry in the 'minor crimes' register. Many years later he would become instrumental in booking my band at Bushey Police Club.

I was given a new home as a single man, at Elliot House 'Section House', in Crawford Place, Marylebone W1. It was a pleasant place to live and was surrounded by some fine pubs. We all had single rooms and shared communal showers and toilets. Women were strictly forbidden to enter the living area of the section house. However, it was rumoured that it was possible to bung the Section House Sergeant a ten-bob note, to take your girlfriend up the back entrance.

I quickly adapted to Paddington Police life, walking the 'beat' and then enjoying the days off, when I could go back to the serenity of family and village. Euston Station was never more beautiful than when I was going home.

Times were exciting for my impressionable young mind. You relied on each other, arrested criminals and backed each other up. Lifetime friendships were forged. Many of the old PCs wore medal ribbons from the Second World War, including gallantry awards. I also enjoyed the rugby football, as 'D' Division fielded the best side in The Met and I was lucky enough to be selected, playing alongside several quality county players.

One of the first 'toys' I bought for my room in Elliot House, was a second hand, Phillips reel-to-reel tape recorder from a junk shop in

Praed Street. I was always into music and listened to the latest chart sounds, especially the Beatles, whenever I got the chance. I used my little Bush radio that Mum and Dad had bought me for my 13th birthday, as I could now afford the batteries.

One evening, when reposing on the bed in my room and thinking of what fun and games I could get up to with Linda on my weekend off, I heard a familiar 'twanging' noise from the room next door. Not suspenders snapping against thighs but the familiar sound of an electric guitar. Somebody was strumming out the classic Everly Brother's hit, 'Dream'.

I tapped on the door. It was Gus Mackenzie, a PC at Marylebone Lane. He invited me in and I saw a nice 'Hofner Committee' sunburst guitar. He told me it was around ten years old. It sounded beautiful. He played some more Everly Brothers songs as I sat on his bed and sang harmony to 'Walk Right Back'. I didn't stay long as I was on early turn in the morning but it made me think, contrary to my promise to Linda, that I should soon treat myself to a nice acoustic guitar.

Two days later, I was in Elliot House canteen around 5pm and eating my basic diet of beans on toast for my evening meal, in order to save money to get married. I had asked Linda to marry me. To my amazement, she actually agreed. It would happen in the Spring of 1969. I decided I could not possibly splash out on an expensive acoustic guitar. It was the cost of a honeymoon.

I finished my beans and was toying with the idea of going over to The Windsor Castle for a Guinness. I was gagging for a beer and could allow myself one bottle. I walked into the foyer and could hear 'Morningtown Ride', a Seekers' song, sang in nice harmony, coming from the gym.

I noticed the redoubtable 'Rip' Kirby, who had taken me learning beats, standing in the foyer with a pained look on his face and fingers in ears. 'It's them fucking traffic wardens. Fucking racket. Are you coming over the Castle?' I told him I might see him later. I needed to investigate the live music.

There were three cops and two traffic wardens. Dennis Gillon, Dave Skull and Vic Russell. The two women were quite good singers. Gloria and Doris, I guessed, were both in their 40s. The brunette, Doris, was lead singer and she looked like she kept a full fridge and possessed a grand pair of noinkers. Her voice was remarkably like Judith Durham's.

I watched them perform. They were lacking a guitar but the singing was great.

The following morning, I saw Vic Russell in the canteen at Paddington Nick. I said I liked his 'band' and he said that music and performing was 'his thing'. I told him I could 'back his vocal group on guitar' if he wanted, but I needed a guitar. He told me to go to Blank's Music Store in Kilburn High Road and tell the proprietor, David Blank, that Vic Russell had sent me. He said that he was 'GTP' (Good to Police) and I would be well looked after. I thought about it and decided I could not afford it. I needed to save for a honeymoon.

A couple of days later, I was on my beat and wandered onto the concourse of Paddington Railway station. At the news kiosk, I saw *Beat Instrumental* magazine. I used to get this great publication in my school days, which advertised all the latest guitars and amps. No harm in looking, so I bought it and tucked it beneath my tunic. That afternoon, I lay on my bed in the section house drooling over Fender basses and Gibson acoustics. The *Mayfair* magazine Rip Kirby had lent me, lay redundant. I needed to get an acoustic guitar.

Next day I was late turn, so that morning I jumped on a no. 16 bus and took a ride to the Kilburn High Road. I got off the bus, which conveniently stopped outside Blank's Music Store. There were guitars of all makes and shapes in the window.

I ventured inside and was immediately confronted by a trendily dressed, little man. He spoke, 'Can I help you?' I said, 'I am looking for David Blank. My name is Jon Nicholls and Vic Russell sent me. I am interested in an acoustic guitar.' He looked me up and down, smiled and held out his hand. 'Hello I'm David. Are you a policeman as well?' I replied in the affirmative. 'You are far too young to be a policeman!'

His Jewish sales patois had reeled me in. 'Have a good look around and try any guitar you like, I will give you a nice discount.' I had my Barclays Bank chequebook in my pocket. I made a beeline for a beautiful EKO 12 string jumbo. It was brand new at £29.00. It cost more than Linda's engagement ring.

I picked it up. 'Here you are, sit down on this chair,' said the pushy David Blank. 'Here's a plectrum. These guitars are made in Italy and are the best recording acoustics going. *Everyone* is using them. The Beatles use them… Acker Bilk too.' 'Who?' I replied. 'Oh never mind.'

I played the chord of 'E Major' the guitar was surprisingly in tune. It had a lovely, 'fat' tone. Twelve strings were no harder to play than six. I loved it. 'I'll do that for you at £25.00. You can keep the plectrum and I will give you a strap and bag for it too.' I played 'A Major' and went into 'Summertime Blues'. I bought it there and then.

So started a long and friendly association with David Blank and his music store. I quickly discovered that many of his customers were the Irish dwellers of Kilburn and they were country music lovers. I would become one of his best customers.

'How the hell was I going to tell Linda?' was my thought as I carried it back on the bus to Elliot House. The guitar was half the cost of a honeymoon to Majorca. As it happened, I never told her about the guitar until we moved into our new home at Macready House, Marylebone, courtesy of the Commissioner. It was a spacious, three-bedroomed apartment, not far from Oxford Street. We were young and lucky. She was so excited she never questioned me about the cost of the guitar.

In the meantime, at Elliot House, I went to the next rehearsal of the The Blues and Twos and added the subtle sounds of the new jumbo acoustic guitar to 'A World Of Our Own' and 'The Carnival Is Over'. It sounded great and I was in the band. We rehearsed a few times and did just the one gig at Chelsea Hospital, to the delight of those magnificent pensioners, one Christmas afternoon in 1968 and that was it. I had actually 'gigged' again but kept that quiet. My Police career came first.

I purchased a harmonica stand from Blanks, which clamped around my neck. I played an 'Echo Super Vamper', which according to David Blank, was played by Larry Adler and Frank Ifield. These are seriously good Blues harps and I featured it in a few Bob Dylan and Donovan songs. I was invited to do a few gigs at private parties. I was never a good singer but with the big sound of the guitar, it sounded passable.

Four years after joining the Met Police, I had gained valuable experience by working in plain clothes on the Gaming Squad, nicking street fraudsters in Oxford Street, who were playing the three-card trick. Also plain clothes work on the Paddington Green Crime Squad. I was also posted to Wembley Stadium for the 1971 Cup Final to watch that glorious Arsenal victory as Charlie George hammered in that mighty shot that dumped Liverpool out of the game. I had the best seat in the house, sitting on the pitch near the goal and getting paid for it. I was also taught to drive properly. The Police driving course was exciting stuff. I was also entrusted to carry a firearm and was taught how to use it. What a great job!

By 1972 I was ready to take the promotion exam and I passed it with flying colours. On 1st January 1973 I was promoted to Sergeant and posted to 'E' Division, which covered Camden, Hampstead, Holborn and Kentish Town.

I had desperately wanted to go to Hampstead but was posted to Holborn, which was a pain in the arse to get to, especially by car, as there were few places to park. Public transport was also difficult during shift times. By this time, Linda and I had bought our first house at Boxmoor Road, Harrow, for the princely sum of £5,900. We had one hell of a job getting a mortgage, but we succeeded in the end. The vendor was a Sergeant at Paddington Nick and we loved the spacious 'Nash' terraced house. So Holborn was not my favourite posting, as I had to drive across London to get to work.

'E' Division had a powerful rugby team, for which I played. The team was run by Don Evans, a kindly Chief Superintendent and ex-Welsh rugby player. He later made me captain of the team the following season. By this time, I was also playing weekend rugby for a cracking civilian club, Harrow Rugby Football Club, where I made many good friends. Several Met cops played for them too.

However, using the old adage 'It's not *what* you know, it's *who* you know,' I spoke to fellow player, Steve Wilkinson, in the bar at Bushey Police Club, one Wednesday afternoon after a game. He was a big, amiable 19 year-old, who had just joined the 'Job' from the Metropolitan Police Cadet Corps. He was also a talented rugby player. As it happened, his Dad was my Chief Superintendent at Holborn Police station.

Conversation thus, 'Here Steve, could you have a word with your old man and see if he could get me a transfer to Hampstead, as I don't like Holborn.' Steve replied, 'Yeah Mate. Leave it to me I'll speak to him tonight.'

Result. Next morning, I am early turn at Holborn Police Station and having beans on toast at 9am. In breezes Chief Superintendent Wilkinson. He comes over to my table. 'Sergeant Nicholls, I am sorry you don't like my police station so I've transferred you to Hampstead.' Thank you Steve and 'Dad' Wilkinson. Great people. *Rugby* people.

'Happy Hampstead' was the best 'Nick' that anyone could wish to serve as a police officer. It sat on Rosslyn Hill, near Hampstead Heath and was a colourful place indeed. It also regularly sent officers for duty at Highbury, where Dad used to take me when I was a boy. Good old Arsenal! What a bonus!

Hampstead was a busy Nick and the job got done. There I met some of the best cops and finest human beings I could ever wish to work with. I never had so much 'fun' as I did at Hampstead. There was never a day without laughter and there were no grim faces as portrayed so miserably and poorly acted as on 'The Bill'. The majority of Hampstead residents were a bizarre collection of arty-farty *Guardian* readers that voted Labour. It was a village, blessed with more than its share of idiots.

My regular pub, frequented after Late and Early turn, was the Sir Richard Steele in Haverstock Hill. The 'in' drink was 'Vodka and slim.' It was in this busy pub that I met characters and actors, like Norman Rossington, Ronnie Fraser and the vastly underrated American singer, PJ Proby. He became notorious for splitting his trousers on stage but his voice on 'Somewhere' was world class.

Around Christmas 1974, I did a solo gig with my Donovan-Dylan set at a private party at the large Stanmore house of Colin 'Nosher' Adams, a Paddington Police officer, who had left the Met to work for British Airways Security. I had walked the beat at Paddington with Nosher, a dead ringer for Clement Freud and found him a funny and incredibly witty man. He had worked for many years on the vice squad at Paddington. He was, however, permanently broke and a restless soul. He was always looking for a cheap deal. He told me he was 'managing' a band called Travelling Lite and I told him that I used to play bass guitar in a band before joining the Job.

One afternoon in June of that very hot summer of 1975, I was on night duty and relaxing in the garden sunshine, when he rang my doorbell. 'You know you said you used to play the bass? Can you help us out in a couple of weeks time as our bass player is in New York?' I told him I no longer had a bass guitar. He said, 'We will lend you one.' It was all his bloody fault.

I explained to Linda, that it was for *one* gig only. 'This band at the airport want me to do a paid gig at Staines Rugby Club in two weeks time and I am off that Saturday night, so I can do it!' Her face dropped.

I said, 'You can come too!'

A rehearsal at 'Cranebank' British Airways Training centre, was fixed by 'Nosher' for the following Sunday. I took Linda with me and we had a pleasant drive there in our Austin-Healey Sprite, a tidy little sports car, which I had recently purchased via the 'Job' Newspaper.

There I met the friendly lads of Travelling Lite. The only real musician in the band, as I would soon find out, was Ralph Lewin. I immediately hit it off with him. I found him an intelligent and friendly guy. Like me, a Grammar school boy.

Ralph takes up the story,

> The Band was called Travelling Lite and was formed sometime in 1974, when some friends got together to play a few songs for a British Airways party at Cranebank. I could play guitar and had been teaching Steve Bateman and Ralph Jones to play. It went down reasonably well and Colin Adams, a former Met Policeman, who was now a BA Security officer, suggested we formed a band and he be the manager. So we decided to do just that. No keyboard player, just myself and Steve on guitars and eventually, Ralph Jones on bass. Pete Allen was the drummer and Keith Young and Ken James were the singers who had roots in the 60's era of music. Soon, we had our first gig booked by Colin – or 'Nosher' - as he was known when in the Police. Ralph the bass player did a lot of courier work in the USA and he was not available for this gig, which was at Staines Rugby Football Club in the June of 1975. Nosher said he used to work with some bloke who was still a copper and used to play bass guitar. How about he brought him along? So one Sunday afternoon along comes Jon Nicholls and his wife Linda, to Cranebank. I liked his bass-playing and at some point, I can't remember exactly when, I said, 'How about you join the band?' What I *can* remember is Linda saying, 'Oh no! Here we go again!'

Ralph was a brilliant guitarist, much influenced by Hank Marvin and he could play any Shadows tune and capture that mesmerising, 'Wonderful Land' sound. The guitar Ralph was using when he joined the band was a Jedson named after J.E. Dallas, a London guitar maker. I formed the opinion that it had been made by gypsies. It was a semi-solid guitar with what looked like a Sturmey-Archer tremolo arm. This was played through a Canadian Traynor 30 watt amp. Either way, it sounded good but not as good as the lovely sunburst Fender Stratocaster he soon purchased from ABC Music in Addlestone. Surrey.

In those early days when we rehearsed, the two male singers would squabble over who was going to sing what. It was a constant problem, which was carried over to the first gig at Staines Rugby Club. The PA they sang through consisted of two Sound City 4 x 10 Columns driven by a Hiwatt 50 watt amp.

We went through our set of Shadows' hits and into the Everly Brothers set, which soon got the crowd on its feet. Some of the band had the collywobbles, as it was their first 'proper' gig. The shy rhythm guitarist, Steve Bateman, playing a new Fender Telecaster, stood with his back to the audience for the whole performance and at several points hid behind the temporary stage curtain, as he banged out his chords. No amount of cajoling could get him to face the crowd.

Talking of Telecaster guitars, I thought them the perfect guitar. They had a unique 'raw' sound and were favoured by my guitar heroes, James Burton, Mick Green and later, Wilko Johnson. Keith had brought back the guitar for Steve when on a security trip to New York.

For that first gig at Staines RFC, I was given a cherry-red Burns Sonic bass through a hired Vox Foundation amp, the inefficient loudspeaker of which, farted most of the time. The band did a nice gig, although the aforementioned bickering of the two singers as to who would sing what, was unprofessional. I took the top harmonies in the Everly Brothers' numbers, because they could only sing in unison. Things would have to change if the band were to go out for proper paid gigs.

I suggested a 'meeting' at Cranebank. Regular meetings are essential in a band, when you can bring in new ideas and sort out problems. Equipment is always a good subject for discussion, music content and then niggles. The problem with the band was that it contained two male singers who I suspected did not like each other.

One would have to go. Two males who couldn't sing harmony was unnecessary baggage. The main question I asked at this meeting was, 'Does this band want to do paid gigs?' The reply was a resounding, 'Yes.' In which case, I stuck my neck out and said that I would find us work as our 'manager' Colin Adams, had not produced anything apart from one forthcoming gig, at Albany Street Police Station's annual dance at Bushey Police Club.

I immediately decided to ask the 'Job' for official permission to do paid gigs. Policemen were not supposed to 'Moonlight'. I duly applied on a 'Form 728' where I correctly stated that the band intended to do charity gigs, Police and HM Service's events. This went up to the hierarchy at New Scotland Yard and to my surprise and delight, was approved.

The main condition was that I did not do gigs, 'whilst on duty'. This permission to conduct a business interest, caused a bit of resentment among some of my fellow sergeants at Hampstead Division. It cost me numerous bottles of malt whisky when I asked them to swap shifts on a Saturday. As much as I enjoyed being a policeman, there was more to life than just living for the 'Job' every day. Although I did the job to the best of my ability, I wanted to succeed as a bass player and bandleader, although I had not yet taken over the leadership of Travelling Lite. I had the 'band bug' back and was looking to the future.

At this meeting, the name of the band was discussed. I did not like it. Travelling Lite implied that we were a Cliff Richard tribute band. Which to some extent we were. Most band meetings often developed into a row and this was no exception. Ralph again takes up the story,

> After one of our many band rows about God knows what, Pete Allen went home and told his wife about it all. She said, 'I've got *mixed feelings* about you being in that band.' In fact, that's what you ought to call yourselves, *Mixed Feelings!*' Pete told us this and the name stuck!"

What I liked about the name, Mixed Feelings, was that it implied changes of emotions and encouraged music 'variety'. I was learning fast and I quickly discovered the knack of getting re-bookings. It was this. Your opening song should be impressive and your last song should leave your audience not only wanting more but with an unforgettable tune going through their head.

One of the best songs we would eventually incorporate to finish with, was 'Everlasting Love' by Love Affair. We added to that, the final sequence of 'Music' ('Music was my first love, it will be my last'), by John Miles. Superb stuff.

Our first major paid gig, at a packed Bushey Police Club ballroom, was for Albany Street Police and went very well. We started with the Shadows' 'Flingel Bunt' then into 'Foot Tapper' and 'Wonderful Land', which brought much applause directed at Ralph. Then I would announce the 'Stars of the Show' and introduce Keith and Ken with 'Gee Whizz It's You' into 'When Will I Be Loved' and 'Walk Right Back'.

We had been told by 'Nosher' that the band was getting a certain fee which I later found out was not the case. It was actually a lot more and he had taken a handsome commission, for which I challenged him. I was under the impression that it was equal shares for all, including the manager. He called me 'a fucking wanker', which disappointed me as we had previously got on well. But 'Nosher' turned out to be a poor business man and we parted company. *I never saw him again.*

I took over the management of Mixed Feelings in the autumn of 1975. The first thing I did was to tell Ken James he was leaving. He had a reasonably good voice but could not sing harmony to Keith who was the better of the two singers. He was OK about it, as he knew his limitations and left without a fuss. *I never saw him again.*

The shaping of the band continued. I was not happy with Pete Allen's plodding drumming on his plum-red Premiere kit. He simply could not keep up, especially on fast stuff like, 'Route 66'. He became visibly knackered and slowed the song right down. The opportunity to get shot of him arose when he went on holiday a few weeks later, when the band was booked for a private gig at Hawker Siddeley Aviation, Hatfield.

I already had a 'dep' drummer lined up. I had been given his phone number, by friend and fellow bandleader, Dave Bedford of 'The Silver Heart Band'. Fellow bandleaders are few but they are good for gig-sharing, equipment loaning, musician swapping and above all mutual sympathy. The conversation usually coloured with swearing about, 'fucking singers'.

Dave knew a lot of musicians. He told me I would have a 'diamond' in Dave Gibbon. He was not wrong. As a bandleader, you must always remain ahead of the game and like a football manager, keep a good 'bench' of players.

Dave Gibbon was a jovial Barnet Council caretaker, who did a fine 'dep' on drums. His right-footed bass drum playing was masterful and it was a real pleasure to play bass alongside him. We all realised what we had been missing. He was also a good singer with a catchy, soulful, voice.

After the successful Hawker event had passed, I consulted Ralph and we agreed that Pete must go. I informed him after the gig on 17 April 1976 at Acton WMC that we wanted to keep the 'dep' drummer. Pete packed up his drums and went home without any argument or fuss but feeling understandably disgruntled. I simply wanted to make Mixed Feelings the best semi-pro band in London and I needed good musicians and singers with a positive attitude. The best were those who had a day job and who loved playing. I liked Pete Allen as a person and at least he didn't want to fight. *I never saw him again.*

I had already asked Dave Gibbon whether he wanted the job and he jumped at the chance. So began another step up for the band. Although Dave had a tatty, Olympic drum kit, he was a fine drummer and 'tightened up' our sound. Dave also had a unique voice, remarkably like Dennis Locorriere, of Doctor Hook and the Medicine Show.

Now was the time to bring in songs like 'Sylvia's Mother' and 'A Little Bit More', which Dave sang brilliantly from behind the drum kit. This visibly irked Keith as it stole his thunder. He would consequently, stand at the side of the stage with his arms folded and a long face. I soon learned that a 'singing drummer' gave a band a distinct advantage.

Dave Gibbon was also a very funny man and great company. I was given the sound advice, 'Never trust a man who doesn't drink' early in my Police career. I enjoy the company of people that enjoy a drink and make me laugh. A lot of time is spent together 'on the road', behind the scenes and before a show starts. No point in driving a hundred miles only to sit for hours with a miserable sod.

Dave Gibbon was a mine of dirty jokes and had us in tucks of laughter. He would have a few beers but then progress to Smirnoff Vodka. This was unfortunate, as it would eventually lead to his demise. Nevertheless, his on-stage commentary to audiences was legendary. He was a funny compere, 'Evening all. Welcome to our show. We are called The Symbolics, that's Sym, on the bass', and alternatively 'Novak and Good'. Then, 'This is a *Mary Hinge* number'. Plus, 'Now we have a *Betty Swollocks* song'. This was funny at Watford Ex-Services club but not at a wedding.

I had several undertakings as the new Bandleader. I needed to smarten the band up for a start. So, I went home and bought us satin shirts from Linda's *Freeman's Club Book*. The order of the day was black trousers and black shoes. Jeans and trainers were out. We also practised our music parts at home for the new stuff that Ralph was busy arranging.

At the Police Station, there were telephone directories galore and *Yellow Pages* for London and the Home Counties. I took many of these directories home, spending hours listing useful addresses. The first thing I did was turn to the pages, stuffed with Entertainment Agents for that particular area and write to them. I also went to the pages of Working Men's clubs, Football clubs, Rugby clubs and Golf clubs. Soon I had over two hundred useful addresses to mail-shot. So with A4 envelopes at the ready, I prepared an introductory letter. The next thing we required, was absolutely essential. Publicity photographs.

We were just six years in Harrow when we decided to move to Carpenter's Park, near Watford. Linda was working at an estate agent in Kenton at the time, so she was instrumental and most useful in finding and bargaining for our new property. The boy next door to our new house was a budding amateur photographer and our first photo shoot was in my back garden. This produced a selection of effective, black and white photographs, the best of which was selected and promptly sent off to 'Walkerprints' with the accompanying wording to go on the back of the pics, plus the cheque, which worked out about £45 for 1,000 'repros'.

I would eagerly await the delivery of the heavy parcel of publicity and that very day, assisted by Linda, place a repro pic. with letter into the envelopes and stick on the address label while she licked the 2nd class stamps. This method of sending out publicity was expensive but I reckoned, worth it. If only one person booked us, I got my money back. I sat back and waited for my phone to ring. It was red hot.

Entertainment secretaries for Working Men's clubs thought themselves 'important' people and had a badge to show it. The Football clubs also began to call, Police clubs and Golf clubs. Entertainment agents too. Soon we progressed from two gigs a month to ten. Working Men's clubs all had a limited budget of between £45 and £60. They were usually good fun to play and you were finished by 11.30pm but the function room was always a tobacco smog, which caused me to stink of cigarette smoke, much to Linda's disgust. Unfortunately everyone in the band smoked, apart from Keith and myself, nevertheless, we were slowly climbing the ladder.

This is how the diary read for December 1976

Fri 3 Wealdstone Social Club £35

Sat 4 Trinity Social Club. Canning Town (B Kember) £50

Fri 10. Hertfordshire Arms. St Albans Rd Watford.

Shaw & Kilburn Dance £70

Sat 11 Deerfield Club West Hendon. £50

Sun 12 Deerfield Club West Hendon £40

Wed 15 Langley Staff College £45

Fri 17 Sun Printers Watford £75

Sat 18 Cartners Dinner Dance, Travellers Rest. Kenton £60

Tue 21 'Done Our Bit' Club; Maygrove Rd Kilburn. £50

Fri 24 Meriden Community Centre, Garston. Watford.

(B Kember) £130

The agents at the time who kept us busy were Bob Kember, Johnny Laycock, William Wren, Claude Brooks and the delightful, Diane J Rowley. It was sometimes difficult for me to get time off from the Police. So, I would need a good bass-dep. In my rare absence, Ralph led the band and our regular bass-dep player in those days was Jim Rodford, a St Albans man who was a member of Argent and went on to play in The Kinks. Later, we 'borrowed' Stuart Milner from local band Tapestry, ran by my pal and fellow bandleader, Gerry Howe.

Our lead singer, Keith Young, also worked as a long-haul security officer with British Airways. He was an ex-Thames Valley Police officer. Tall and handsome he had the 'sixties' voice of Cliff Richard and Bobby Vee. He also owned the PA system. He would often bring his wife Paula to the early gigs at clubs and pubs. She would dance with Linda when the band started and the two mini-skirted girls would be first on the dance floor.

I enjoyed it when Linda came to see the band as I valued her common-sense, advice and observations. I soon found, however, that as the standard of the band got better and our gigs got more prestigious, it was just not possible to take wives and girlfriends to gigs. I soon made this a solid rule in Mixed Feelings, much to the dismay of some love-struck musicians who always wanted to bring their partner to events. One musician turned up at a posh event at a Heathrow Hotel with his wife, her sister and her Mum and Dad! Just imagine the exasperation of the client, when a ten-piece band turns up for his daughter's wedding and *everyone* in the band brings a partner. No way.

Although I liked Keith's singing he could be a prickly bugger. He would argue about songs, money and clothes. He was always reliable and immaculately dressed but was old-fashioned in style and outlook. He was also getting annoyed with Dave Gibbon and his vocal & vodka antics.

Keith hardly drank at all and would only have the occasional shandy. The rest of the band were constantly searching for real ale, although we respected the traffic laws and certainly in my case it would mean losing my job as well, if captured for 'drink-drive'. Keith was getting problems at home and he wanted to spend more time with his young family. He stipulated he would only do *one gig* a week, preferably Saturday nights. Dave would sing lead vocals from the drum kit on other nights. Dave was great for the first half but his voice started to wander when he hit the Smirnoff.

The absence of the lead singer, as in Keith's case, became a problem when a client booked the five-piece band and only four appeared. Some singers seem to possess a lack of loyalty. Ask any function bandleader and he or she will agree. *Singers sell the band.* If a client sees a band with a good front singer, he or she books that show *as seen.* If, on the night of the event, the singer is not there, either through illness, WT or lack of loyalty, he or she lets the client, band and bandleader, down. It can also leave you liable to be sued.

In 50 years of being a bandleader I cannot get this simple message through enough to singers. 'If you are not there, then you let us all down and fuck the show up.'

4

HERE WE GO AGAIN! (1975-81)

In the hot summer of 1976 we had moved from Harrow to Carpenders Park but saving for that deposit on the house was hard even though we were both working. Plus, I was constantly on the prowl for another bass guitar. On stage I was using a second-hand, single pick-up Gibson EB0 bass, which I had purchased from Blanks Music Store at £70. Beautifully made, it played well but I was disappointed with the 'pudding middle' so typical of the Gibson bass sound. Plus it constantly went out of tune especially in hot weather and I was forever fiddling with the pegs on stage, tuning it by ear too.

To break the monotony of the quiet Sunday night shift when I was working at West Hampstead Police Station, I would often drive up the Kilburn High Road and park the police car outside Blanks Music Store and salivate over the guitars. There were no shutters. None needed. Kilburn High Road was well policed.

I had seen a lovely Sunburst Fender Precision bass in the window. It was brand new, USA made with a maple neck and priced at £180, which I thought a good deal. These beautiful beasts usually went for over £200. A few days later I called in at the shop while I was on early turn and must have caught David on a good day. I had cash in my pocket too. 'How much for that Fender Precision?' 'I can do that for £170 to you,' said David. I produced £160 in cash and waved it under his nose, 'I've only got £160 on me.' He smiled and said, 'Oh go on then, I'll take it.'

I'd got myself a Precision! It had a nice velvet-lined hard case and strap included too. The sweet smell of new carpet and polish when you open the case is never forgotten. I sat in the lounge with the new guitar on my lap. Labels still attached. The Marshall 4x12 and 100 watt top stood in my hallway. I connected it up and plugged in the guitar. It sounded a treat. The wide, maple neck I was not used to, after playing the Gibson. It was a little wide for my average size hands and the 'action' needed adjusting a little. All new guitars need setting up.

'And where did you get that thing from?' asked Linda as she came in from work. 'Blanks Music Store,' I murmured. She looked at me, 'I hope you are not buying expensive guitars, as you know we are saving for a deposit for a new house. So how much was it?' I looked down and lied. 'Err, fifty quid.' 'You little liar!' she chirped. 'I bet it was over three times that. Besides you've already got a bass guitar!' I looked up, 'Yeah I know, but it's rubbish. This one will do me now. I'll sell the other. I've got money in the bank too.' At this point, I would advise any married musician, *always* have separate bank accounts and *never* be afraid to fib to your wife about the price of gear.

I was playing rugby the next day, on Saturday afternoon, at Harrow Rugby Club. We were playing local club Barnet and it was a nice win for Harrow. I enjoyed a comfortable game in the centre and scored a try. Afterwards, in the bar, hooker Paul Davies, asked me how the band was doing. He told me he used to play bass and had his old Hofner bass in the boot of his car. He had brought it along to see if I would like to have it, as he was clearing out clutter in his house.

'Have it? I would love to have it!' He brought the bass into the bar. Among the predictable shouts of 'Give us a tune,' I noted that it was a solid, dark cherry red Hofner 182, made in 1962. 'Are you sure you don't want anything for it?' I asked him. Paul assured me he didn't. 'Just treat it nice.' What a kind guy. For the price of a pint of Grotneys, I now have three bass guitars. Bloody hell! What would Linda say?

I tried to smuggle it into the house but she spied it. 'So, how much did you pay for that one? You've already got *two* bass guitars, what do you need another one for?' I explained that a chap at the Rugby Club *gave* it to me. I could see that she didn't believe me. 'He *gave* it to you? You bloody liar. Do you think I'm daft or what?' 'What?' I asked…

The Hofner scrubbed up lovely. 'Just like my mother-in-law.' I joked to a scowling wife. The paintwork was hairline-cracked but I used 'T cut' to make it glow. I discarded the old flat-wound strings and gently passed a flat, carborundum stone over the frets to rub out any indentations. I then polished the frets with Brasso and treated the neck with Three-In-One oil. I fitted a new set of Rotosound round-wound strings. The Hofner played a treat. It smelled like a car engine but the action was smooth. It sounded great too.

The next day, Linda reminded me that we should go house hunting. We saw a nice house in Penrose Avenue, Carpenders Park. A modern Watford suburb, with a notorious reputation, made famous by Leslie Thomas in his book about wife swapping, *Tropic of Ruislip*. I joked that I could swap her for a Fender Jazz Bass.

I reluctantly placed ads in *Exchange & Mart*. I decided to keep the low budget Hofner and sell the expensive other two. It will boost the house deposit fund and gain me lots of house points.

Exchange & Mart came out on a Thursday. On Thursday lunchtime, my home phone rang. 'My name is Trevor Bolder from "Spiders from Mars" and I would like to come and see the Precision bass.' Due to my ignorance, I didn't notice that he said 'Spiders from Mars' which was David Bowie's band.

A big silver Mercedes pulled up outside the house. I opened the front door and towards me walked two fur-coated, satin-shirted 'Rock gods' with back-combed hair and mascara eye make up. Linda simply described them as 'weirdos.' I invited them in. Trevor Bolder was a jet-black haired, guy with colossal sideburns.

I invited them into the lounge where they asked if they could smoke. Permission was granted while Linda made them a cup of tea. I had both the Gibson and the Fender set up, both plugged into a Marshall 100 bass top and 4x12. Trevor looked at the Gibson and says, 'I've got one like that. Is it for sale too?' I told him it was. He picked up the Precision and turns it over, looking for any blemishes or scratches. He squats down to one knee, plugs it in and plays a walking bass scale. He says, 'It's beautiful. Why are you selling it?' I tell him the truth. I need the money for a house deposit.

He passes it to his mate, also a member of the band who played a slick riff. He does not quibble the price and hands me a pre-written Nat West cheque, 'Spiders from Mars' for £180. It was backed up by an office address on the back. I really wanted cash and the policeman inside me, asks for more guarantees. Trevor tells me that, 'Surely, David Bowie's band is good enough? Phone the office.' They light up again and I phoned the 'office' and spoke to a male who confirms the identity of Trevor Bolder. To further endorse their cred, they gave me a copy of their latest single 'White Man Black Man'. I still have it.

Trevor asked me about my band and what sort of music we played. He was a nice guy who seemed genuinely interested and he gave me some kind advice. 'The best bass speakers are JBL. So if you can load an old cab with JBLs they won't blow. HH are good too. Always use fifteen-inch speakers. Never twelves for bass.' He also tells me some things I did know. 'Use Rotosound strings and sell the Gibbo. It will go out of tune.' The cheque went through without a problem and the next thing I heard was that Trevor Bolder had joined 'Uriah Heep.' He was still using 'my' bass until his death in 2013.

I sell the Gibson to a big Rastafarian, 'Winston' from Westbourne Grove, who plays in a Reggae band. He loves it and tells me he has built a 4 x 18" speaker cabinet, out of an old wardrobe, to throw out the sound when his outfit plays the Notting Hill Carnival. Hells Bells. I might see him there.

The move to Carpenders Park that summer was effortless and I now had a garage to store equipment. There were two main reception rooms at the house, one of which we would use for rehearsing on Tuesday nights.

We would often learn five or six new numbers at each rehearsal, which Ralph and I would choose beforehand. The secret was to perform the new songs within a few days, while the music was still fresh in the head. Ralph wrote out the simple chords and I just followed the guitar parts. Bass lines were lost on me. I just did not have the time to learn to read bass music. I thought I didn't need to, but then we started backing cabaret.

It was also the heyday of the Irish Dance clubs and one of these huge ballrooms was in the Kilburn High Road, which just happened to be on my police 'manor'. The National Ballroom was owned by the Carey

Brothers, who were fast making a multi-fortune in the construction of the new city of Milton Keynes. Hundreds of Irish labourers would be seen waiting at the bus stops in Kilburn High Road at 6am every morning, where they would be collected by coach and conveyed up the M1 to their respective building sites.

They would return at 6pm and spend their hard-earned cash in the local pubs, such as The Black Lion and the Sir Colin Campbell. Later in the evening, they ventured to the National Ballroom, which was fast gaining a reputation as one of London's top music venues and which saw regular appearances of the great Irish show bands.

As a police officer, I was occasionally called to beer-fuelled fights at the National Ballroom. In spite of the efficient doormen, these sometimes spilled out into the street. I soon learned to let the Paddies swing it out before stepping in. It was always a straightforward fisticuffs and they never kicked their opponent in the head when he went down. Fighting with knives was unknown and confined to the jungle. Invariably, it would all be settled by making the scrappers shake hands and they would obediently salute me and go home when so ordered by the 'Garda', as they respectfully called us. Arrests were rarely made.

This simple method of common sense policing impressed Seamus O' Brien, the friendly manager of the National. He and I soon hit it off and the offer of a pint of Guinness was always there. There were rumours afoot at the Police station that collections were being held for the IRA, within the confines of the National, but I never saw it. I was met with nothing but respect and always a warm Irish welcome. I just happened to mention to Seamus that I played in a band and he immediately gave us some gigs as support band to famous Irish names such as Brendon Shine, Big Tom and the Mainliners, Philomena Begley, Jim Tobin and Firehouse and the American singer Billy Jo Spears.

These Irish Show Bands were terrific and consisted of excellent musicians and singers, who had the knack of keeping the dance floor full. They were a great influence on me. Seamus returned to Ireland and was replaced by Gerry Smithers, an impish cheery little character who welcomed the local police to the premises. Furthermore he loved our band and gave us a bigger spot with more money. He did insist however, that we played the Irish National Anthem at the end of the night.

I soon became well known to the formidable doormen at the National. Little did I know, one of them would later enter the music business and become a major sponsor of the band and a personal friend. Graham Logue was a stocky Scot who collected vintage guitars. He also lived in Hemel Hempstead.   Graham takes up the story,

> We soon got to know the local Sergeant, Jon Nicholls, and he was often in the foyer at chucking out time. Surprisingly for a cop, he played in a very good band that performed here. Before I got to know him, he was here in plain clothes one night and got in an altercation about Irish politics, with one of the local yobs, which ended up with a punch-up in the foyer. Myself and another door-man unceremoniously threw them both out, down the steps and into the street but the manager, Gerry Smithers was horrified and said 'For fuck's sake don't throw him out, he's the local sheriff! Go and get him back!'

I was lying on the pavement when I was suddenly yanked to my feet by Graham, dragged back in and brushed down. He apologised and said he didn't realize I was a cop! So I gained fame by being the only person to be thrown *out* of the National Ballroom and thrown back *in*.

Charity nights were often on the cards at the National Ballroom, many in aid of local children's charities. In turn, we also performed at charity events at the Royal British Legion club in Lithos Road. West Hampstead. At this point, I must say that charities, when you are a semi-pro band and you have a 'day job,' were often done with no charge to the charity concerned, or maybe a 'free bar', which was a dangerous practice with Mixed Feelings.

As time went on and the band progressed to a superb, 'professional' status in the mid-nineties, charity events were always charged at a reduced price but nevertheless, a sensible one, as you needed to pay musicians who did this for a living.

In November 1977, Linda and I went to the Hampstead Police annual dinner dance at Bushey Police Club. The band was Mike Jones and the First Impression and the lead singer, Mike Jones, made a good 'first impression' on us both. He was immaculately dressed and probably 30 years old. He sang through a small HH PA System with an HH 100 watt solid-state amp and pair of Dual Concentric 160 watt, 2x12 cabs either side of the stage. It was the first time I had heard the HH PA and I thought it excellent.

He fronted a four-piece band with the ideal line up of guitar, bass, keyboards and drums. I realised then that a keyboard player was essential to any modern band. I was determined to get us one. Mike sang 'You Make Me Feel Brand New' and 'Betcha By Golly Wow', lovely songs by The Stylistics in a rich falsetto voice. I wanted him in my band.

Due to Keith Young's previously mentioned self-enforced absence because of family commitments, plus the offer of lower budget gigs for a smaller band, we often went out as a trio with Ralph on guitar and Dave on drums and vocals. I would also sing vocals and we would belt out Doctor Feelgood numbers, Status Quo, Johnny Kidd and the Pirates, plus Doctor Hook, all easy to play, catchy material. A full 'meaty' sound was created with Ralph's skilful guitar playing and Dave's solid drumming. Also, without a front singer, we could fall back on our catalogue of Shadows' tunes. We could do them all and Ralph emulated Hank Marvin brilliantly. We even did 'Nivram' with its clever, but easy, bass solo. As Ralph remembered;

> We did this gig at Bushey Police Club and I went to the toilet
> where I heard two guys talking and one says to the other,
> 'This band are miming to the actual records. Nobody can do
> 'Cavatina' that good.' I guess you can take that as a compliment.

On the equipment side, any guitarist or bass player, who was active in the seventies, will remember that guitar leads often used to break, especially those trendy but useless, curly ones. I wasted hours of my life trying to re-solder jack plugs to leads. I actually kept a soldiering iron in my uniform locker in the Sergeants' room at West Hampstead Police station, so that in my refreshment break, I could repair broken guitar leads.

After breaking my second guitar lead in the same week, I parked the police car on a Friday morning, directly outside Blanks Music Store and went into the shop, where I met David's smiling senior assistant, Mr Kay, wearing his usual doctor-like white coat. He was David's elderly uncle and would often help out in the shop. He was the caricature of a tubby Mr Punch. I said to him, 'Mr Kay, Do you have a guitar lead which is unbreakable?' He said to me, 'My boy, my boy, we sell guitar leads which are guaranteed for life!'

He then produced a heavy-duty guitar lead with huge white 'whirlwind' solid brass jack plugs and it looked real, heavy metal. I duly shelled out £12, which included my police discount. It was quite the most expensive guitar lead I had ever purchased. That night, we had a gig at Imber Court Police Club. On our second song, I trod on the heavy lead and the bastard thing broke.

On the Monday morning I took it back to the shop. David was in there on his own. He gave me his usual quick smile but was looking very down. I said, 'I bought this lead on Friday as Mr Kay said it would last a *lifetime*. The bastard broke on Friday night's gig.' He looked at me sorrowfully and said, 'Mr Kay dropped dead on Friday night.'

It was around this time, that I was breveting through a second-hand book shop in Penn, Buckinghamshire, in my never-ending search for bargain-priced, British Regimental histories of the First World War. Another expensive hobby which, on that particular day, I pursued without success. Not wishing to waste my day off I drove a bit further on, to High Wycombe, for a quick 'gander' in The Sun Music Store.

Then I saw it. In the window was a lovely second-hand Sunburst Fender Jazz bass with a rosewood neck. I went in and tried it. It was priced at £190. It was manufactured in 1963. I told the young salesman the neck was slightly bowed and it carried some wear and tear in scratches and dinks. I knew how to straighten a guitar neck by adjusting the truss rod and therefore made an offer of £180 for it, which was accepted and so I left that shop with a beautiful, vintage bass guitar that I would cherish and constantly use on stage for the next thirty years. During those years of constant use, the guitar would go into Ray Cooper's guitar workshop at Ashridge, for two re-frets and two body sprays. The hardware was never changed.

As Ray Cooper, an expert 'luthier' said to me, 'If Leo Fender intended his guitars to have a brass 'nut' he would have fitted one. Do not fuck up your valuable Fender by tampering with the electrics and fitting extra pickups.' In spite of flirting with flashier and more complicated basses, like Status, Wal and Warwick, I remain the eternal Fender fan. They are simply the best.

The gigs were coming in thick and fast and the first day of the New Year, 1978, saw us performing at the Cricklewood Trades Hall; the next day at the National Ballroom. The standard of events quickly improved for us too and continued to do so, through the long summer months.

This workload got too much for Keith Young, who finally threw his toys out of the pram at the Rank Zerox Club at Denham, in the October of 1978. He took his Sound City PA with him. I was not sorry to see him go. He was a family man and although a reasonable rock' n' roll singer, he did not want to keep up with the times. Nor could he sing falsetto. We were also held back by the fact that he would only do *one gig* a week. We also suspected he suffered from WT. *I never saw him again.*

I phoned Mike Jones immediately. Mike was a journalist at ATV Television Studios at Elstree. I rang him at work. I wondered if he would be interested? He answered the phone and within seconds had joined the band. Mike says,

> First Impression did not have the work volume of Mixed Feelings and with regard to that band, I have nothing but warm feelings! Joining the band was a major step-up for me and I felt there was far more unity than just being a front man, as was the case with First Impression. Once I had joined, I loved the variety of numbers we did, especially the Four Seasons' medley as well as the big ballads. Also, the fact we tried to keep up to date, with the relevant chart hits of the time.

I could not wait to tell Linda. 'Mike Jones is joining the band!' Ralph, Steve and Dave had not actually heard of him but took my word for it and quickly grew to regard his fine vocal qualities as another 'step up' for us. Linda was pleased for me and she liked Mike Jones. She always maintained that he was the 'classiest' singer we ever had in the band.

Whenever a new singer joins your band, either by default or the previous singer leaving, you have to adapt to their style. It's no good making a Soul singer, sing Country and Western. I always worked on the principle, 'If somebody leaves then replace him or her with someone better.' I usually did.

Mike was just the sort of singer I needed. Handsome, single and a sports car driving, flash Harry. He was a flirt with the ladies and sold the band times over. Mike was a smoker but had a smooth and accurate voice that could handle The Stylistics, The Chi-lites and The Four Seasons, as well as very powerful stuff, like John Miles' 'Music' and the classic song 'American Trilogy'. He also brought to the band the music of Billy Joel and could effortlessly sing 'Just the Way You Are', 'My Life' and the underrated ballad, 'Honesty'. We were also fans of Neil Sedaka, one of the greatest singer-songwriters of all time and we did a couple of his haunting songs, 'The Hungry Years' and 'New York City Blues'. Without doubt, Mike's best song was Lionel Ritchie's 'Three Times a Lady', which made an excellent opener as the fogies could waltz to it. He lived in Hemel Hempstead and told me what a great 'music town' it was. I would find out, in time, that he was right.

His first gig with the band was at the National Ballroom, Kilburn on Friday 22nd November 1978. It was a good weekend because the following night we performed at the British Aerospace Sports club in Stevenage and then on the Sunday, we stormed Hertford Football Club and got a tremendous reception. The arrival of Mike Jones upgraded our show and netted us real quality gigs. We were a great pub, club and wedding band but had still not broken into the West End on any real scale. We were not yet a *first class* function band. For that we would need a keyboard player and a girl singer.

It was a happy time made even happier for me, because on Sunday 1st October, 1978, Linda gave me the most precious gift any man could wish for, a baby son. It was the best day of my life. Linda was a good mum and in my regular absence from home, being a police officer *and* musician, she took charge and brought him up admirably. My big regret is that I missed a lot of his early years and upbringing. One day, my little boy, Gregory, would manage Mixed Feelings.

We were still restless about the HH PA system we had purchased since Keith had left the band. Although reliable, its 15" Bins and radial horns were too bulky to carry in our estate cars. There had also been a dalliance with a PA company called Simms-Watts but it proved inefficient for vocal harmonies.

One Friday in December 1978, we were performing at the Castle Hall, Hertford, for a company called Rumbelows. The excellent cabaret band on the bill with us was called 'Barley'. We were amazed by the crystal-clear quality of their PA system, also enhanced by a beast we had not seen before, the Roland Space Echo.

The PA was called 'Bose' and we just had to have it. I took one look at Ralph and we both knew what we wanted. A few days later, 'The Bank of Lewin' and I invested in a Bose PA system. Don Larking Audio, of Luton, did a good deal for us with *two pairs* of Bose 802s and stands. This was by far the most expensive but also the best PA system we had yet bought. Ralph spent out even more and bought *two* Roland Space Echoes, one for his guitar and one for the vocals.

As more than one musician and client said, 'Mixed Feelings *must* be good as they have got a Bose PA.' We would later add a pair of Bose 302 bass bins, plus another pair of 802s, for fold-back monitors. Bose proved to be a fabulous, short-throw, PA system. The 802s contained eight mini 4"speakers. Unfortunately a common fault with them was that over a period of time being left in a hot van and heavy use, the cardboard speaker cones would deteriorate and split.

Replacement speakers were expensive at £50 each and there seemed no alternative other than replacement. I thought of an excellent DIY repair idea and pulled Linda's tights off one afternoon. She thought her luck had changed but I simply wanted the nylon material to make 1"square, speaker repair patches. Sealed with her clear nail-varnish, they did the trick and the 'linnypatch' saved us a lot of money.

A word of warning here about Bose PAs; *never* stack one on top of the other, on the stand without a ratchet strap. At a Heathrow hotel, a punter carrying a tray of drinks from the bar, tripped over the tripod legs of our Bose PA stands on the edge of the dance floor. Like slow motion, the top PA cab fell off the stack and hit him square on the head. He kept hold of his drinks and stayed on his feet, putting them down on a nearby table before collapsing unconscious. Fortunately he recovered and we thought it bloody funny. No such thing as 'elf and safety.'

At this time, we were doing a lot of work for Diane Rowley, a lovely lady and highly successful agent from Chesham. She was a long-time friend and fan of Mike Jones, so now that he was established in the band, Mixed Feelings became her number one choice for gigs. She came up with some top quality, corporate work and our reputation climbed another notch on the music scene.

In those days, it was fashionable for a company to book a band, disco and half-time cabaret, for their annual party or event. The cabaret was usually an up- and-coming comedian who also 'sang a bit'. The condition of our contract was that the band had to 'provide PA and musical backing for the cabaret'. This was in the days before taped or digital backing tracks, so cabaret acts relied on the band to play live music backing.

Most comedians thought they could sing. Most couldn't. Bradley Walsh was an exception. He could actually sing Elvis, Sinatra and Cliff very well. He was also an impressionist who could take off my favourite funny man, Norman Wisdom. He was a local lunatic who previous to going on the road full time, had worked at Rolls Royce with a future drummer of the band, Terry Wilson. Brad was mad, hyper and fun to work with. We backed him on several occasions at the Hilton Hotel, Watford and the Rolls Royce Club at Leavesden.

We also provided backing for many of Diane's other cabaret acts, such as Lew Lewis, Jimmy Crawford, Mike Lee Taylor, Aden J Harvey and Garry Anderson. We also backed on two occasions, Michael Barrymore – who I found to be a very nice guy who treated us kindly. He was also a great act.

The powerful vocalist, Joe Longthorne, we also backed at Imber Court Police Club. He had an astounding 'mimic' voice and would ask the audience to call out a singer. He would deliberately choose an easy song of – for instance – 'Elvis Presley' and turn to us and say, 'It's Now Or Never, lads!' So, we got away with it, as there were only four chords. To our delight, some berk in the crowd would shout, 'Cliff Richard' and so we would do 'Living Doll', an easy, three chord-trick. Shirley Bassey was a challenge! We did however master the challenging 'Something', written by George Harrison.

One of the acts we did come unstuck with was Roger de Courcey and his stupid bear. It was at Bushey Police Club when 'Nookie' turned around to us and said, 'This fucking band are useless. If you can't read music then fuck off.' So we did and promptly slunk off the stage, to the amusement of the baying crowd. It was not the first time we would get sacked. Nevertheless, I was fuming and waited backstage to give that fucking bear a good kicking.

I could write pages on backing cabaret and the cock-ups. The problem was, at this time in the life of the band, we didn't possess a keyboard player. As brilliant as Ralph was at improvising and providing piano-like sounds on his guitar, if piano backing was needed, we would ask local lad 'Sparky' Harrison to 'dep' with the band. He could read music well and I soon realised that we urgently needed a keyboard player to expand our sound.

It was at Imber Court Police Club that we began a long and delightful association with a madcap act, known as the Mini-Tones. I became a friend of Kenny Baker, the very funny pint-sized midget who would also star at the controls of R2D2 in *Star Wars*. His partner in crime was Jack Purvis, who was a couple of inches taller than Kenny. Together they made a hilarious act. They would also feature in the crazy film, *Time Bandits*. Kenny was a brilliant harmonica player and he would sometimes turn up at Mixed Feelings events and play harmonica with the band, much to the amusement of the crowd.

On this particular occasion, the client asked the band at 'cabaret time,' to have 'whatever' we wanted to drink. He had come into the dressing room and gone away with our expensive order of 'five large Remy Martins', that particular brandy being Mike Jones's favourite. The Mini-Tones were on stage and bringing the house down. Fortunately, they were largely self-contained and did a stand-up comedy routine for the first 20 minutes, before the band came on stage and played some simple music backing, for Kenny and his harmonica.

The five triple-sized brandies had been delivered one inch deep in glasses like goldfish bowls and we decided to drink them at the end of the show. Another mistake. When we eventually came off stage to a rapturous applause for our final song, 'American Trilogy', we walked into the dressing room to find five empty glasses. 'The fucking Midgets have drunk our brandy!' Dave Gibbon fumed. Indeed they had. Another lesson learned, *never trust Midgets*.

My diary reads; *Thursday 18th June.1981 Dave Gibbon sacked.*

I really needed a girl singer if we were to crack the West End. For now I was totally happy with our new star vocalist, Mike Jones. I was pleased with the progress of the band and simply loving my dual role as a police officer with a fantastic hobby, that also made me a bob or two. But nothing in life is easy and I noticed a mounting problem with friend and drummer, Dave Gibbon.

Thereby lies another mistake. As a 'professional' bandleader, you should never get too close to anyone. Purely in case you have to sack them. I was never 'professional' and I just loved those guys who were in my band. I was close to Ralph too. He would come to our house most

Sundays for a roast dinner and during the summer of 1980, Ralph, Dave and Mike joined us for a summer holiday on the island of Minorca. So that threw the 'rule book' out of the window. Although I suspect Linda was not impressed with our brandy-fuelled beach antics, pissing contests off bridges, human pyramids, pedalo capsizing, drunken cricket matches, Dave being sick in the hotel pool and brawls with Germans.

Holidays aside, Dave was continually hitting the vodka bottle and regularly bringing a bottle of Smirnoff to gigs. This would result in a noticeable, slurring of vocals and more ruder innuendos between songs viz;

'Mary had a little lamb, she kept it in a *bucket* and every time it got away, the Bulldog tried to put it back.' But then would add in his North London accent, 'It was the cat that tried to fack it.'

Plus, 'Old Mother Hubbard she went to the cupboard to get poor Rover a bone, but when she got there, the cupboard was bare, so he gave her a bone of his own.' To crown the evening off, over the microphone Dave would say, 'Mixed Feelings would like to thank you all for coming. Now would you all please, *fuck off,* as I have got a paper round in the morning.' This was not funny at Richmond Hill Golf Club and Jimmy Tarbuck told me so. When I told Dave to 'leave it out', he said, 'And you can go fuck yourself Mr Plod.'

In the Police *Instruction Book* there was a directive which reads, 'Idle and silly remarks will be ignored.' But Dave's bawdy comments did not pass unnoticed by Inspector Bill Glindon, the sullen but efficient, manager at Bushey Police Club. He said to me quietly, 'I should get rid of that wanker before he loses you work!'

I am always concerned when good people hit the vodka bottle, for their regular tipple. The trouble with vodka is that it is moreish and easy to drink. That makes it dangerous. I have drunk it myself and got through a whole bottle, diluted with fresh orange juice in a single two-hour session. You think you are OK but you are, in Dave's words, 'absolutely bolloxed'.

Dave Gibbon was a great character but I could no longer suffer his drunken antics and mood swings. For no apparent reason he would burst into tears. I suspected WT. Not only that, vodka caused him to 'decelerate' on the kit. 'Johnny B Goode' would start at a frantic pace only to slow right down, not unlike a train pulling into a station.

The time came on that fateful Thursday night gig at Wandsworth Working Men's club. I told him to his face, that his tenure as drummer in Mixed Feelings was over. He cried. I was sad too, as our friendship was over. He quietly packed away his drums, gave me a hug and left. *I never saw him again.*

Stepping in on drums temporarily with the band was Hugh Grundy, who was the drummer in the iconic sixties band The Zombies. He was also a founder member of Argent and was another solid player, but too loud! He was unable to play quietly during dinner music. He clattered through the rock songs with ease but was not good on the 'strict tempo'. It was simply not his sort of music. Nevertheless, a nice guy who showed great foot technique with his bass-drumming. We were what Hugh would later describe as a 'local dance band'. He was an eternal 'rock star' and would keep his status. The search continued.

I had a replacement drummer earmarked. A young professional from Leighton Buzzard named Geoff Gammon and he ticked all the boxes. He had been the drummer in the house band at London's renowned Rhinegold Club. He had a great voice too and looked and sounded like Leo Sayer. Geoff could sing most songs, so was a useful asset. He had a higher vocal range than Dave Gibbon and a lower alcohol consumption. He remembers,

> I enjoyed my time in Mixed Feelings. They were an excellent band and we played some memorable songs and instrumentals like 'Toccata', 'Who Loves You' by The Four Seasons, 'All By Myself' and I think we also did, 'Davy's On The Road Again' by Manfred Mann. I know harmonies in Mixed Feelings were a big thing.

He also brought a shiny black Rodgers drum kit with him and I liked the sound of his Sound Edge high hats, which really cut through. Geoff was a solid drummer and looked the part, although he seemed a restless soul and unfortunately only stayed with the band a few months. I suspect he had done enough late nights in the West End and the monotonous travelling to countryside gigs with Mixed Feelings got him down. Nevertheless, Geoff remained a good dep for the band, should we need him and helped us out on a number of occasions, so between him and Hugh Grundy, we soldiered on. I continued to look for the right drummer, but in the meantime we desperately needed a keyboard player.

I faced up to this in February 1979, when keyboard player 'Doctor Don' joined the band. I had been given his phone number by Sting's 'minder', my pal Ronnie Mann, a likeable north London rascal. Ronnie 'gave me' one of Sting's valuable fretless basses, a gorgeous white Fender precision. He said I could 'keep it for as long as I wanted.' I took it on one gig and in spite of the lovely action and tone range, quickly decided that I couldn't play a fretless bass.

It was hard enough singing harmonies without having to look down and see where my fingers were. Dave Gibbon had been quick to tell me, 'You are fucking shit on that bass. Tell Sting to stick it up his arse.' I duly returned the bass guitar, with thanks, to its celebrated Hampstead resident owner, less Dave's heartfelt message.

Besides supplying me with cheap 'Nike' trainers, Ronnie assured me that his old china, 'Doctor Don', would do us proud on keyboards. Using a Logan String Machine, which was perched on top of a Wurlitzer Stage Piano, this young trainee doctor at Guy's Hospital opened up a new world of sound and pushed Steve Bateman further towards redundancy. He carried a good sense of humour too and was quick to diagnose my athlete's foot, but refrained from looking at Dave's 'Farmers'.

Don was in the band for just six months but was often unavailable, due to his doctor's shift work at the hospital. It was bad enough having me working shifts and juggling my police duties, without another 'shift worker' to worry about. He fully understood when I told him it was not working out and stayed on until November 1979, when we 'signed' Richard 'Dick' Henninghem, from The Crazy World of Arthur Brown.

Dick had replaced Vincent Crane in Arthur's band and had returned to the UK after a final American tour. He was now living in Hertfordshire and was holding down a sensible job as an Art Teacher at Stanborough School, Welwyn Garden City, while raising a young family. He had seen our advert for a keyboard player in the *Melody Maker* and phoned immediately. Things were looking up. He also possessed one of the greatest portable pianos ever to hit the rock stage.

Dick says,

> My 'audition' for the band, consisted of Jon, Ralph and Mike
> Jones visiting my house in Essendon, Herts where I invited
> them to my studio (ie. garden shed) where I proudly showed
> them my new Fender Rhodes stage piano and demonstrated my
> piano skills. We then went to the local Pub for a beer. I got the
> job.

I liked the pipe-smoking Dick. He was an intelligent, reliable and
well-read man but could carry the mantle of 'difficult fucker' as was
described by all of his band mates. A plus point was that he liked real
ale and so we would often discuss the merits of Wadworth 6X and
sample a few jugs before taking the stage. I admired him because he was
a schoolteacher and maintained the 'stiff upper lip', when in one single
year he collected more black eyes than I would collect in the whole of
my Police Service. I found this of course highly amusing, much to Dick's
annoyance, as my chosen profession certainly invited violent assault.

As Dick commented;

> Although playing in function bands is pretty tedious, especially
> hacking up and down the motorway at 3am, we did some good
> gigs and usually got fed well. Once, when asked by my young
> daughter how the gig had gone the night before, I answered
> the question 'Not bad, it was roast beef!' Musicians being
> musicians, (and historically bracketed with mummers, thieves,
> vagabonds and cutpurses) usually managed to extract some fun
> out of any situation and we did have some good times.

I now realised that our rhythm guitarist Steve Bateman, a dependable
and nice guy, had become surplus to requirements. He was another
financial mouth to feed and in August 1981, after a gig at Langley Village
Club, I steeled myself to tell him he was no longer required in the band.
It was hard but I suspect he was expecting it and left quietly. He would
not be short of cash, as he had the back up of his car repair workshop
but I would have to look elsewhere to get my car serviced. *I never saw
him again.*

I needed to settle the drummer position urgently. During this time,
through agent Diane Rowley, I had met Gerry Howe who ran a tidy
four-piece band called Tapestry. Based in Hemel Hempstead, the

excellent drummer and vocalist was Vaughan Rance. Sometime during the autumn of 1981, I saw the band in action at Hemel Hempstead Pavilion.

Gerry played keyboards and sang lead vocals. He was sales director at Mills & Boon and had no intention of ever turning professional with his band although he had some excellent musicians around him. He did it purely for fun and turned out to be a reliable friend. Such was the big demand for Mixed Feelings, I passed gigs over to Gerry if we were unavailable and Tapestry always did a great job. But I wanted his delightfully mad drummer.

I offered Vaughan a live audition for Mixed Feelings at Bushey Police Club in March 1982. Live auditions can well go tits up but I was confident that he would not fail. I had previously seen him play and he duly arrived with Gerry, who had been invited with their wives to have dinner and watch the show. Vaughan was excellent, but fartingly nervous and sped through the numbers he chose to do. He recollects,

> Geoff Gammon was on drums on the night of my audition.
> I think he'd already quit the band but was filling in to help
> you out. I do recall being very excited and auditioning on
> 'Celebration' and 'Ladies Night', (Kool and the Gang) I also did
> a lead vocal test on something like 'Lying Eyes' as well. I was
> mad keen to get the job. I think what helped me was my ability
> to pitch decent third harmonies and vocally it sounded so much
> richer and fatter than other bands.

All of us liked 'Born' as my little son called him. Indeed his third vocal harmonies with Mike Jones and myself added a superb new dimension. His voice and harmony singing were much like Graham Nash of The Hollies. Never had a Hollies medley and Four Seasons medley sounded so good. He played a big Ludwig drum kit with a giant open-fronted bass drum, which I suspect he slept in as he kept a sleeping bag in it.

He was also a very funny man and a natural mimic. He could take off other band members and would imitate Dick's squeaky voice and did a wonderful impression of Mike Jones dragging on a fag. I did not pass unscathed, as his 'Mr Plod' accent was directed at me when he asked, 'What Beat am I on Sarge? Fast or slow?' As Vaughan said;

In Tapestry I was earning £30 per gig. When I joined MF it went up to £70-£80 per night so I had certainly landed on my feet. I had never earned so much money from something I loved doing. It got to the stage when I was paying the cash into the Abbey National and eventually the inquisitive girls on the counter gathered around me and said, 'Excuse us asking, but we are intrigued as to what you do?' I said, 'I play in a rock band.' They asked what it was called and I said Mixed Feelings and they knew of us!

We now had the ideal all-male, five-piece band that would take us further forward. Clothes-wise I decided on a mixture of white jackets and black trousers and this proved to be a good combination, but Dick kept his pipe and tin of St Bruno, in the side pocket of his new white jacket. Soon the area above the pocket was one huge piss-coloured stain. Vaughan suggested that he get leather patches sewn on to the elbows of his jackets, as most schoolteachers do. Dick took it in good stead, even when the band performed at a PTA Ball at the Chancellor School, Brookman's Park and Vaughan accused him of searching behind the bike sheds for juvenile smokers.

The Deanbeats at Buckingham Town Hall 1964. The Deanshanger Oxide Works Dinner Dance
L-R Malcolm Taylor, Nick Gould, Stan Matthews, Jon Nicholls (playing Rosetti bass guitar
into home-made amp) Note the Watkins Dominator 17 Watt Amp as PA

'Old Hocker' The Rev. Paul Hoskin
Benefactor of the band

The Fenton Weils 1966. Stoke Bruerne Locks
L-R Stan Matthews, Dave Crooks, Alan Leeson, Jon Nicholls

Deanshanger House 1966.
Note the Selmer 100 Watt Amp (Supercharged)

The Metropolitan Police Sports & Social Club Bushey. 'Where it began and ended'

Mixed Feelings. The first real 'lineup' 1976
L-R Keith Young, Steve Bateman, Ralph Lewin, Jon Nicholls, Dave Gibbon

Mixed Feelings 1979. L-R Ralph Lewin, Dave Gibbon, Steve Bateman,
Jon Nicholls, Don Rogers. Centre. Mike Jones

Ralph Lewin & Fender Stratocaster
Hemel Hempstead Pavilion 1979

Mixed Feelings. The Brighton Grand Hotel 1982
Rear. Jon Nicholls. Mike Jones, Ralph Lewin
Front. Vaughan Rance, Dick Henninghem

Barry Elliott
'One Voice'

Top
Mixed Feelings 1983
Centre Barry Elliott
Rear. Dick Henninghem, Ralph
Lewin, Vaughan Rance,
Jon Nicholls

Bottom
The Keith Blakelock
Memorial Concert
The Palace Theatre.
Shaftesbury Avenue
Tuesday 12 November 1985

First Girl Singer
Debbie Lee
'They were heady, crazy days'

Photo Kevin Hill

Michael Black
'A friend in need is a fucking nuisance'

Photo 'The Stage'

Mixed Feelings 1989. L-R Jon Nicholls, Nikki Brightman, Dick Henninghem,
Ralph Lewin, Terry Wilson.
On floor, Mick Mullane
(The suspects arrested for attempted murder)

Ashridge House 1993 L-R Jon Nicholls, Jeremy Moore, Lisa Grahame, Dave Howard, Terry Wilson, Kathy Edge, Jamie Hardwick, Pete Callard
Photo Marissa

Hemel Hempstead Pavilion
A great music venue
Sadly demolished in 2002
Photo. Hemel Gazette

On Stage Hemel Hempstead Pavilion 1993 L-R Pete Callard,
Jon Nicholls, Kathy Edge, Terry Wilson, Dave Howard, Jamie Hardwick
Note. JN playing Kubicki Bass. Bose 802 Stage Monitors

Helen York, Dave Howard & Sue Acteson
'The girls were our main selling points'

5

DULL IT ISN'T

'Dull it isn't,' was a catchphrase, coined to recruit more officers to the Metropolitan Police in the early 1980s. Nothing could be more true! My time at Hampstead Police Station was certainly happy and I crammed as much adventure into my life as I could. I was doing quite a bit of plain-clothes work, including postings to the Divisional, 'Q' car, which entailed chasing criminals in and around central London. I also worked on several murder squads. All of these nice postings left my evenings free for gigs.

I still did a bit of shift work and always saw the funny side of Policing. I saw people at their best and at their worst, which was something that the useless politicians never experience. One summer's night, I disarmed and arrested a mad French chef, who attacked me with a 12" carving knife in the Finchley Road. He was drenched in blood, having just stabbed an elderly woman to death and it took all my strength to subdue him. He duly went on trial at the Old Bailey for murder. He complained that I had hit him over the head with my truncheon during the scrap and then *stolen* his 'best knife'. The all 'ethnic minority' jury believed him and found him 'not guilty' even though it was revealed *after* the trial he was wanted in Paris for knifing another unfortunate woman to death.

I was nevertheless, commended by the Commissioner but I lost faith in the criminal justice system. I got even more flippant with police work and I started to write a book called, 'Short cuts to Police duty'. The art of which, I became notoriously expert.

This frivolous attitude did not go unnoticed by Alison Halford my acting Chief Superintendent, who noted on my annual appraisal;

> PS NICHOLLS is one of Hampstead Division's best sergeants.
> He is always immaculately turned out and his attention to detail
> and general knowledge of station procedure cannot be faulted.
> He has a pleasant way with people and yet is a very able leader.
> However, despite these glowing accolades, I suspect that PS
> NICHOLLS lacks the necessary drive to take him to the next
> rank. He has all the personality and skills required to hold
> the rank of Inspector and even higher but he seems reluctant
> of grasping the nettle of seeking advancement. *This lack of
> motivation doubtless, stems from his keen interest in music.* He is an
> accomplished guitarist and plays in a group to raise money for
> charity. NICHOLLS feels that he will have to forego this most
> pleasurable pastime as it will conflict with the rank of Inspector.

During my time in the 'Job' I worked with some great characters, some of whom became lifelong friends, including the Met's first black police officer, Norwell Roberts QPM. We were both sergeants on the same relief. He was quite one of the nicest and funniest men I have ever met and we never stopped laughing at his practical jokes, like setting off a 'laughing bag' when I was giving evidence at Magistrates Court. He is worthy of another book. He soon became a fan of the band and remembers;

> Jon was the leader of a band called Mixed Feelings, which
> played at several local venues 'on the manor,' when he was
> not working of course. On one particular occasion, he was
> performing at the National Dance Hall in the Kilburn High
> Road. As I was the Section Sergeant on night duty, I wandered
> in to see him. One of the songs the band did was a Doctor
> Feelgood song, 'Back in the Night.' Upon seeing me standing
> at the back of the hall in full uniform, he changed the words
> to 'Black in the Night' much to the amusement of all those
> present, including me!

Indeed, working night-duty, with, 'Nozzer the Cozzer, the smooth talking Rozzer' as he announced himself to an astonished jury at the Old Bailey, was an absolute pleasure, although ordinary daily occurrences could be turned into sheer bedlam. Nozzer would scare away difficult people at the station counter by using Tippex as war paint and talking mumbo-jumbo. Nevertheless, the job got done and no-one complained. The laughter almost killed me, if one could die from split sides. All that is another story as Norwell fondly remembers, 'I can honestly say that my time spent working with Jon taught me so much and my life is much richer for the experience.' Mine too.

In September 1982, I was working as a temporary Detective Sergeant on a murder squad at Mill Hill Police Station when out of the blue, I was called to the telephone. It was about the band. It was a John Jenkins, an inspector for HM Inland Revenue. This was nothing to do with murder. He introduced himself and politely asked in his rich Welsh accent, how I was. Then came the thunderbolt. 'What can you tell me about a band called Mixed Feelings?' I was not on blood-pressure pills but soon would be.

Declaring my extra earnings to the Inland Revenue was something I had been fully intending to do but I had stupidly, just never got around to it. 'They' had finally caught up with me. Fortunately, I had kept diaries and recorded every gig in the previous seven years, in a Cathedral account book. I had written down how much the band had earned and how much I had spent on gear, fuel, clothes etc. I had also kept all the contracts and receipts.

We had also performed for free at many Army, Police and Hospital charity events. I reckoned I was well out of pocket but that was no excuse. This phone call caused my heart to miss a beat. There are three stages in the life of a musician. *Stage one.* You do it for love. *Stage two.* You do it for love and money. *Stage three.* You do it for money. I was still on stage one and putting one foot on stage two.

I nervously explained to Mr Jenkins, that I had only earned 'expenses' with the band and he advised me, 'You must always tell us about your extra earnings. Have you kept records of what you have earned?' I assured him I had. 'That's good then Jon. Have a word with your mates in the band and find your self a good accountant and let him sort it out. You will have to go right back from when you first started earning 'expenses'. You can offset it against what you have spent on guitars, amps, fuel and clothes. We might end up paying you money. I look forward to hearing from you.'

It was a scary call but that tax inspector could not have been more decent about it. Now I needed a good accountant to sort this out. I didn't want the 'Job' to find out I had been 'captured' by the IR, or I would be in serious trouble.

I immediately phoned Rod Crowe, a friend who managed a club band in south-west London. He had previously told me about this brilliant accountant, named Geoffrey Hull. 'He's right up your street! He reads the *Daily Telegraph* and the *Daily Mail* ! He gave me his phone number.

I immediately called Geoffrey Hull. It was 6pm. I was still in a sweat. A female answered, 'Ivy speaking.' I announced myself to what sounded like a very 'vexed' Ivy and asked to speak to Geoff. She said, 'Geoff's having his dinner, so call back at 6.30pm.' In the meantime, I phoned Ralph. He had just got in from work. He deserved to be frightened too. 'We have been rumbled.' I told him.

I called Geoff back. He answered the phone. As Rod predicted, he was 'right up my street'. He said he liked policemen, soldiers and musicians. He said he hated politicians, especially Neil Kinnock, lawyers, vets and strangely enough, accountants. He asked me to come and see him the next morning and bring my 'books'.

At this point in time and following the birth of my little son who was now three, we had finally decided to move from our town house, in Carpenders Park, further out into rural Hertfordshire. Much influenced by Mike Jones, I wanted to move my family to Hemel Hempstead, which was conveniently situated near the M1 and nearer to our families in Deanshanger.

We were further encouraged by the Commissioner's decision to extend the limit to where Met Police officers could live, to 25 miles from Charing Cross. Hemel Hempstead was now within reach. It also attracted me because it had a great reputation as a 'live music town' with its famous 'Pavilion' plus good schools, pubs and sensibly priced properties.

I particularly wanted a house with a big garage for the storage of equipment and for rehearsing etc. We found one in June 1982 and made an offer for the spacious detached house in pleasant, Wootton Drive, with a huge four car integral garage and rooms underneath. It was perfect for a budding bandleader and ideal for rehearsing.

When we moved into our new house in the late summer of 1982, I was excited about it but quickly found that there were flaws in it which would require spending money. I was the only source of income and the extra cash from Mixed Feelings would be handy. I was also the proud owner of a one-year old Golf GTI, a beautiful car which I only kept for a month before selling it on to a friend. We needed the money and the sale of the car helped to pay for extras on the house.

Ralph was selling a car, which he had bought temporarily, to see him over when changing jobs. So I bought his reliable, Datsun automatic. The car had no street credibility in the eyes of my four-year old son but it had a huge boot. Perfect for humping PA cabs to gigs and it was economical to use. Besides I had plans to buy a small van, when finances allowed. This brings me to Geoffrey Hull.

As directed by him, I turned left at the Penny Black pub and found his house up a private, leafy lane in picturesque Byfleet village. It was 11am as I pulled on to his wide gravelled forecourt and parked the Datsun next to a nice Mercedes saloon and a new Volvo Estate. I got out of the car and admired his large detached bungalow, set in woodland. Standing on the step, in front of the open front door, was a distinguished looking man with a full head of white hair. I would guess around 60 years old. He was smoking a cigarette and held a folded copy of the *Daily Telegraph* under his arm.

'Geoff?' I asked. 'It's me, Jon Nicholls.' He gave me any icy stare. 'Yes I know who you are. Get that heap of Japanese shit off my drive.'

I moved the car further back down the lane and parked it up. From that moment on, I found the best accountant and friend any man could wish for. His handshake was firm and he invited me in as we sat in his spacious lounge. I said to him, 'I guess you don't like the Japs then?' He said, 'I hate the yellow bastards.'   I found out that he held the *Burma Star*. So did my Dad. That spoke volumes. When I told him Dad held the same medal, his eyes lit up. 'I won't have anything Japanese in this house. They were a cruel and barbarous race and responsible for the death of several of my mates.' I cast my eyes quickly around his lounge looking for any Japanese gadget. His huge colour TV was a Phillips.

I told him that I liked his cars. He replied, 'They're not mine. They belong to a couple of the lads in Jethro Tull. One belongs to Ian Anderson. He leaves it here when he's in the States.' He told me that he had recently come back from a USA tour with the band. He was their finance manager and accountant.

Geoff skipped though my accounts book. He never took the fag from out of his mouth except to flick ash into the ashtray. Soon the sun was casting rays through swathes of blue smoke. 'Always write down your finances in pencil.' He looked over his glasses at me. 'Then we can alter them if need be.'

As the chattering budgerigar in the corner of the lounge, constantly repeated, 'Kinnock is a pillock, Kinnock is a pillock,' Geoff smiled and said 'He only speaks the truth!' He then asked me for the name of the tax inspector who had called me. He phoned him there and then. 'Hello John. It's Geoff Hull here. How are you doing? I've got Jonathan Nicholls with me. You spoke to him yesterday. I am taking him on and you will get his returns in a few days. Thanks Mate!'

'Do you know him?' I asked incredulously, 'Yes. I know most of them.' Geoff replied. 'He works in the Public Department in Cardiff. He's a good bloke and providing we are honest with him, you won't get any problems.'

Two days later, I received a bill from Geoffrey Hull & Company, Chartered Accountants. It was for £250. 'Bloody Hell.' I thought. 'That's a lot of money!' I was gutted. The bill came fast but I paid it immediately, posting off a cheque by return of post. Geoff had told me that second to hating Japs, he hated, 'Fuckers who didn't pay their accountant's bill immediately.' Two weeks later I received a cheque from the Inland Revenue for £1,200.00.

Soon, the whole band was under the wing of Geoffrey Hull. Most got tax rebates. Especially Ralph, who had spent more money on PA equipment than anyone and was the main patron of the band. Geoff and Ivy Hull were not only our accountants but became real fans of the band and came to see us perform on several occasions, especially at nearby Imber Court.

They loved that great American singer, Billy Eckstine and requested that we learn a certain song, 'Passing Strangers' (a duet with Sarah Vaughan) especially for them. Once we had acquired a competent girl singer, we performed the song. It remains one of the great songs of all time. Whenever I hear it, I think of Geoff.

Furthermore it showed how good the singers in Mixed Feelings were, to carry that number note perfect. Geoffrey Hull was not only a fabulous accountant but a diamond of a man. His constant letters to *The Telegraph* were a revelation. Castigating editors and politicians alike, about the correct use of English. Such a master of the English language was he, I asked him to proof read my forthcoming book, *Cheerful Sacrifice*. He remained my accountant and friend until his death in 1989. I miss him.

In December 1982, we performed at fourteen major Christmas events but only one, the Café Royale, was in the West End. We had also made big inroads into the lucrative Jewish market after a fellow police sergeant had asked us to perform at his son's Barmitzvah party, which was held at Hutton Grove Synagogue in Finchley, where we had gone down a storm and my phone was even hotter.

Vaughan again,

> We were new on the Jewish scene and our first real Jewish gig was at a posh synagogue, The King David Suite, at Great Cumberland Place, Marble Arch. We had to play the 'Hatikva' and Ralph only knew the first verse. He didn't know the middle bit, so when we practised it before the punters arrived, we got stuck on the 'middle eight' and the client came over and tried to hum it to us. He didn't know it either, so he called over to one of the Jewish waiters and asked him how it went. The bloke hummed the first bit - which we knew – and then stopped. The client said, 'You've only sung half of it!' and the bloke replied, 'I'm only half-Jewish!'

We weren't Jewish and so needed to learn the essential catch songs for 'Simcha' dancing. Help would soon come in the form of Howard Robbins, a young London toastmaster on the scene. He took the time to record the songs for us and he gave this to me on a cassette tape. Howard would become a great friend and fan of the band.

I long suspected Mike Jones of being a Freemason, as since he joined we seemed to be picking up a lot of Freemason's gigs. Freemasons are that secret society that today, remains an enigma. I have several good friends that are Freemasons such as Norwell Roberts, who carries the high rank of 'Almoner'. I started to get lots of enquiries from Freemasons to perform at their Ladies Festival event.

One was a certain Chief Inspector when I was a sergeant at Hampstead. He offered me the chance to join his lodge, which was The Lodge of St James, a Met. Police Lodge. He told me that it would 'benefit' me as a bandleader and police officer. I had to pay in a lump sum of money to join and then attend several dinners and meetings a year. Although I remained a 'suspected Freemason' among my colleagues in the Met, I had declined his offer. I simply did not have the time.

Mike Jones had a mate called Harry Allenby who was a Freemason. Harry called me one winter's morning and enquired if we could perform at a Ladies Night at the Brighton Grand Hotel. One thing I have learned over the years is that Freemasons always plead poverty. They raise millions of pounds for worthy charities but expect entertainers to appear for peanuts.

Over the years we have performed at many Freemason's events and although the money was mediocre, Freemasons were always good value as customers and generally filled the dance floor quickly. They were receptive and appreciative and often gave us a few beers on the firm. An essential requirement for any band at a Freemason's Ladies Festival was to be able to perform the 'Masonic Grace' and 'The Ladies Song – Here's to their health in a song'.

So, I agreed to go to the Brighton Grand Hotel on a summer Saturday night in 1982. A couple of days before the event Harry Allenby called me and asked if we minded backing the cabaret. 'Who is it?' I asked him. 'Susan Maughan,' he said. 'Yeah, of course we can!' Harry promised me a free bar. Being a child of that most exciting '60s music period, I remembered Susan as a 'one-hit wonder' with 'Bobby's Girl', so I immediately went to the cellar with my bass and learned 'Bobby's Girl'.

Harry phoned me on the Thursday night before the gig and asked if we could be ready to sound check with Susan at 3.30pm. I agreed and gave Ralph, Vaughan and Dick a call to get them to the Brighton Grand for 2.30pm, in order to set up in good time for the sound check. Dick and Vaughan were OK about it but Dick as usual, took a bit more persuading. 'Who is going to pay for parking?' was one of his whines. 'I am,' I told him. 'What time does it finish?' and 'Are we getting fed?' were his next regular questions.

Now to be fair to Dick and to any musician who gets a gig in Brighton, it is a real 'happy' place to perform. Over the years we played it many times, the two main venues for party events being the Grand Hotel and the Metropole next door but it was a real pain in the arse for parking, especially on a Saturday in summer, when many people head for the pier or the beach.

Brighton was also a surprisingly violent place on a Saturday night, where I saw more bloody fights after midnight, than I ever saw in the Kilburn High Road. However, I considered it most rewarding to perform there, but I did sympathize with Dick and his moan about driving to Brighton.

Everyone got there on time, including 'Biggus Dickus', as Vaughan had now named him. Parking outside the side doors at the Grand was always difficult although there was a small 'pull in' which was subject to tickets from the wardens.

We were fully set by 3.30pm and eagerly awaiting the arrival of star cabaret, Susan Maughan. We were on stage and ran through our opening tribute to 'War Of The Worlds' and 'The Chances Of Anything Coming From Mars' 'Forever Autumn' and more. All great fun and a thrill to play and I noticed the waiters stopping to watch us. We had an amazing sound and as Ralph says;

> Dick was not into synthesisers, which were at that time taking the music scene by storm. We needed a synthesiser sound on some of the tracks we did, so I did it myself. For a guitarist I think I had a more complicated set up than Andy Summers! A Casio PG 380 Guitar Synth and a Fender Stratocaster. Three synth modules and a midi router with Data disc!

It got to 4pm and Susan Maughan had not arrived, so we went around the corner to our favourite 'Gay' pub appropriately called The Queensbury Arms and reputed to be Brighton's smallest pub. Over a period of time and on account of the amount of gigs we did at the Grand and the Metropole next door, the cheerful landlord and his merry men got to know us well and always made us welcome. Being a Free House, they sold good ale and so we sat down for some band banter and enjoyed a couple of pints of Sussex Bitter.

We ambled back to the hotel at 5pm to see if Susan had arrived. Yes she had. Standing in the middle of the dance floor, with arms folded was a track- suited little lady with a face like a spanked arse.

'Are you my backing band? Where the hell have you been? I have been here half an hour waiting for you! You were supposed to be here for 4.30pm.' 'Hold on,' I said, 'Who are you?' 'Well who do you think I am?' she yelled. Vaughan muttered, 'Helen Shapiro?' Unfortunately, she heard him. 'I'm Susan Maughan and I am the cabaret this evening!' I refrained from saying, 'Never heard of you!' as I knew it would piss her off even more.

To my dismay, I noticed great heaps of music charts piled on the stage. For keyboards, bass, guitar and drums. She had Mike Jones's SM58 mic we had set up for her and was on the dance floor facing the stage and ready to go. I really needed a music stand and made a mental note to always carry one in future. I went and got a chair from one of the dining tables, as did Ralph and we plonked the heavy charts on that.

Now firstly, I couldn't read bass music but I usually got away with it by reading the guitar chords. To my horror, these charts were all 'dots' and to crown it all, her opening song was the awful, 'What A Difference A Day Makes' with four key changes. What a totally shit song but it got worse, the next song to my horror was 'El Bimbo'. 'Never fucking heard of that,' murmured Ralph. 'Fuck me.' I said to myself, 'I'm gonna have to *wing* it.' Now the majority of professional bass players - apart from Paul McCartney and me - can read music. This was where I should have paid attention to 'Hog's music lessons at school.

She clicks her fingers and off we go, the intro is eight bars and it's a *bossa* beat. Susan was warbling away. She was actually a good singer. I was OK for the first two lines then fucked up. 'Stop, stop,' Susan calls, waving her arms in the air, 'Somebody is fucking up!'

'It's me.' I reply, 'I don't know this one but I know 'Bobby's Girl',' She looks at me hands on hips. 'This is my *opening* song and we are doing it! Right, again from the top.' She clicks her fingers and off we go again. I am OK for the first two lines then 'fuck up' again. She looks at me and says very irked, 'You can't read can you?' I splutter, 'I know 'Bobby's Girl'.'

'Piss off. I'll get a *proper* bass player!' She says. This is immediately followed by a colossal guffaw from Vaughan. 'And if you think it's funny, you can piss off too!' Result I say! 'Come on Vaughan, let's go back to the Pub. We were doing this for free anyway. Fuck Bobby's Girl.' 'That's first prize in the raffle,' says Vaughan.

Dick, who can read music, is not going to miss out on the beer. 'Hang on boys! I'm coming with you. Fucking rude woman.' He switches off and abandons his keyboards, jumps off the stage and follows us to the door, followed by a red- faced chuckling, Ralph. He is looking like a naughty schoolboy who has been sent out of class. 'She has sacked the lot of us,' says Ralph. 'Bitch doesn't deserve us,' says Dick. 'Real Ale Twats' would be a better name for the band.

We get back to the Grand Hotel around 7.45pm. Dickie-bowed, moth-ball smelling males, escorting salad dodging wives, are milling around the tables. We hear the usual clinking of wine glasses and the sounds of four silver-haired old men, sitting on the stage reading music. Susan is still sound checking and has brought in her own backing band at her or Harry Allenby's expense. They are doing 'Bobby's Girl' and using our gear but we don't mind. It sounds great.

Susan Maughan's manager was Howard T'loosty (who also managed Frankie Vaughan) He advised me;

> Female acts are generally difficult to manage. They can be temperamental and unpredictable. Susan Maughan was a good performer and I liked her a lot but she only had the one hit, 'Bobby's Girl' and dined out on it. If it wasn't for that record she would not have worked on the scale she did. And yes, I guess she could swear a bit!

However, during the busy December of 1982 a heavy shock was on the near horizon. New Year's Eve was looming as well as a sell-out gig at the huge Electrolux Factory Social club in Luton and there would be no Mike Jones.

According to Vaughan, Mike had found a new woman and was 'fanny-struck'. He would also announce his 'retirement' in the New Year. His excuse was that he had the 'flu but the truth was that he was conniving to 'bury the ferret' on New Year's Eve. This had led to another acute rise in my blood pressure, not for the first time with singers.

Vaughan was simply *told* he was singing lead vocals from behind the drum kit. It was certainly squeaky bum time for him but I knew he could do it. This was all provided he could be serious for once, stop fucking about and keep the essential lyrics in front of him. In all honesty, Vaughan would have been perfect for a comedy show group, like the Black Abbots or Baron Knights.

We got together in the spare bedroom at Wootton Drive, the night before the event. It was too cold in the cellar. We had set up a small HH combo, with just guitar and bass, a dozen essential cans of McEwan's and got stuck into a frantic rehearsal. It was impossible for Vaughan to learn all the lyrics in time for the event, so we had to write them down by hand. This was in pre-computer days, so copies of sheet music were produced from my modest collection and Linda was sent to the kitchen and ordered to use her secretarial skills to speed write the words in big format, to more than thirty songs.

There is a worn-out saying, 'It'll be alright on the night'. As it happened, it was. The event went well without our missing lothario and Vaughan carried the show magnificently, after several visits to the karzi. I sang the easy Chuck Berry stuff such as 'Route 66', 'Johnny B Goode', Johnny Preston's 'Running Bear' and more. Vaughan sang the hard stuff and even managed 'You'll Never Walk Alone' at midnight. The dance floor was crammed and the cigarette smoke like a Mersey fog as the drunks joined in the Scousers' lament. It's surprising how many Luton people support Liverpool. I think it is the Irish element. Or were they just fans of *Carousel?*

To our relief, the client was delighted with the four-piece band and didn't dock the fee of £600, the most we had ever earned. Vaughan got an extra tenner plus the £100 that we were all paid. A fair-sized lump of the rest went to our agent, Diane Rowley, who received a good report from the client. I told her that Mike had been 'F-struck'. When she asked what that was, I said he was 'Flu-Struck'.

So, with Mike Jones wanting to leave, I became despondent that we would never find a singer as good. Mike promised to stay on until we found someone to replace him. So we planned our first audition for male singers and thanks to an advert in *The Stage,* my phone started to ring and soon we had over twenty applicants. The audition was fixed for a mid-week night and it was then that I embarked on a learning curve about auditions and how *not* to conduct them.

The new house had a sizeable basement area which ran the width of the house and was perfect for band rehearsals. I had the room cheaply carpeted and equipped with a small Sound City PA system, a battered SM 58 microphone and an Orange 4x12 bass cab, with an old Hiwatt valve top and a HH 100 guitar combo amp. There was a vintage Olympic drum kit too, which I had picked up from another ad in the 'Job' newspaper.

As the night of the big audition loomed closer, I thought up a method of selection which would determine the best singer. A song that was popular at the time, was Frank Sinatra's 'Send In The Clowns' so I decided I would get all applicants to sing this song 'acapella'. Which means no backing instruments.

First to respond to the ad and first at the door at 7pm prompt on the night, was a good looking blonde-haired Geordie lad. I could hardly decipher his strong Newcastle accent on the phone but he gave his name as Barry Elliott.

I made the first mistake in conducting auditions by supplying free beer. There was an ample supply of Double Diamond, Newcastle Brown and McEwans bitter. Barry and his fellow Geordie mate, Ritchie, who generally accompanied him everywhere, did not hesitate when told to help themselves.

The front doorbell kept ringing and the room was soon heaving with chatter, laughter and the sound of cans popping. Singers and musicians soon made friends with each other in the haze of cigarette smoke. Some even knew each other. Dick and Ralph had turned up and Vaughan volunteered to be 'door man'.

At the time of this first audition, I was paired with an experienced detective, by the unusual name of Jack Shults. He was an interesting individual, who possessed the primary requirement of a Metropolitan Police officer – a good sense of humour. He was the great grandson of a German immigrant who had arrived in London just prior to the First World War and the family had dropped the 'Z' in Shultz, due to anti-German sentiment.

His grandfather, Jack Shults, had been killed on the Western Front in 1915 while serving as a sniper with the British Army. I had, the previous year, taken Jack to the lonely grave at Quarry Cemetery in France. I had mentioned to 'Von Shults' that I was auditioning for singers that night and he said he would 'Send his boy along as he was nineteen and just what we were looking for.' I said, 'What's his voice like?' He said, 'Elvis.' His son John had arrived at the house soon after Barry and they were soon getting on famously and tearing into the beer

With the room buzzing like a saloon bar, I announced we would draw lots for the order of auditions. I had penned the lyrics to 'Send In The Clowns' in huge print on the back of a roll of wallpaper and pinned it to an old door, which was propped in the corner of the room. Lots were drawn and some of the guys were visibly nervous, but Barry just stepped forward and said, 'I'll go first.' He never bothered to draw a ticket.

At this point Vaughan was upstairs in the kitchen on the phone to some keen Caruso, who had got lost en route to Hemel Hempstead. He remembers,

> There was this dipstick on the phone, who was asking for directions to the audition. He had got lost in Tring. Then I heard this voice from below. *Isn't it rich? Are we a pair? Me here at last on the ground, You in mid-air, Where are the clowns?* I said to the dipstick, 'Don't bother coming mate!' and put the phone down. Linda and I rushed down the stairs to see who was the possessor of that fabulous voice.

The room was stunned to silence as Barry Elliott sang all four verses of 'Send In The Clowns' without looking once at the lyrics. The hair stood up on the back of my neck. It was brilliant. He started the song in the key of D and finished in D. There was huge applause. I looked at Linda and her face told me we had found the singer to replace Mike. Ralph was facing me and simply mouthed, 'Fucking hell.' I said, 'Who's next?'

John Shults bravely stepped forward. 'I can't follow that.' He said meekly. 'But I'll have a go.' Four or five blokes promptly left. As one said, 'No way can I follow that Mate! Take him on now.' Young Shults had a go and merely confirmed the fact that his Dad had a sense of humour.

Mike Jones left the band being FS and with absolute WT but on good terms with us all. His last gig was Saturday 12 February 1983, at the Bedford Moat House Hotel. He fondly recollects;

Mixed Feelings was a great team of musicians and good friends. I had a great time in that band and to be perfectly honest, with hindsight, I wish I had remained longer.

The following Saturday, Barry Elliott walked on to the stage at Mountbatten Pavilion, Thorpe Park, to a packed house. He opened with the Neil Diamond song 'Hello Again' then went into 'I Write The Songs', part of a classy Barry Manilow medley, arranged by Ralph.

People were simply stunned by his opening set and those not dancing stood to applaud. His voice made the hairs rise at the back of my neck. He had the audience baying for him and as Linda commented, 'If Mike Jones was the classiest singer, Barry was the sexiest.' As one female fan commented, 'He can park his slippers under my bed, anytime.' Could Barry take us into the West End?

We had a blinding Summer of 1983, performing at over sixty events, none of which were in the West End, The big bands still ruled. We were still a five-piece band and at the end of 1983 our main agents were: Enterprol, Templar, Diane Rowley and Crown Entertainments.

December 1983 looked like this:

DECEMBER
Friday 2 Crest Hotel. Heathrow.
Sat 3 Beverley School New Malden.
Wed 7 Met Police Club Bushey. Harrow Rd. Christmas Dance.
Fri 9 Boreham Wood Civic Hall
Sat 10 Luton Chiltern Hotel
Tue 13 Spread Eagle Hotel. Thame.
Wed 14 Spread Eagle Hotel Thame.
Fri 16 Bushey Police Club. (Ruislip Police)
Sat 17 Bushey Police Club. (Paddington Police)
Wed 21 Waggon & Horses Shenley. (Lynton Electrical)
Thu 22 Holiday Inn. Swiss Cottage.
Wed 28 Luton Chiltern Hotel.
Sat 31 Bushey Police Club

It was all massive fun and I was now on 'stage two', (love and money). I have *never* regarded being a musician as 'hard work', even when we were travelling hundreds of miles every weekend. We were doing something we loved and if anything, it was 'tiring' but *never* 'hard work'. Any musician or singer who regards the job as 'hard work' should not be in the profession. In all honesty, we earned good money from a 'hobby' and like all hobbies, practised and practised until we came good. I always looked forward to the next gig, planning how it would go, what clothes we should wear and learning the bass parts for new songs; for the further we got the less we rehearsed.

Vaughan Rance, not always generous in his praise, said,

> I knew then, I wanted to be in a band and getting into Mixed
> Feelings which was the best band on the circuit – and known
> for it - was the pinnacle of my music career. The band of
> course got to where it was because of Jon's drive, tenacity and
> determination, unmatched before or since.

1984 started well and during January we did our first gig at the Pressed Steel Fisher Club, Oxford. This later became the Austin-Rover Club and boasted a massive ballroom, which could accommodate a thousand people.

We were introduced to the venue by the Harrow-based agency, *Enterprol*. The main booker at that oddly named company was Joanne Tremayne, a friendly lady who knew the entertainment business inside out. She also loved our band. Over the years we did many gigs at this great 'Factory Club' venue in Oxford, including the 1999-2000 Millennium Ball. We often backed singers and supported bands, including The Fortunes, Freddy and the Dreamers, The Rockin' Berries, Gerry and the Pacemakers and The Merseybeats.

On this first occasion at the club, we were backing Dave Berry who had a string of top ten hits in the '60s such as 'Memphis Tennessee', 'The Crying Game' and 'Little Things'. He was quite dour and kept himself to himself, turning up for his sound check smartly dressed in a nice suit and overcoat, carrying a brief case.

He would also don a leather jacket when he went on stage to hide his microphone, which was part of his act. In the dressing room I noticed that when he opened his briefcase it contained a bottle of Johnny Walker. He never offered us 'sippers' but sat there quietly, acquired a glass and drank the lot himself. It didn't seem to affect his act.

As usual, the best singer at the event was Barry, who stole the show and got us further lucrative gigs at the venue, some of which were for Oxford Police and the organiser, Constable Wally Cox, assured me the gigs would, 'Keep coming as long as we had Barry!'

Like all the other function bands we never wrote our own stuff but did everyone else's songs, for which we had to complete the usual Performing Rights slip at every venue. We would discuss what new songs we should do and I would then play them to Linda, who would dance to them. 'If it's not danceable, don't do it,' was her straightforward advice.

Ralph reminded me that Dick Henninghem hated playing waltzes and quicksteps, but our audiences consisted of a high proportion of 'strict tempo twats', so it was good form to open the show with a waltz. 'Moon River' and 'Are You Lonesome Tonight?', both in the key of C, slotted together nicely. Properly sung, it would instantly win over the crowd, as Barry never failed to do.

Ralph also commented,

> Dick threatened to resign when you announced we were going to do 'The Birdy Song!' He point blank, refused to play it! But friendly persuasion on your part, like hiding his pipe, finally got him to play it.

Sometimes I felt like ramming the pipe up his arse but I did sympathise with his assessment that it was 'a fucking dreadful record.' Some sort of silly German 'Oompah' tune, but it got the crowd doing the stupid actions and wagging their elbows in the air. Thankfully the fad didn't last long and we soon dropped it.

As for Dick, I wrote in my diary, 'Biggus Dickus is an awkward fucker and refuses to wear a Kippah for the Jewish National Anthem. He says he will play it, but not wearing a fucking hat.' I commented that Dick looked a remarkable understudy for Fagin. Vaughan more scathingly said 'He looks like a rat poking his nose out of a hedge.' Dick saw the funny side and reluctantly wore the Kippah, generally after being plied with lashings of 'Vera & Phil'.

In the August of that year, we shared the stage at the Twickenham Rose Room, the HQ of the English Rugby Football Union, with Luton based band, Footz. The lead singer was Nikki Brightman, the sister of Sarah Brightman. I decided, there and then, that I would have to get a female singer for Mixed Feelings. It would add an extra string to our bow and probably allow me to achieve my desire of gigging in the West

End. I took her telephone number but could see she was quite happy in her own band. It would be some time before I could steal her.

I was also friends with bandleader Mike Jordan, from Harlow in Essex. I spoke to the chatty Essex boy Mike, most days and went and saw his band on a number of occasions. Mike's wife, Vanessa, fronted the band and was a powerful singer. Mike was the guitarist and also sang lead vocals.

When I stopped off to see them on my way home from 'Late Turn', they were performing at the Watford Hilton Hotel and they started their show with the song 'Chanson D'Amour', not my kind of number for opening a party, but beautifully sung. 'Nessie' also ran a busy entertainment agency and they started to give us a lot of gigs. The name of their band was, JJ Flame, a name I really liked, but they later changed it to the mundane Spotlights.

Mike was an experienced bandleader, having been through the holiday camps. I learned a lot from him. He mentioned a London agent and impresario, Michael Black and gave me his phone number, suggesting I call him.

Within a month Michael Black had us booked in the West End. We were at the London Hilton Hotel. It was a Friday night gig and Michael paid the band the sum of £250. We were on in the main ballroom and appearing to a thousand people from a City bank. Michael brought his sweary secretary, Marcia, with him and she showed me to the Green Room.

She was running the show, although Michael kept us entertained with a supply of blue jokes while we were setting up. We enjoyed a nice dinner of lamb chops and roast spuds. We had already changed when Marcia appeared in the doorway, 'You're on! You're on! For fuck's sake! Come on! Get on that fucking stage!' Impelled by the level of obscenities thrown at us, we left the dressing room at top speed and ran down the stairs to the ballroom. As we were about to go on stage, she said to me, 'Have you left a tip for the waiter?' I replied in the negative. 'You always leave a fucking tip for the waiter!' So I ran back up the stairs and left a five-pound note on the table. When I got back to the stage she said, 'Where the fuck have you been?' I said, 'To leave a tip for the waiter.' She said, 'I didn't mean now you silly fucker! Get your fucking arse on that stage and get going!'

We got going all right. Lesson learned from Marcia. Always leave a fucking tip for the waiter. Otherwise as Michael rightly advised, 'He will piss in your fucking beer.'

In spite of the tantrums from Marcia, both she and Michael liked the band, who did a storming gig and left the crowd baying for more. They booked us back immediately, for the following year. Michael was also impressed with Barry's powerful voice. 'Where did you find him, Son?' But not impressed with Barry's tattooed fingers, one hand spelling 'Love' the other spelling 'Hate'. From then on, Michael insisted that Barry covered the tattoos with stage-make up whenever we worked for him. 'We can't have him looking like a fucking drug dealer, Son!'

So began a lasting relationship with Michael Black and we stayed closely in touch until his death in 2018. We hit it off, probably because I was a police officer turned bandleader, the notion of which he liked. He name-dropped several senior Scotland Yard officers who he claimed were his 'best' mates. Michael enjoyed his legendary status as an old-fashioned agent and pantomime villain. He was one of the last of the 'old school' characters to grace the West End. There were very few like him that had his vigour and zest for life. He told massively, exaggerated and funny stories about the music business. No-one knew more about it than Michael Black. He was always immaculate and had represented the best of British and American stars. Having virtually cornered the market for 'high-end' bookings at many of London's leading hotels, he acquired the nickname of 'Champagne Charlie, the King of Park Lane'.

I will always remember one gig at the Hilton, when he walked on to the stage and wrote the cheque out for the band while we were actually performing! He tore it out of the book and stuck it in my top pocket. Next on stage was the '60s band, The Searchers. He did exactly the same, writing out the cheque on the stage, in the middle of 'Needles & Pins' and sticking it into Mike Pender's top pocket, before flamboyantly replacing the top on his fountain pen.

Michael was a 'Water-Rat' and married to Julie Rogers, the '60s singer who had a monster hit with 'The Wedding'. He was the elder brother of the lyricist, Don Black. He also told me that he used to be the booker at Cesar's Palace at Luton, the California Ballroom at Dunstable and the Palace at Wolverton! He had been good friends with Brian Epstein and had attempted to buy The Beatles from him over lunch in

1963, for a million pounds. According to Michael, Brian had told him to 'Get fucked!'

There were very few stars who didn't know Michael Black, whether they liked him or not is another matter, as he was the self-proclaimed 'Jewish Robin Hood'. 'I rob the rich to pay myself!' At one time, he represented Bruce Forsyth, Shirley Bassey, Dave Allen, Des O'Connor, Jimmy Tarbuck and Tom Jones.

As an agent I found him ruthless. He always came straight to the point. 'What you need is a girl singer, Son. Then we can really talk business.'

We were well into 1985 and Mixed Feelings were playing all types of events but only breaking the ice in the West End. I had spoken to Ralph and we both thought a girl singer would give us extra 'clout' (in more ways than one). Barry was doing magnificently and everywhere we performed they wanted us back.

However, there came a very sad occasion, not only for the Metropolitan Police but for the British nation, when on Sunday, 6th October, 1985, PC Keith Blakelock was savagely murdered at Broadwater Farm, Tottenham, during a riot. The dust had barely settled after the tragedy, when it was suggested that a fund-raising concert for Keith's family should be organised.

I initially suggested Bushey Police Club as a venue, with the object of Mixed Feelings doing a series of money-raising performances there, but this was going to be far bigger than that. I was promptly elected on to the advisory committee with a search for a suitable 'free' West End Venue. Andrew Lloyd Webber came to the rescue and offered his magnificent Palace Theatre in Shaftesbury Avenue. He had an available changeover date from one musical to another, which was Tuesday 12th November. We grabbed it.

Soon there was an array of stars all wishing to give their time for this worthy cause. It was difficult to know who to leave out. The show, ably directed by Colin Burring, was an emotional occasion.

Mixed Feelings were limited to just two songs and for one of those we had to back a singing Met Police Officer, Ken Palmer, who was a Neil Diamond mimic. His chosen song was 'Love On The Rocks'. For the one song we were to do, I chose a song by Barry Manilow, which I hoped would have a dramatic effect on the 1,400 strong sell-out crowd.

I wanted the theatre lights to be turned down for 'One Voice Singing In The Darkness', leaving a single spotlight on Barry.

The band was introduced by compere, Jimmy Tarbuck, with the words: 'It's always nice when Police and civilians get together to form a band and there is no better example than Mixed Feelings.'

Were we nervous? Yes, terrified, but Barry sang brilliantly and the three-part harmony with Vaughan and I slotted in beautifully. The sound was great too and we got thunderous applause. It was a massive venue and Dick Heninnghem remembered;

> It was a full house but I was not nervous until the curtain went up and I realised that the audience didn't stretch backwards but upwards, which made you feel like a fish in a goldfish bowl. However, I enjoyed the finale and standing alongside Sir Harry Secombe singing 'Land of Hope and Glory', backed by the London Philharmonic Orchestra.

There were many stars on the bill and the first half, compered by Jim Davidson, gave a chance for the Met Police to show off its hidden talent. I was talking to Jim, with whom we would do many more shows, in the wings and he asked me if I knew his brother, Billy, who was a detective at Wood Green. The second half featured several popular acts of the time, including the cast of *Eastenders*. There followed a nice 'after show' party, attended by Elizabeth Blakelock and the boys, Mark, Kevin and Lee. We all tried to be cheerful in view of the circumstances. As Jim Davidson said to the audience, 'With Maggie's help we'll get it right.'

We took a lot of spin-off gigs as the result of our brilliant performance at the Keith Blakelock Memorial Concert. Many were for Police events and we naturally preferred to do functions for the Police, during those dangerous days of IRA atrocities, in the relative safety of a Police Club.

There were four good clubs in the corners of the Metropolitan Police District. Our favourite and most local, was Bushey in Hertfordshire, then there was The Warren in Kent, Imber Court in Surrey and Chigwell in Essex. We performed at many enjoyable events at all four venues over the years, but I was sometimes concerned when a 'Nick' chose to hold a Christmas Party at a civilian venue.

Such was the case when we were booked by Holloway Police to perform at their Christmas Party on Thursday, 5th December, 1985.

The event was to be held at the Gresham Ballroom in the Holloway Road. This was another Irish dancehall, far scruffier than the National Ballroom at Kilburn.

The stage was filthy and the room stank of stale beer and piss. Nevertheless, the staff seemed 'friendly' towards the local police, as they arrived with their predictably attractive women, in small clusters, shuffling around to find a suitable table. In the tradition of warm Irish hospitality, we were given several pints of Guinness as we set up our gear.

As the evening progressed, I noticed that the event had been gate-crashed by several suited males with big sideboards and bellies, drinking at the bar. We played the usual background pop music over our sound system and stood at the bar as the 150 plus crowd tucked into a Christmas dinner.

We played our usual first half set with a mixture of popular hits from the '60s and present day but this crowd were bloody hard work. No one danced and they simply sat there in the chilly damp surroundings, supping Guinness and eying us suspiciously as if to say 'Go on then, entertain us. Let's see how good you are.'

It was one of those rare gigs where you want to get it over with as soon as possible and go home. Usually we loved performing and showing off but even Barry was a bit subdued as he necked the free brandy. At the welcome interval, there occurred the typical Police raffle, which consisted mainly of donated bottles of spirits, the usual portable colour TV and a pair of free tickets for the next Arsenal home game.

We went over to the crowded bar and one of the wholesome female bar staff asked Barry to sing 'something Irish' in the second half. She gave her name as Dolores and she possessed eye-riveting 'jubblies' which mesmerised Barry, who was a confirmed 'tit man'. I promised her we would 'play something Irish'. In response we were given more brandy and Guinness.

Towards the end of the evening, as there were still very few people on the dance floor, I announced 'a song for Dolores' and Barry sang a beautiful version of the famous 'Londonderry Air'. It drew scant applause from the grumpy Old Bill but the red-faced infiltrators of the Irish fraternity cheered, whistled and clapped. Then as Vaughan Rance remembers;

> All of a sudden there was a massive punch up with some of the
> local Paddies in the bar. Apparently, it was caused by the band
> playing a certain song, which stirred up Irish Nationalism. The

Coppers took the piss out of it and violence followed. A few days later, I was interviewed by a senior London, police officer at my home. He was dealing with a serious complaint of assaults on the Paddies by some police officers at the event. He asked me, 'What was the actual song you played that sparked off the fight?' I replied, 'I can't remember.' He said, 'Look I'm not supposed to say this but does "Danny Boy" give you a clue?'

We never got booked back.

6

WHAT KUNG FU DAT?

To say I was disappointed when Vaughan dropped the bombshell that he was leaving the band is an understatement. He seemed happy and had earned himself enough money to buy himself a nice Ford XR3. He was a good mate and I greatly enjoyed his company. But money is not everything. I suspected he had WT. He remembered,

> It was a decision I didn't make lightly. But I felt I wanted to spend more time with my wife and babies. Mixed Feelings were getting very busy and taking me away from home. Three nights a week was great for the extra cash when you are bringing up a young family and need the money. But I was missing my family.

There were plenty of drummers out there. Most kids with musical ambition at some time want to be a drummer. It seems an easy ride to bang a drum along to the latest pop tunes, but drums are not the easiest of instruments to properly master. The sort of drummer I was looking for in Mixed Feelings would be like Vaughan, brilliant and daft. One who could make me laugh. I had already discovered that *all* drummers were bonkers.

The search continued, while Vaughan continued to hold the fort. Linda, as always, reassured me I would find someone as good. Mixed Feelings was a five-piece band with one male vocalist and I was the only backing singer. We needed a top harmony voice. We tried out other drummers.

Vaughan, who was 'standing in' when needed, phoned me. 'All correct Sarge. I have located a brilliant drummer! He can sing and he likes real ale. His name is Terry Wilson and he lives in Hemel too!' 'Is he as daft as you?' I jokingly asked, 'He is as silly as fuck!' was Vaughan's reply. He was not wrong.

I phoned Terry Wilson immediately. He was playing in a local band called Bootleg and they were booked into the Heath Park Hotel on Saturday lunchtime. On Sunday, Terry was performing in a local Jazz band at Snooks Bar, which was located under Hemel Pavilion. It was a weekend off and I would go to both venues and watch him play.

I watched Bootleg, which was a four-piece band fronted by Martin Constable, on guitar and lead vocals. Terry seemed a good rock drummer and sang 'Lucille' which was in the key of C and very high. His voice was very good but I couldn't tell from Bootleg whether he could play all styles. I didn't say much to him but went to see him next day at Snooks.

The smoky Snooks Bar was a popular Sunday lunchtime venue in Hemel Hempstead, as it held Jazz sessions. It was a good council-run bar. More like an English pub, selling Charles Wells Bedford ales and well-run, by witty ex-school master, Mick Jones. Children were banned too, an excellent plus.

I got to like Snooks Bar and the people that ran it. A great music venue, with superb acoustics but the Jazz was simply 'OK' for me. I was not a Jazz lover and never have been. I found it boring to the ears although I greatly respected the musicians who could play it. Jazz is 'music for musicians'. I have never appreciated it and never listen to it at home.

Snooks was almost empty, with probably twenty people or so, scattered around. I noticed that the Hemel Jazz fans purchased their clothes from charity shops, were usually bearded and purchased a half a pint of Eagle bitter, which would last them two hours. Some were even drinking tea or coffee. Sacrilege on a Sunday lunchtime! (A pub is for drinking beer!) Just the sort of customers a pub didn't need. The takings behind the bar must have been abysmal but who cared? Staff wages were paid for out of the public purse.

The Savill Row was an excellent 'mainstream' jazz band and I saw a different Terry Wilson. The band was run by Dave Savill, a superb local trumpet player and consisted mainly of local musicians. There were seven of them and they played all the American Jazz standards. I watched Terry closely. He was certainly a great Jazz drummer. He played a tiny Gretsch kit with only one tom-tom. He did a drum solo, doubtless to impress me, which lasted for two pints of Bombardier.

After a beer with him at the bar I warmed to him. He had a cheeky 'David Essex' face and when he laughed, you laughed with him. I needed to know more about this chirpy little feller and invited him to my house for a beer the following night.

Linda and the boy had gone to bed when Terry turned up as agreed at 9.00pm. He was a spot on timekeeper, although not always on the drums as I would soon find out. Especially after he had guzzled four pints of London Pride. He brought a dozen bottles of Becks 'Frau-Basher' with him. Scoring points all the time.

Soon his tongue was loosened and he told me how chuffed he was to be considered for the position of drummer in Mixed Feelings. He would of course have to give Bootleg a month's notice, to find another drummer and although they were only a club band, they had a few gigs. Loyalty I would find, was one of Terry's attributes. As Terry said,

> I liked Jon and we hit it off immediately. I knew he ran the best band for miles around and they were doing top events. I told him I would eventually get a Yamaha kit if I got the job. I was excited at the prospect. We had a few beers and I asked him if he was interested in some 'blow'. He said that he 'might be' and asked me what I had got and where I had got it. I told him I had some 'Black Afghan' in the car, which I had got from a mate in Snooks. I also asked him if he liked porn. Fucking stupid question I suppose. What man doesn't? He said he did, so I shot out to the car and brought back a dozen or so videos and a bag of blow.

'Here you go,' he said. 'This lot is for you!' He dumped them on the sofa and then asked me what I did for a day job. I replied, 'I am a Sergeant in the Metropolitan Police.' His face went white. He said 'You are fucking joking!' He held out his wrists and said, 'Fucking hell, Sarge nick me now.' I told him he had got the job and he could keep the dope.

When I looked at the VHS film titles, I was amused to see one called *Down on the Farm* and another called *Donkey Sanctuary*. A daft and 'deviant' drummer had joined the band.

Terry said,

> Joining Mixed Feelings was my dream come true. All the years of drum practising as a kid had paid off. I couldn't wait to tell my friends and family. It was like winning the lottery.

Terry's first gig with the band was on Saturday 8th February, 1986 at the Wolsey Hall, Cheshunt, where we were performing for the local Post Office. We were still a five–piece band which consisted of Dick Henninghem (keyboards) Ralph Lewin (guitar) Barry Elliott (vocals) Terry Wilson (drums) and myself on the bass guitar.

Our show was a challenge, with numbers and medleys that most semi-pro bands would never attempt, including 'War Of The Worlds', 'Toccata', 'Music' (John Miles), 'Electric Dreams' and still, 'American Trilogy'. In spite of my limited skills on bass, we even did a good version of Paul Young's 'Come Back And Stay' and I managed to emulate the sound of a fretless bass on the Fender by slurring the strings and reducing the treble and bass controls, thereby producing an earthy, 'wooden' tone.

It was easy to change the tone of my superb Fender during a live performance and it never failed me. Our adventurous choice of music was testament to the keyboard skills of Dick Henninghem and the guitar wizardry of Ralph Lewin that ensured the phone kept ringing.

I was still hankering for West End gigs but for this, we would definitely need a girl singer. Terry suggested we should get one with 'big tits and nice arse' as he would be sitting behind her. Plus, he said it would 'sell the band'. As it happened he was not far wrong in ideas of salesmanship. Barry didn't want a female in the band, 'Why-aye man, what da ye wanna fucking bird in the band forrah? She'll be a load a fucking trouble.'

I placed an ad in *The Stage* newspaper in the summer of 1986 and several girls turned up at my house for an audition. We auditioned twenty in one night, but only one was any good. Debbie Lee had the warmest voice of the lot. I was however, totally inexperienced at managing female singers, although not at managing women. Women police officers were usually easy to manage, self-disciplined, smart and reliable. Female singers are a different species and often carry baggage.

Debbie was no exception. She couldn't drive and would require a lift to gigs and a lift home. If someone was London-bound then that could be arranged. Sometimes her partner, Kevin, would drop her off and stay to watch the gig. To get Debbie home safely to north London, was a huge responsibility for me as a bandleader. I felt liable for her safety. From then on, I made certain that all applicants for Mixed Feelings had their own transport. Nevertheless, Debbie dressed the part and looked sexy on stage; she was a pretty girl with a great voice. There were certain songs she sang brilliantly. Especially 'Till', a powerful Tom Jones, ballad.

We changed the show around and opened with songs like, 'Heartbreaker', which pissed Barry off, as he was the star of the show and never wanted a girl in the band in the first place. No way was any woman going to steal his thunder.

Fellow bandleader, Dave Bedford, endorsed the quality of Debbie's lovely voice, describing it as 'golden'. Previously she had sang with his band Silver Heart. Debbie remembers,

> I saw an advert in *The Stage* and phoned you. Kevin and I came to see Mixed Feelings at a gig at Hemel Hempstead Pavilion. I remember we were knocked out by Barry's performance. Barry's opening number was the Brenda Lee song, 'All Alone Am I', then into the Skeeter Davis hit, 'End Of The World'. I know that I went on to sing that medley on my own, when I joined and it became a firm favourite of mine. I finally got the job when I came to your house in Hemel Hempstead to audition and we went to the basement where the band was all set up. After I had sang a couple of songs, your wife heard me from upstairs and came down to listen to more. She seemed impressed.

As Debbie said herself, 'They were heady, crazy days' and she fitted admirably into a macho hard-drinking band. Our first gig with Debbie was at Morris Motors, Oxford, on Saturday 20th September, 1986. We enjoyed a good autumn of gigs that year and she certainly added another spectrum of talent to the band. From then on, we were never without a female singer on major events.

Debbie enjoyed a drink too and in spite of Barry's misgivings about girl singers, they seemed to get on well. On stage she was always immaculate and with her good selection of transparent stage clothes, she could hold the attention of the men in the crowd with her sexy dancing and her golden voice.

Eventually she got rather competitive in the band 'drinking forum' and began to match Barry in the guzzling stakes. She was 'one of the boys' and was a good laugh. We were often given a free bar at many events, a nice perk which would sometimes lead to mayhem within the band and affect performance.

Barry was never a 'real ale twat' like the rest of us but preferred a dangerous French drink, called brandy, as he was under the illusion that it was, 'good for his voice'. Sometimes he would mix it with a generous measure of port. He would often sup from a large glass of lemonade and brandy, which looked like a pint of lager. A short raffle break would often see Barry guzzle a half-pint of Courvoisier (if it was free) which would cause a dramatic change from a smooth voice, to 'I can shout the loudest' during the second half of the show.

A few derisory 'fucks' would be thrown in too, mainly aimed at me, who was calling the shots. I managed to keep Barry under control for most of the time but he didn't need much encouragement to have a drink. The new drummer, as brilliant as he was, was no help either. He soon hit it off on the gulping stakes with Barry and the pair of them became a pain in the ass.

Following one or two off-stage 'vodka and bitter lemon' fuelled rows with Barry - as to who would sing what - it eventually became noticeable to all, that Debbie was also pressing the self-destruct button. Barry would jokingly mock her new stage dress and she would take the bait and a flaming row would ensue. Debbie was also very funny when she had a drink. On New Year's Eve at Bushey, to the amusement of the crowd, she lay on her back and peered up the piper's kilt.

It was worrying me and although I liked a drink, if it continued on the dangerous level attained, then one of them was going to have to go as they were continually sniping at each other. I just didn't have the nerve to sack her. I was saved that headache on Saturday 24th January, 1987 when the band had been booked to perform at a corporate event at the Hatfield Lodge Hotel.

The band had torn through the first half with terrific renditions of Giorgio Moroder's 'Electric Dreams' and 'Never Ending Story'. The dance floor was totally packed in that mediocre venue. At half time we had gone to the bar, where for some reason Barry got stuck into a furious row with Debbie who had burst into tears and ran off to the bedroom allocated to us for changing, with a cry of 'You wait till I tell my Kevin!'

With just five minutes to go until the second half, I went to the room accompanied by Terry and Barry, to ensure Debbie was OK. I had a spare key and we found that Debbie had locked herself in the en-suite bathroom. 'Are you gonna sack her tonight?' asks Barry. 'No I'm not.' 'Why-aye man! Then let me fucking do it! 'I've already fucking telt her at the bar she was fucking sacked!' He then shouts, 'Oy! youse in there, ya fucking bitch, youse is fucking gannin from this band youse is!'

Did I need this? The band is due back on any moment. Barry bangs on the bathroom door, 'Oy! I need a fucking piss and if youse don't come out, I'm gonna kick the fucking door in.' With that, the door flies open and there stands Debbie, changed into her silver mini-dress, with tear-stained mascara running down her cheeks. She promptly administers a high kick, straight into Barry's Jacobs. Barry goes down like he is shot and curls up on the floor, 'Ooya bastad! Ooya fucker!' If that's what you get for sacking a girl singer then count me out.

The show goes on and both singers surprisingly got on with it. Barry needed another half bottle of Courvoisier to settle himself and belted out the very high, 'Everlasting Love', remarkably in tune. Maybe the bollock adjustment worked. Love Affair it wasn't but as Terry remembered, 'it was the funniest thing he ever saw.'

Debbie left the band soon after to spend more time with her baby son. She says she cannot remember much of what happened in those 'crazy days' but in spite of the drunken rows, she remained friends with Barry, who eventually found lodgings with her. I never saw Debbie again but her son Kevin is now a roadie for Mixed Feelings and a singer in his own band. Debbie was a brilliant singer and remains a fond memory plus lesson learned about female singers. *Always* put your hands over your valuables when sacking one.

On Sunday 28th September 1986 I had put a note in my diary, 'Ivan acted up last night'. On the night in question we had performed at the Oakley Court Hotel in Windsor Great Park. 'Ivan the 'orrible', as named by Ralph, was our first 'roadie' and had been recommended to me by Dave West, a local bass player who had performed in Wham.

A busy band like Mixed Feelings needed a roadie, provided we could afford one. These useful utilities come in all shapes and sizes, male or female. For many years we had an excellent female roadie who was romantically attached to my son. Very few of these 'Edweak Armstrongs' hold a driver's licence. Many wore a Hawkwind T shirt.

Ivan was a strange one. Barry had also met him at 'The Horns' pub in Watford. A chunky little chap, aged about twenty-eight, clean shaven with a flat-top hair cut. He was highly combustible, especially after drinking Stella Artois.

He told me he had once been a roadie for Wham, whereby his pay had been five quid and six cans of lager per gig. He said he had been sacked for fighting. So I thought he might be useful if we ran into any trouble.

The Oakley Court was a pleasant place to play, although hardly geared up for Rock bands. It was classed as 'posh' as it lay on the edge of Windsor Great Park and on this occasion, we were to perform in a small marquee on the lawn.

The previous weekend we had played at a raucous Essex wedding and the stage had been 'invaded' by several macho males and a few tangerine-tinted, female Bacardi Bruisers. They all thought they could sing better than Barry. One had to incorporate 'friendly persuasion' to get them leave the stage.

Drunks, who climb uninvited onto the stage, are in layman's terms, a fucking nuisance. They are a danger to the musicians, as they are unpredictable and are usually carrying three-quarters of a pint of lager, held at such an angle it would be spilled into the vocal monitors. 'I wanna sing, Johnny be Good ' was the usual demand.

There then usually followed, 'Gimmee that fuckin' mic.' The immediate reaction of any bandleader was then - and still is — 'Get the fuck off my stage!' Bearing in mind, you have *every right* to throw the intruder physically off the stage. Not only are they invading your space and threatening your valuable equipment, they are a danger to life.

In all practicality, I had developed a knack of talking 'nice' to the unwanted guest and they would leave the stage with no problem. The only exception allowed was the client who was paying the band, or maybe the bride and groom who would be invited up by the band to say or sing, goodbye.

There are further scary stories of stage invaders later.

This was Ivan's first gig and he was keen to make an impression. I had told him that part of his 'duties' as a roadie was to ensure the safety of the stage. 'If anybody steps onto the stage and you get the nod from me, you are to come and remove them by speaking to them nicely.' Ivan grunted, 'Righto Jon!'

They were a predominantly 'senior' crowd at this event, so I chose to open with a waltz, 'Three Times A Lady' is an easy one, whereby a bass-playing bandleader could play the lines without concentration and look to the next song.

The ambience at the Oakley Court was pleasant. Several silver-haired couples were abundantly showing off how well they could waltz, quickstep and dance in formation. Dozens of black-suited, black-tied males, with their wives glamorously attired in colourful satin ball gowns came spinning and sweeping past the band. This was a posh event where Freemasonry reigned, so I decided to slip from one waltz to another, a simple one, 'Moon River.'

The couples were all vying for the centre of the 'Come Dancing' floor, when a dear old boy of about eighty or so, who looked like Bruce Forsyth, tripped over the corner of the stage in his oversize patent shoes and dragged his elderly wife down on top of him, both of them sprawled on the stage.

It was so comical, but suddenly our Ivan was among them. It was like a loose maul at Twickenham. He had the old man in a headlock. He then proceeded to drag him off the stage by his head and along the dance floor with the old girl rolling off the stage and kicking her legs up like an overturned wood louse. Thereby Ivan, released his stranglehold and stood there sticking out his chest and mouthing, 'Fuck off or you'll get some more.'

Other concerned guests helped the shocked dancers to their feet while Ivan pointed at me as he brushed his hands together and said, '*He* told me to do it.' Thankfully no one was injured and I sent over a bottle of the cheapest champagne to their table, which was met with agreeable nods.

The compensation culture had not yet been conceived.

Ivan did a few more gigs with us but had a thirst for lager on a massive scale. He finally got his marching orders after getting pissed at the Twickenham Rose Room, after which he chased Barry around the car park. Barry had used the Geordie vernacular, 'Howay man, ya fucking thick bastad,' which Ivan had interpreted as a good reason to murder him. 'Don't you ever call me fick!'

I had long admired Nikki Brightman and cannot deny that being the younger sister of Sarah Brightman was not an influence on me. I would love her in my band. Properly marketed, she would sell us. I had long regarded the signing of singers and musicians as like scouting for football players. If you could offer them better money they would usually come.

There was something unique about Nikki with her Gothic looks. Good to look at and listen to, she had her own transport too. I had mentioned to her at the 'Twickers' gig if she might be interested in joining Mixed Feelings and she replied in the affirmative. She also said she was bored with her day job at David Doyle's Estate Agents in Boxmoor, Hemel Hempstead. The amount of gigs that Mixed Feelings were doing meant she could give that up and become a professional singer.

I duly turned up at her quiet office the Thursday morning after Debbie had left and Nikki was the only one there. She made me a cup off coffee and we enjoyed a chat. She joined the band.

Nikki proved excellent on her first gig, which was Friday 30th January 1987 at Kempton Park Racecourse. She knew stacks of songs and easily handled the Tina Turner belters, although she soon found Barry impossible to harmonize with, as he would just sing louder. Her voice was very different to the shrill voice of her famous sister and in my opinion far richer. I asked Barry what he thought of Nikki. 'Why aye man. She's got lovely big tits.'

Ralph told me that he was getting fed up with Barry's boozy antics. I could well understand why. I never could comprehend why so talented a singer would want to self-combust. Barry was now lodging with Terry who was hit with WT and had become single again.

As long as I could keep Barry off the brandy it would be OK, I told myself. But it was not to be and I was fighting a losing battle. I was half expecting the phone call, when he rang from the pub. He was pissed and said he was moving back to Newcastle. I was so disappointed and I had another sleepless night. He had been in the band for four years.

As Howard Robbins, London Toastmaster commented,

> Barry was undoubtedly the best singer on the circuit at that time. His voice was just unique. I will never forget his rendition of 'I Should Have Known Better' by Jim Diamond. He actually sang it better! I can remember the catering girls drooling over him. He certainly put you in the frame for many Jewish events. I loved his voice and fast became a fan of Mixed Feelings. You were without doubt, the best band around at that time.

Barry was also a good mate and had lived with me for nine months after turning up on my doorstep one Sunday afternoon, carrying an acoustic guitar and a plastic carrier bag containing his total earthly possessions. He had finally, been thrown out by his long-suffering partner. His only comment was, 'Ooh Jon. There's hell on!'

Barry would spend the next few years living temporarily between Edgware, Hemel Hempstead or Newcastle, wherever he could 'lay his hat'. He kept singing, as it was his only source of income. He kept in touch with me and before long he would be hankering to come back to the band.

So I advertised again in the good old *Stage* newspaper for male singers. I was worried. I never thought I could replace Mike Jones let alone Barry. I have never suffered from depression but I was certainly dejected. People were paying honest money for the band based on Barry being there. I could not let them down. I had to find a good male singer and quickly.

The day *The Stage* ad appeared, Mick Mullane called me. He sounded a real upbeat guy and turned up at for his audition driving a 1937 Austin Seven. I liked him immediately and he was just the tonic I needed. A good-looking lad with an adaptable and accurate voice, with which he could switch from Frankie Valli to Elvis Presley. He was a former member of the Stutz Bear Cats, a vocal group, that I had seen on TV.

I offered him the job immediately and he instantly hit it off with Nikki. He was the first singer to bring an element of comedy to the band. His Stan Laurel antics and expressions tied many an audience in knots of laughter. My brother Mark remarked,

I never thought you could replace Barry but each time someone left, you went one step further with a better and a different style of singer. Mick Mullane was brilliant, had a wonderful voice and made me laugh. His antics on stage were just brilliant. I remember him 'tossing the caber' with a long cardboard carpet tube at Hemel Hempstead Pavilion. It was almost as if Mixed Feelings had become a comedy band.

Mick did the first of his many gigs with the band, at the Spider's Web Hotel, Watford on Saturday 25th April 1987. A major difference from Barry was that Mick was a natural harmony singer and could sing an incredible falsetto with Nikki. The brilliant song 'I Know Him So Well', from the musical *Chess* sounded just like Elaine Page and Barbara Dixon. I suggested to Nikki that we should do some songs from *Phantom of the Opera*. At first she was a bit reticent as these were her brother-in-law's songs, but she agreed to it, as it would perhaps further sell the band.

Ralph spent many hours writing out the arrangements for the three songs featured to open our show. The 'Overture', 'Music Of The Night' – which Mick sang superbly - and the lovely duet, 'All I Ask Of You'. We took great care to emulate the actual sounds in the musical, with Ralph's Casio guitar synth and Dick who created a superb cathedral organ for the 'Overture' on his Roland Juno 60 keyboard.

Other bands must have thought us self-indulgent and bonkers for featuring songs from musicals but this was special and I thought, another feather in our cap. Opening the show with this was a big seller, which I really enjoyed playing. Nikki, appropriately, wore a long black dress for her part of Christine and I had procured a Phantom mask for Mick. Our Jewish clients loved it and the word soon spread that Sarah Brightman's sister was singing in the band.

That was until we played to a more down to earth audience at Bushey Police Club later in the year. Not everyone liked *Phantom*. Police officers are notoriously difficult to entertain and on this occasion we were playing for Hampstead Police. As we stylishly launched into the 'Overture' the formidable wife of the Chief Superintendent marched across the dance floor and stood there, hands on hips, glaring very menacingly at me throughout the whole of our 8-minute medley. At the final flourish of the epic cathedral organ, there was a storm of applause from the seated audience and she said in a loud voice, 'Never mind all this shite! Play something we fucking well know!'

I immediately launched the band into 'I Will Survive'. The dance floor was promptly packed. One can never fail with this song. I always found it amusing to watch the women dancers wagging their fingers at guilty-looking husbands and singing, 'How you did me wrong!'

So lesson learned. If you want lots of gigs you cannot be too indulgent as a band. It's nice to do one or two 'production' numbers but you *must give the audience what they want.* (Even if it means the awful 'Birdy Song'.) To be honest, the vast majority of the public know little about pop music and most never gave a toss what we played as long as they could dance to it.

Terry was forever complaining about playing a 'Disco beat' of 120 straight bass-drum beats to the minute, with the 'off beat' snare. 'It's fucking boring.' He would continually grouse. He would try to bring in some rock footwork to 'We Are Family' and 'I Will Survive', but it didn't work.

I discovered that 120 beats to the minute is the fast pace of the dancer's heart and it never fails. It was also the secret of binding songs together and creating a non-stop dance show, which Mixed Feelings soon gained a name for. *The Stage* newspaper journalist Colin Findlay, was present at the Entertainment Agents' Association Ball we performed at and wrote, 'This band will keep your dance floor packed all night.'

We now had a powerful line up of singers and musicians. Gigs in the West End had started to trickle in but we were still in the 2nd Division and I wanted us in the Premiere League. In spite of the exciting activity with Mixed Feelings throughout the summer, I had managed to hold down my day job in the Metropolitan Police, refusing all transfers to other stations and eventually being posted to the CAD room at Hampstead Police Station, after being totally *banned* by the Chief Superintendent, from doing Custody Sergeant duty.

This was due to me inadvertently locking the (pain in the arse) civilian, 'Lay Visitors' in the cells for four hours, when I 'accidentally' forgot all about them. They were imprisoned with a smelly vagrant on a very hot day. 'Serve the tossers right,' said Inspector 'Geordie' Warren who thought it highly amusing. This welcome suspension, was much to the annoyance of some of my fellow sergeants, one of whom said, 'You did that on purpose to get out of custody work, you jammy bastard.'

I looked at the banning as a 'gift from above', as it enabled me more free time to play with the band and time to put the finishing touches to my first book, *Cheerful Sacrifice*, which I had presented to the publisher Leo Cooper, in the spring of 1987. He immediately accepted it for publication and invited me for lunch. There began a lasting friendship with a great guy but that's not for here.

1988 was turning into yet another busy year for the band but I suffered a massive blow in June, when my dear Dad died suddenly from a ruptured aorta. He was only 67 years old and much loved. I know he had been proud of what I had achieved and had been a massive fan of the band. He would come to see us whenever appropriate and loved the voices of Mike, Barry and later, the antics of Mick Mullane. The last Mixed Feelings gig he attended was at Hemel Pavilion on Saturday 25th June. The cabaret was Richard Digance and it was a Round Table event.

The great thing about Hemel Pavilion was the 600 balcony seats where 'private' guests of the band could sit unnoticed. There was a bar in the balcony too. There was however, a major design fault to the building; the toilets were three floors down in the basement and there was no lift. On that particular night, I saw Dad struggling up the stairs after visiting the toilets and he was breathless. His heart was worn out. I put that down to the War years, when everyone smoked. Dad liked a good drink too. 'Press on Regardless, Cyril.'

I was treated pretty decently by the senior officers at Hampstead Police Station and was given two weeks compassionate leave to sort out Dad's funeral. I found much comfort in Linda and my little son. Never did a man have better friends. Terry stood on his head in his underpants and tried to drink a pint. Even Dick bought me a beer. Three days after his death, we did a gig at RAF West Drayton and Nikki said kindly, 'I think you are brave to do the gig. I would be in bits if it were my Dad.' Being with family, friends and mad musicians is a great healer. The show must go on.

We had a great summer and performed on HMS Belfast, on the main deck of the old battle cruiser in July. The sound of the band had carried across the Thames as Ralph remembered,

I well remember that gig on the deck of HMS Belfast. It was
a hot summer night and we played beneath a canvas awning.
One of the security staff from the Tower of London phoned up
to say that the noise of the band was pissing off the Ravens and
if we didn't turn it down we would arrested and locked in the
Tower.

HMS Belfast is not the easiest gig in town. It is run by the Imperial
War Museum and to assist in the running costs of the old ship, it is let
out for private events, one of which is the Oxford v Cambridge Boat
Race Ball at which we performed for many years and the Varsity Match,
Rugby Ball. On this occasion it was a private party. The problem with
this gig is getting gear on and off the ship. It has to be 'humped' along
a hundred metre gang plank. The humping didn't stop upon arrival at
the deck either. If you were booked to perform in The Wardroom, the
gear had to be carried below decks, down a ladder. So, I am back to the
recurring problem of 'roadies'.

On this occasion I made the mistake of recruiting five police officers
from Hampstead Nick with the lure of free beer. They were thirsty lads,
one Lancashire lad was known as 'The Ferret' and another as 'Beaker'
(because of his striking resemblance to *The Muppet Show* lab assistant)
and they cost me a small fortune in beer. From then on, I found it
cheaper to pay one roadie good money.

The lads turned up early and helped us aboard ship with the gear.
Only a small Bose PA for the Belfast. We were all set within 45 minutes
and as guests had not yet arrived, I took them to the nearest pub. Five
pints of London Pride later and we were required to leave after The
Ferret had stood on a table and recited Rudyard Kipling's *Gunga Din*,
which had 'offended' someone.

At the next pub, The Ferret raised his glass and said, 'Here's to the
Great Fire of London,' and using his cigarette lighter, set his hair on fire,
which caused a dreadful stink but was promptly extinguished by Beaker
who poured a pint of Abbot over his head. Again we were required to
leave and it was only 6pm.

From the lofty gangplank and in full view of the champagne reception
guests, The Ferret pissed into the river. We were then stopped from
boarding the ship. It took a lot of explaining to the Naval Security
guys that we were the band. After much grovelling, the good-natured

old matelots eventually allowed us on board, after The Ferret had convincingly told the guys that his Dad had served on the Belfast and 'fired the last shell at Bismark.'

The band were doing a cracking gig to a wild and very pissed, crowd. I made another error when I announced a medley of Village People hits for the benefit of the 'sailor boys'. The song following 'YMCA' was the rowdy, 'In The Navy'. The crowd went ballistic, jumping up and down and clapping in time to the gay intro. There was a bit in the middle eight where I announced, 'Who put sand in the vaseline?' and 'Would you like a parrot or a cockatoo?' to great cheers. To my horror, the cavorting road crew stripped off. One of them had disappeared and a few minutes later I saw The Ferret being escorted off the ship in his underpants. He had been caught in the out of bounds 'A' Turret, attempting to load the 6" naval gun, which he said he intended to fire at the Houses of Parliament as 'Margaret Thatcher had stopped his school milk.'

'It's that bloody band,' was the comment from the ship's crew. We never got that gig back and received a formal complaint from the agency about the 'disgraceful naked dancing of the road crew, who had drunk all the rum punch.' Lessons learned. Never use police officers as roadies. Would I learn this lesson?

I loved doing gigs for HM Armed Forces, as I was so interested in the regimental history of the bases and seeing the regimental silver at Officers' and Sergeants' messes. Most of these gigs came by way of agents who specialised in military gigs, namely Don Maxwell, Howard T'Loosty and Mike Malley. I found the Sergeants' mess the more friendly of the two, as 'The Ruperts' were as mean as hell. The Sergeants' mess steward would often give the band a free bar. They also did their own catering and the food was superb. There is nothing like an Army curry.

We were on a roll of gigs for HM Armed Forces during the eighties and the diary shows Summer Balls in 1988 for RAF Brampton, RAF Henlow, RAF Halton, HMS Warrior and RMA Sandhurst. These gigs were great fun, once one had got through the strict security at the camp gates. They were also very tiring, as a typical event would start at 6pm and finish at 7am next day. There would often be two or three bands involved, plus a disco.

One particularly hot summer's night, we were booked at HMS Vincent, a Royal Navy Officers' mess in Kensington. We had set up our equipment on the small stage in the corner of the wardroom and the kindly mess president said to us, 'Have what you want to drink lads. You can help yourself to the buffet when the guests have been served.' Happy days.

A sumptuous buffet was brought out about 6pm by the Navy chefs and laid out around the room on several long tables. The guests were due to arrive at 7pm. It was a baking hot night and I noticed that besides the usual chicken legs and lamb kebabs, there were lobster tails, prawns, crawfish and crab claws all laid out on silver platters, garnished with slices of lemon and rapidly melting ice in the room which was not air-conditioned.

At around 9.30pm the band were told to help themselves to the buffet. We were starving as usual, after being to the pub. I had noticed that there was lots of seafood still out, the ice having long melted in the heat, so I warned the guys not to eat it, as it might be 'high'.

Within two minutes, Terry had a plate stacked high with lobster tails and crab claws, which he carried into the small 'green room' adjoining the wardroom. I said 'Don't eat that crab or you'll shit your pants.' He then promptly ate the lot, belched noisily and came out with his usual comment that he was 'as full as a vicar's sack.'

The Naval officers and their wives looked magnificent in their medals and finery and the dance floor soon filled up with our opening song, 'Love Lift Us Up Where We Belong'. Then we broke into 'Hot Stuff' and suddenly there was a smell of eggy sulphur so bad it cleared the dance floor. People eyed us with utter disgust. Holding their noses. It was as if someone had let off a stink bomb.

Terry looked up at me from the drum kit and shouted 'Jonny, I've shit myself and need to go to the loo!' I stopped the band at the end of 'Jump' and Terry crimping his arse cheeks together, hobbled off the stage and limped up the stairs to the first-floor washroom. So what song could we do without a drummer?

'If' by David Gates was perfect. Fortunately the windows were open and a breeze had partly cleared the malodorous air. Couples eyed the band suspiciously before drifting back onto the dance floor. The song lasted about three minutes. Terry was back in time to tap out the last few bars. He said,

I thought it was a fart but it wasn't. I also had a terrible pain in my guts and had to leave the stage. I should never have eaten that fucking crab. By the time I got to the toilet on the first floor, I sat down and it was like a flock of pigeons being released. I managed to wash my arse in the washbasin but I threw my dirty under-crackers out of the window.

The band finally finished at 2am and many of the guests were leaving. As we were breaking down the gear the mess president said to me, 'Well done mate! The band did a great gig. Everyone is happy apart from the Admiral.' I said, 'Why is that?' He said, 'Some dirty bastard has thrown a pair of shitty underpants onto the windscreen of his Rolls Royce.' We never got that gig back.

The autumn and winter of 1988 saw an amazing step up in gigs. Nikki and Mike were selling the band together with a good song selection. Our diary for December reads;

DECEMBER
Thu 1 Grosvenor House Hotel. Ballroom.
Fri 2 Chiltern Hotel Luton
Sat 3 Chiltern Hotel Luton
Tue 6 Great Fosters. Egham.
Wed 7 Mead Crystal Rooms. Brentwood.
Fri 9 Bushey Police Club (Ruislip Police)
Sat 10 The Beverley School. New Malden.
Wed 14 Excelsior Hotel
Thu 15 Holiday Inn Slough.
Fri 16 Chiltern Hotel Luton
Sat 17 Bushey Police Club (Hampstead Police)
Wed 21 Middx & Herts Country club. Stanmore.
Thu 22 Chiltern Hotel Luton
Fri 23 Chiltern Hotel Luton
Fri 30 Chiltern Hotel Luton
Sat 31 NYE Rolls Royce Watford.

For a long time, I had been on the Hampstead Police 'Social Club Committee'. Meetings of this small group of four or five officers were usually chaired by the Chief Superintendent and sometimes held in the Rosslyn Arms at his behest. The Social Club would organise and finance events such as day trips to Brighton or the Newmarket races, which were highly popular with the Irish publicans from the Kilburn High Road. Battlefield tours to France were also financed. Thus came about the founding of the legendary Hampstead Pals.

Naturally, some officers objected to funds being spent this way but they were the usual grumblers who supported bugger all. We would also organise the popular children's Christmas party at Bushey Police Club plus the annual dinner dance. All these events were poorly supported apart from the aforementioned, kid's party. I soon discovered that my fellow police officers loved 'Smoking Concerts' which were men-only events. The only women allowed were the strippers.

I acquired a shady reputation for organising these popular money-raising events for local charities. They were much loved by the rank and file police officers, who would clamour for tickets which went on sale at £10 and were usually sold out within 24 hours. The price of the ticket also included a fish and chip supper, wrapped and delivered by 'Jimmy the Greek', the dependable proprietor of the excellent Nautilus Chippie, next door to West Hampstead Nick.

The entertainment usually included a required, foul-mouthed stand-up comic and two or three female strippers. Sometimes as the 'gentlemen rankers out on a spree', arrived for the event, they were serenaded by the subtle tones of the Mixed Feelings trio. We were never paid for these little gigs, 'just free beer and a free horn,' according to Terry. At some men-only events, we often backed singer and blue comedian Mike Felix, in his revamped line up of the 'Migil Five'.

One such event was held on a Tuesday in March 1988 at the local British Legion Club at Lithos Road. The advertisement was sent out to surrounding stations, via the Police night despatch and by 4pm the next day the event was sold out. On this occasion I was looking for something completely 'different'.

Previous events had entailed 'Jelly Wrestling' whereby naked females would wrestle in an inflatable paddling pool, filled with strawberry smelling, red jelly. This was all terrific fun, until an Inspector was thrown into the jelly by the two strippers. It was even funnier when they sat on his face.

Other attractions included 'Snake Charming' which featured a corset-clad stripper, who carried onto the stage a python in an Ali-baba basket.

This eight- foot long reptile would be produced to the baying audience and trained to slither down the underpants of a blindfolded Scottish volunteer, who was sitting on a chair blissfully thinking it was female finger tips massaging his tackle and promptly got a 'dickus erectus'. He passed out after the blindfold was removed and he saw that he was being 'gobbled' by a snake. He had to be revived with a large measure of Talisker and assured it was a *female* snake. There was nothing 'queer' about him.

My outrageous charity-raising activities had not passed unnoticed by the Metropolitan Police hierarchy and I was formally 'warned' by the Hampstead Chief Superintendent that, 'sexual exhibitions' were 'politically incorrect' and 'were to cease forthwith'. I thought I would have just one more go.

I had read about 'Dwarf Throwing' or 'Dwarf Tossing' in the *Daily Telegraph*, apparently it was very popular in Australia. So I enquired as to where I could procure volunteer dwarfs for the occasion. I made a call to music agent and friend, Dave Nash of Bromley based, Crown Entertainments. He was my usual supplier of strippers and comedians for stag shows. As usual, he came up with the goods and I was given the name of compere, Danny Bamford, who would bring the dwarfs for the event, plus two strippers. He would also bring mattresses, which would serve as a landing ground for the tossed dwarfs. He was to be paid £700 in cash for the whole package.

To add a unique touch, I telephoned Kenny Baker and asked him if he would open the event. He was immediately up for it. I had managed to obtain a police uniform from our ever-helpful stores man, Peter Russell, which I had taken to Alan the Tailor's on Rosslyn Hill and had it suitably altered to fit Kenny, who looked hilariously smart as the Metropolitan Police Commissioner, Sir Kenneth Newman, who was not much taller.

I had also 'borrowed' the Chief Superintendent's cap as it had 'scrambled egg' on the peak. He was unaware that I had a spare key to his office. (At this point I have to say it was not me who locked the station cat in his office for the weekend) There was no shortage of volunteers to lift Kenny on to the table to make his speech, which I had written for him, nor carry in the heavy mattresses for the dwarf throwing.

The compere started the show with the usual dirty 'one line' gags and piss-taking of the police. The strippers did their first-half act to the usual cat-calls and obscene comments. The fish and chips were delivered on time, most of which were thrown across the room to the despair of manager Billy Keating who would have to sweep the mess up in the morning and I will never forget one unfortunate officer sitting there with a piece of battered cod, splattered on his bald head yelling, 'What Kung fu dat?'

At 10pm the main part of the event began. The two fit-looking dwarfs came on to the floor. One was white and clad in a black mini-flying suit and the other was black and clad in a white flying suit. Both wore motorcycle crash helmets. There was a strong custom-made leather harness around the upper body, with a huge carrying handle on the back, which enabled one to throw them.

The noise in the club was tremendous as I stepped forward and was the first to 'toe the line'. The line of mattresses ran for about 24 feet and terminated at the lounge wall. Kenny Baker announced the contest, 'Gentlemen you can choose who to throw, the white or the black. They both weigh the same.'

The dwarf named 'Ali,' lay face down on the floor, arms outstretched as if about to dive. I picked him up. Bloody hell! He was heavy, probably about 10 stone. I swung him once, twice and then threw him. The best I managed is about halfway on to the first mattress, a mere seven feet. I hear shouts of 'Wanker' as the noise in the room reaches a level higher than Highbury.

Everyone wants a go, it has been announced the winner will receive a free flight to Australia to enter the world dwarf-throwing championships, providing he can throw a dwarf further that 20 feet. The competition gets fiercer and there are some big guys throwing the dwarfs. Noel King, the powerfully built Irish publican of the Black Lion on Kilburn High Road, takes the lead by throwing 'Roger' on to the third mattress – about 18 feet. The commentary and competition is getting hotter when up steps a very big man. Constable Jan Leloch is a man mountain, weighing in at 30 stone and 6'9" tall.

He picks up Ali and swings him once and the dwarf extends his arms into the dive position. He swings him twice and lets go. The little lump flies through the air like a rocket. He hits the far wall with a resounding 'bonk'. So that's why they wear crash helmets! Jan Leloch is the outright winner and presented with a bottle of Malt Whisky. He has thrown the dwarf 25 feet and it is announced he will 'represent the Metropolitan Police' in the World Dwarf Tossing Championships in Adelaide. He is the new UK Champion. As Jan remembered,

> I was not allowed to go to Australia to represent the Metropolitan Police and Great Britain in the World Dwarf Throwing Contest. I wonder why? I remember the evening well. What a brilliant night! In particular PC Brian 'Wan' Kerr RIP trying to throw the dwarf but he'd had too much to drink and kept landing on top of him. I think his best throw was about 3ft. The other great memory was the fantastic amount of money we raised for charity that night. They were great times and nobody took offence to anything.

The next day I am summoned to see the Chief Superintendent. He has received a call from Scotland Yard and I am ordered to 'Stop this bloody Dwarf Throwing forthwith.' Hampstead Police Station and the Metropolitan Police were fast getting a bad name. I was threatened with a transfer to Brixton. 'Whatever next?' he bellowed at me. I replied, 'Donkeys.'

7

RIOT

I had taken a fortnight's annual holiday, commencing on a day that will long stay in my memory, Friday 21st July 1989. The following day, accompanied by Linda and young Greg, we were going to drive to France and explore the battlefield of Verdun before driving on to Metz, to meet a French police friend, Paul Nicolas.

It was a hot, balmy night and the band had been booked to perform at an Eastern Electricity Board dinner dance at Fanhams Hall, an old Jacobean manor house turned conference and banqueting venue near Ware in Hertfordshire.

Since the HMS Belfast debacle, I had promised myself never to use police officers as roadies again. However, a long-time mate and fellow police officer at Hampstead was Michael 'Dusty' Miller. To earn 'beer money', he became a temporary roadie for the band and he made a good one too. He was not a big man, but strong, and looked upon being a roadie as good training for football. He was certainly the fastest roadie we ever had and could lift anything put in front of him. He soon became pals with Nikki Brightman and would regularly wind her up with his Geordie wit. He also lived in Hemel Hempstead, which was handy as we could pick him up on the way to gigs.

I drove my new car to this event; it was a flashy, one year old, Vauxhall Cavalier SRI, which I had purchased with the little bit of money Dad had left me. He had been dead for one year now and my grief was still raw. I was not drinking alcohol at this event as I was driving home in the early hours of the morning. Then after a couple of hours rest, I planned to drive to Dover for the ferry crossing to France.

The night was a hot one and the band arrived in dribs and drabs at the venue. Ralph, with a face like a baboon's arse in the evening heat, was glaring and swearing as usual, 'Fucking Friday night fucking traffic!' and slung his guitar on to the stage area from a full 12 feet away. Fortunately, it was suitably cased and Leo Fender had designed his wonderfully tough Stratocasters for just such irritable musicians. The comment 'Bunter's got the hump again' did not help matters.

So we set up in one of the window alcoves of the hall. I set up the one pair of Bose 802 cabs on their chrome stands, either side of the recess. This small system I carried in the back of my car and was adequate for most events, together with my 1x15" Trace Elliott Bass combo. I knew this popular venue well and I guess there were 250 persons in attendance. It was our regular band of Ralph Lewin on guitar, Dick Henninghem on keyboards, Terry Wilson on drums with Mick Mullane and Nikki Brightman on vocals.

A very lively crowd abounded on this night, lots of noisy laughter and tribal yelling. They had been drinking heavily at the free bar since 7pm. One mixed table of builders and plumbers near the stage area were particularly rowdy and according to the venue management had consumed four bottles of whisky before the starter and had got very bothersome during the act of a mysterious hypnotist. I am convinced he hypnotised two or three heckling members of this disruptive table, just to shut them up.

After the hypnotist had finished his act to a disrespectful chorus of boos, the dance floor instantly filled as we launched into 'All Night Long' and 'Dancing On The Ceiling'. I also noticed that several clowns in the crowd had stripped off. I recognised some of them as the hypnotised male volunteers who had gone on stage and sucked lemons believing it was melons, then snogged each other.

The organiser of the function came onto the stage and asked me to stop playing immediately. He stated the obvious in a forthright manner that, 'Many of the guests were drunk and stripping off.' He further warned that if we didn't stop now it would kick off.

At 12.45am, we finished early at this welcome news and left the hot and humid ballroom to get changed. Some of the guests were indeed, down to their underwear. We trooped into the dressing room, which was just off the main courtyard and got changed out of our sweaty stage wear and I donned cotton shorts and a T-shirt. During this I could hear a woman screaming, 'Sing us another fucking song!' Who was she referring to? I packed my clothes away and went back across the courtyard. Then I saw a female cake-detective, shouting at Dusty the roadie. 'Sing us another fucking song!'

I made my way gingerly, through the heaving foyer, which was clogged with about a dozen pissed men and women all arguing, swearing and aggressively pointing fingers at each other. Not a rare sight at the end of an evening and not the first time I had seen a husband and wife dispute. I guessed they were waiting for taxis. One fat mini-skirted woman blocked the doorway.

I squirmed my way through them and went into the smoky ballroom to retrieve my guitar and speakers. There was the usual table of drunks refusing to leave with one kilted, sweaty individual, standing on a chair singing, 'Flower of Scotland.' If ever there was a more depressing *dirge* written for a nation with an inferiority complex, it was that shite. At least it's better than American Pie.

As I carried the guitar out, the doorway was still blocked by the slapper. She was puffing on a fag and deliberately obstructing anyone from leaving, whilst unloading her stock of obscenities at a sweating Dusty, who was trying to carry out equipment. By now, it was 1.35am and I guessed she thought Dusty was the singer in the band, as she demanded another song.

We started to load equipment into the back of my Cavalier, which was parked on the edge of the courtyard and I again returned to the ballroom via the congested foyer. Dusty remarked that, 'It's gonna kick off.' By this time, I was getting a bit concerned.

We collected the last bits of gear and went back to the foyer where lard ass had shut the door and stood with her back to it from the inside. Dusty was standing in front of me with two bags of leads. She jabbed a finger at him. 'He won't sing another song so I am not letting him out.'

Dusty then helpfully said, 'No songs for fat girls!' She then screamed 'Don't you call me fat!' I then said 'Move your fat arse!' With that, a pissed male pointed his finger at me and said, 'Don't you speak to my fucking missus like that!' His finger pointing was a little close as he managed to poke me in the eye so I dropped my clothes bag and punched him on the chin.

Then it really did 'kick off'. Both of us were attacked by what seemed a pack of mad dogs. At first it was an exchange of punches, then the fight spilled into the Gents toilets and Dusty and myself, heavily outnumbered, ended up on the floor being kicked about the head and upper body. I noticed that Dusty was bleeding from a cut over his eye. I looked at him and said, 'we're gonna have to get up, or die!' So we managed to stand up amid another flurry of punches. I noticed that the cow who had started all this trouble had taken her shoe off and was trying to bash Dusty's head with her stiletto heel. I noticed the shoes were new as I could see the price tag on the arch.

The only two members of the band involved in this brawl were Dusty and myself. The rest had sensibly run away as the fight spilled into the courtyard and the cry went up to 'Kill the band.' As Terry Wilson said,

> It was all caused by that fucking Hypnotist who I'm convinced, deliberately hypnotised that table of builders. Then that big old tart refused to let us out of the door. I bet she had been cocked more times than Dick Turpin's pistol. Then it all started with a massive punch up in the foyer and in the courtyard. Jon told us to 'run away' so we did, especially when someone shouted that they've got knives. That's me out of it! I ran and hid in the field then found my car and scarpered but the police stopped me.
> On reflection I should have stopped to help Dusty and Jon but I thought, 'Fuck that.'

I was boxing with one idiot when I saw Dusty run over to a builders' skip in the corner of the courtyard and grab a couple of lengths of 4'x2". Conveniently cut and about the length of a baseball bat. We were both bleeding from head wounds, as he threw one to me and said 'Defend yourself Jonny, they've got knives! At no time dared we announce we were police officers. We would have certainly been murdered.

'Here they come again!' shouted Dusty, as at least ten of them charged across the courtyard, one carrying a carving knife, which the staff later confirmed had been taken from the kitchen. The guy with the knife shouted 'Cut the bastards!' That was the last thing he said, before he was brained by Dusty with an almighty smack with the timber right across the bridge of his nose. Down he went, followed by one after another, as my fearless roadie, swinging his bat like Ian Botham, knocked them all down. It all seemed very theatrical but some never got up.

Meanwhile, I was engaged in single combat with a shaven headed troll, who had taken his shirt off and had also armed himself with a piece of wood from the skip. We swung at each other like medieval swordsmen but I had simply run out of steam. My arms had turned to jelly and I tripped backwards over a low kerb, thereby dropping my lump of wood. The troll was on me like a bull terrier, with his piece of timber across my neck and was kneeling on it. Some of his surviving mates had aimed kicks at my head while I was on the deck and it took all of my remaining strength to try to lift him off me. I had to resort to pulling him off, by tearing at his ears and grabbing the sweaty rolls of fat at the back of his neck as he punched me in the face. I was unable to shift him so I turned my head to one side, unable to breathe due to his weight on my neck and chest and so prepared to die.

Never did a Geordie accent sound so sweet, 'Move your hands, Matey,' I dropped my hands from his neck and immediately heard a very loud 'clop' like a cricket ball on the willow. I was promptly showered in what seemed like hot water. The Troll flopped forward onto me unconscious. It was blood.

Dusty had applied his best cricket swing to the back of his head. In doing so he had scalped him. A saucer-sized lump of flesh had spun across the yard like a Frisbee. In the light of the morning, a police forensic officer had found it gruesomely stuck to the dressing room window. Dusty Miller had saved my life with that well-timed blow but had almost taken another. We were in the shit.

Loads of flashing blue lights tore up the drive as the police arrived. Herts Constabulary had never seen such excitement since a cat had got stuck up a tree in Ware. 'A riot at Fanhams Hall' had been the call and police units from far and wide had attended. All of us, including Nicci were promptly arrested and taken to Hertford Police Station. Five of the opposition had been ambulanced to hospital. Three were detained with one in a serious condition.

In the charge room at Hertford Police station we were treated professionally. 'The band had beaten us up' was the allegation made by the opposition, eight of whom had been arrested and taken to Bishop's Stortford Nick. The police believed them.

The first thing I did was to tell the custody sergeant that there were only two of us involved. The five other members of the band should be released forthwith. The request was ignored. When Dusty and I were ordered to turn out our pockets pandemonium ensued at the production of Metropolitan Police warrant cards.

'Fucking hell. Get the Guvnor out of bed. We've got two Met Police officers in here, for attempted murder,' said the sweating custody sergeant, mopping his brow with his hanky. He reminded me of Rod Steiger from the film *In the Heat of the Night*. In all reality, the Herts lads treated us well. The incredulous looks soon turned to smiles, 'If you Met boys think the charge of attempted murder is so funny, then so do we.' After being searched, all seven of us were placed in separate cells. It was hot in those cells too. Soon I was joined in the cell by a friendly Scottish detective inspector, who was definitely not suffering from an inferiority complex.

Looking at Gerry McQueen, I could see he was close to the end of his service. He was not overly enthralled with being called out in the middle of the night but this was exciting stuff. It's not often two Met cops could be on a murder charge. Plus, this was a good 'earner' for him. We hit it off immediately. His handshake was firm as he said, 'Jon, we need to get this sorted out now. You be straight with me and I'll be straight with you.'

I looked him in the eye. He smelled of Old Spice and his hair was still wet from the shower. He was not wearing a jacket, just a collar and tie. Through his pressed white shirt I saw the outline of a regimental tattoo on his upper arm. 'You were in the Black Watch then?' 'Yes I was son, how the hell did you know that?'

We were getting on splendidly as I talked and he made notes. He said, 'I believe you Jon, but you will have to convince a jury if this bastard dies!' He then went to interview Dusty.

I shouted down the cell corridor to Dick, Terry, Mick and Ralph, 'You guys all OK?' and then the old lie I had told many prisoners, 'You'll be out of here in a jiffy!' I then started to sing 'Jailhouse Rock'.

The others joined in. Nicci could hear us in the female cell. Other prisoners woke up and were soon clapping along. 'Everybody in the whole cell block was dancing to the Jailhouse Rock.'

At 5.45am the night duty custody sergeant was relieved and replaced by someone I knew well. Sergeant Ian Ronson was an old friend. A fellow member of the Western Front Association and one, who in his spare time, 'moonlighted' with Club Cantabrica and drove our Hampstead Pals coach to the battlefields of France. He was grinning like a chimp and thought it hilarious to find me in the cell for attempted murder. He soon arranged for a cup of tea and a *Daily Telegraph* to be brought down the cells for Dusty and me. It was police nepotism at its best. The others got fuck all.

Fifteen hours later we were all released on police bail. Due to the repeated blows to my head I had been seen by the police surgeon and the cuts repaired. I was advised to attend hospital as soon as possible, for an X-ray. I had been due to go on holiday that morning with Linda and little Greg. Both had been mad with worry. Just after 6pm we all met in the pub just down the road from the nick. Never did Abbot Ale taste so good.

Dick Henninghem would never forget the 'Riot at Fanhams Hall'. It was certainly not his weekend,

> It was part of my weekend equivalent of an *Annus Horribilis*. On Thursday I left my ex-wife, to organise her departure with our children from the family home, staying at my sister's house nearby. On Friday night I played a posh tuxedo function for the Eastern Electricity Board at Fanhams Hall in Ware. For some reason, a bunch of Enfield plumbers took a dislike to us and, by one o'clock in the morning, I had been arrested and thrown into a cell, along with the rest of the band, leaving my equipment in the open air in the car park. I was incarcerated in solitary confinement (having point blank refused to share a cell with a vomiting drunk) for fifteen hours. I was interrogated and finally let out at five in the afternoon. The charge was GBH. (which according to Terry, was 'Gobbling Behind Hedge') but as the Sergeant said, 'if he snuffs it, it'll be manslaughter.' Charming! All I'd done was run for my life and only just made it by diving headfirst through the passenger door of Terry's accelerating car. (The plumbers and their charming wives had

been taken to another police station and, apparently, half-wrecked the place) On Sunday, I moved back home to find my ex-wife had stripped the place bare and taken both the cats! I really did believe that 'Himself' had it in for me that weekend. I must have done something awful in a past life to deserve such treatment.

An enforced holiday from the police ensued. Being on full pay assisted to alleviate the stress and implications of being on bail. We fully expected to go to prison, should one of our assailants die, or at the very least, to be found guilty of GBH. My brother Mark was a shining light of comfort and took us on regular fishing trips to Stowe School lakes where he was a friend of the warden. In those beautiful surroundings, we learned to catch big carp. There was no better therapy. We also enjoyed the subtlety of malt whisky. In December we finally got the hoped-for verdict. 'No case to answer.' Through it all, the band played on.

Mick Mullane was becoming increasingly unhappy. After the Fanhams Hall debacle, he thought us a band of hoodlums. After all, this gentle soul had been incarcerated in police cells and had almost collected a criminal record. The word quickly went around that Mixed Feelings had been 'arrested for murder' and 'This band beats audiences up'. The rumours soon reached Michael Black who phoned me, 'Son, your band is nothing but fucking trouble. I've got you a gig for Finchley Boxing Club.'

Mick didn't trust our Geordie roadie, who had been allegedly flirting with his woman. I knew that the sensitive Mick suffered from WT when he had left the stage in a flood of tears, after singing 'I Heard It Through The Grapevine'. I liked him very much. He was a terrific singer and a lovely guy. He finally threw in the towel and left on friendly terms on Sunday 14th January 1990, after three years with the band. So, I had singer problems yet again. He would be difficult to replace. *I never saw him again.*

I needed a singer urgently so I took a gamble and phoned Barry, who I knew was hankering for his job back. Plus, I knew he needed the money. He re-joined for the next gig at the Rover Club at Oxford.

He had been lodging with Debbie's ex-boyfriend Kevin, in North London. We reverted to many of his old songs, especially the Barry Manilow medley. Nikki hated it and she quickly lost interest. Barry, permanently suffering from WT, was pissing her off and she just seemed to give up. She ceased to 'try'. She was walking on to the stage looking, as one Jewish client described, as 'dowdy' and 'looking like she didn't want to be there.'

I mentioned to her that she had laddered her tights and I paid for another pair but she managed to ladder those as well. She also developed the infuriating habit of *yawning* at the audience, when on stage. Huge cartoon yawns like Sleepy the dwarf. As a major fan, the Chief Superintendent's wife commented, 'Didn't she get any fucking sleep last night?' I was disappointed in Nikki and told her so. She simply shrugged her shoulders and left. *I never saw her again.*

The next girl singer to step into the breach was Sara Raybould, a Birmingham girl and a good singer, who lived in Hemel Hempstead with keyboard maestro John Maul. She knew a few Gloria Estefan songs and saw us through several gigs but she was not into the commercial 'poppy' music we were playing. The travelling and late nights also got too much for her and she began to 'cry off' gigs. I decided she would have to go when she let us down again by 'reporting sick' with a sore throat when booked to play at the Kodak annual dinner dance in Hemel Hempstead.

We did the event with just Barry on vocals who got us through magnificently. He was on his own and in his element, receiving a standing ovation at the end of the night when we finished with Billy Joel's 'This Night Should Last Forever' and 'Everlasting Love'. Despite the genuine adulation, the self-important organiser, George Corfield, docked our money in the absence of a girl singer. Lesson learned. The contract is binding and I so wished singers would realise that, before 'crying off' gigs.

Answering the ad placed in the good old *Stage* came Kathy Edge. A red headed, Yorkshire lass with a belting voice. She also had a belting temper. I liked her and could just about handle her. She was fun, professional, intelligent and probably the most forthright talking female singer ever to grace our stage. For a start it didn't take long for her to tell Dick, with his peculiar traits, that he was a wanker. The profanities rolled effortlessly off the tongue of this female Geoffrey Boycott.

She could easily match Barry on vocal volume and no way would she let him stand in front of her on stage when she was singing a lead vocal. This row got to epic proportions and resulted in a line of white gaffa tape being put along the front of the stage and Barry, whom she scathingly referred to as the 'no hoper', was given strict orders not to cross when Kathy was singing, at dire risk of him being emasculated. It was not unusual to hear, 'Do not cross my fucking line!' She would have made a fine NCO in the British Army.

Her first gig was Saturday 13th October 1990, at a Masonic Ladies Night Dinner at the Carnarvon Hotel Ealing. She sang a cracking version of 'One Moment In Time' and the crowd loved her. She was always immaculate on stage, wearing some classy outfits. There was nothing 'dowdy' about Kathy.

It was around this time that the newly divorced Dick and Terry had gone on a sunshine holiday to the island of Malta. Local musician, John Maul had admirably 'depped' for Dick on keyboards and he was so good, that I wanted him and his innovative sounds in my band. So, all I needed now was the 'excuse' from an increasingly, difficult Dick. He would soon present it to me.

A happy Vaughan – also because of his recent divorce from the wife he had left the band for - stood in for Terry on drums. According to Terry, whilst they were in Malta, Dick had been 'Turking some old tart in Valetta' and had moved into her apartment and had not once used his hotel room. This had naturally, peeved Terry who was desperately trying to mend himself after his own sticky divorce and needed some company.

No sooner had Dick returned to the UK, when he telephoned me and said he was going back to Malta the following week, to see this new woman with whom he had become FS. He was going to be away for a full fortnight and would miss some important gigs, including a big Jewish wedding in Woodford Green. I was extremely annoyed as he had let me down but he had actually handed me the opportunity to replace him on a plate. I needed a keyboard player urgently, so I called John Maul and offered him the job in the band with immediate start. He grabbed it. When Dick returned from Malta he had lost his job. He didn't seem bothered.

This was a musical turning point. John Maul lived in Hemel Hempstead and worked for keyboard makers, Roland. He fully understood 'midi' and how to extract the very best from a modern keyboard. Something that Dick – as good a player as he was – did not bother to do. He was a professional demonstrator and great character too, blessed with a wicked sense of humour. He was also – like most keyboard players – acutely deaf. I would call a song and he would cup his hand over his ear and try to lip-read.

His first gig was that important Jewish wedding at the James Hawkey Hall on 25th October 1990. During dinner music, he had masterfully played 'If I Were a Rich Man' to a joyous reception. The Hollies, 'He Ain't Heavy He's My Brother' was the second opening dance request at this event and I was standing alongside John, as Barry belted out the vocals and I became unstuck at a part of the song, with a certain bass note. I suspected it was a B flat but was unsure and not having the music to hand, asked John, 'What's this chord?' He looked at me, holding his hand to his ear and said, 'Ay?' I said again, this time shouting, 'What's this chord?' he replied, 'He Ain't Heavy He's My Brother.' When the elusive note came around for the second time, I said frantically, 'What's this chord?' and John replied, 'He Ain't Heavy He's My Brother.' I shouted at him, 'You deaf cunt!' He replied, 'Is that the next song?'

In the meantime, in the fallout following the Fanhams Hall arrest, the Met had kindly awarded me the 'Police Long Service and Good Conduct Medal', which was presented to me by that very finest of Commissioners, Sir Peter Imbert. I took Mum, Linda and Greg to the lovely ceremony at Hendon Training School.

I had by then served twenty-two and a half years in the Met and as much as I still enjoyed the job I was more interested in making the band a success. We were still climbing the ladder but had a few problems that needed ironing out. Barry was becoming troublesome again and consuming far too much brandy, although crowds everywhere still adored him. We ploughed through 1991 successfully but we had still not made the top level and broken into the West End. So 1992 arrived and was an eventful year in getting the band sorted. I was still not there with the right professional people that I wanted. On 1st February, the unsettled Barry left the band for the final time and moved back up North. I was disappointed, but in a way relieved. He was a brilliant talent wasted.

I held further auditions for male singers in the basement at Wootton Drive. We had a good set up there with a drum kit, guitar amps and bass amps plus a Roland keyboard courtesy of John Maul. About twelve guys had turned up for the auditions. You know that some will not be suitable before they have even sung a note. The 'Three B's' viz. Baldies, Bellies and Beardies were not what I wanted.

At the audition one guy looked very different. He was wearing washed and pressed denim jeans, (nothing looks worse than dirty jeans) a leather jacket and cowboy boots. He had very long permed hair. A different image again. He was real heavy metal, with eyebrows like a forest of spiders' legs. Plus he was extremely self-confident. I had at this time set up a cassette tape deck and had invited singers to bring their own backing tracks. Dave 'Ryka' Howard got the job when he sang 'Living On A Prayer' note for note in the written key. We would adapt the band to suit his voice.

Dave lived in Dunstable, just a few miles away and his 'day job' was allegedly, an electrician. 'Of sorts,' I would find out when he blew me right off the stage at the Dorchester Hotel after re-wiring a lighting desk, much to the amusement of the band. I asked him to disconnect the desk and he pulled out the wrong plug, resulting in me being blown off stage again. I never asked him to re-wire anything else! As Terry remembered,

> Dave Howard looked the part. He was proper heavy metal. This would give us a new theme. So Jon adapted our music and we started doing some songs that suited his voice, Alice Cooper, Bon Jovi, Scorpions and more. He said he was an electrician but that was a joke. I asked him to re-wire my drum studio and when I switched the light on the fuse box blew up and almost set the house on fire.

We would indeed 'adapt' and I decided to finish our first half of the show with a great Bon Jovi song, 'Blaze Of Glory' the theme from the movie, *Young Guns*.

There was no pleasing everyone. Kathy didn't like him for starters. I never fully understood why. Perhaps she never fancied him. I suspect it was because his hair was longer and curlier than hers.

For the vast majority of male singers, performing in Mixed Feelings marked the pinnacle of their careers. Very few, after they left, went on to greater things. I noticed that over the years, the majority of male singers upon joining the band, made it their primary object to shag the female singer. Many tried, some succeeded. Not all with the same singer I might add! Dave Howard was happily married and never tried. He served the band well and modified his vocals to sing some of the finer harmonies with Kathy. He could easily handle ballads like 'Always' and the traditional 'You'll Never Walk Alone', which was always in demand for Round Table events. Most bands can play it. Few singers can properly handle it.

Dave was always pleading poverty. He was earning good money but never bought a round of beers, although he was quick to take a drink from you. Unfortunately, there are some musicians like that. He had given up his day job as an electrician, after being threatened by the Fire Brigade. He was now relying on Mixed Feelings to pay his mortgage. In order to save money, he bought himself a knackered BSA Bantam motorbike, which he would ride from Dunstable to my house in Wootton Drive and park in my garage. He would travel in the band van to the event, sometimes driving it and help to set up the PA and gear.

When we arrived back at Wootton Drive at 3am, he would kick start the noisy old motor bike and wake up Linda who complained that the house was stinking of petrol. He had one of those old-fashioned crash helmets. When he put it on, his face looked like a bum in a bucket.

8

BEWARE OF THE BOOGIE MAN.

In March 1991 I took an important step and purchased a second hand, but tidy, Bedford Midi-Van from a dodgy car dealer in Luton. Most of the band gear, with careful stacking, would fit in the back and it could be left overnight in my garage. There were three seats in the front and if I placed the new TOA bass bins face down, a small mattress could be placed on top, which provided precarious but comfortable seating for another two or three persons.

Being a serving officer in the Metropolitan Police I was forbidden to join a trade union. However, the Musician's Union offered great insurance terms for drivers and equipment protection. Plus, at that time, they gave you a million pounds worth of Public Liability insurance. Rules were made to be broken so I joined the union and kept my mouth shut. Very soon, Terry and myself were elected onto the Herts branch committee, led by resolute chairman and legendary Jazz drummer, Eddie Clayton. The monthly branch committee meeting, held at The Cock in Sarratt, consisted of five minutes of business then a splendid piss-up on union funds.

I recommend any musician, singer, sound engineer, DJ or roadie to join the MU. It is purely worth it as a bandleader, if only for peace of mind. One can obtain the right insurance through the Union's efficient brokers, Victor C Knight, (still operating today). Loss or theft of your valuable gear, even if left in the van, parked in the street overnight, is covered.

This was our first van and rock n' roll! Many glorious 'piss-ups' were held on the way back from gigs, when bottles of Port, Abbot Ale, or London Pride were consumed, usually courtesy of clients and loudly accompanied by bawdy songs.

Having our own group van meant we were really 'On The Road'. It reminded me of the old 'Deanbeats' days. Such fun it was, that musicians would often drive all the way to my house just for the ride in the van and the wild party on the road.

The drawback was who was going to drive it? We took it in turns. We started to experiment with roadies and drivers. The driver would not drink at that actual gig. This was a lot of fun but not for the driver who would remain glum all night. How I hate diet coke.

John Maul thought van travel great fun, as we would pick him up and drop him off in Hemel Hempstead. Lots of laughs and very late nights ensued, especially if we stopped at the Pink Rupee Gurkha restaurant at Cricklewood Broadway, on the way home from a London gig. The strong Everest lager they sold would often result in John 'bailing out' of the van and theatrically rolling on the pavement outside his house, like a Red Devil.

I loved the incredible sounds that John produced from his keyboards. He was an expert *demonstrator* and continued to reveal the latest Roland sounds at every gig. Quite often he would turn up with a brand new Roland keyboard, fresh from the drawing board.

This keyboard virtuoso, failed to impress Ralph however, who due to his high-pressure day job at Guinness, was getting increasingly grumpy. He was also finding himself musically redundant in many aspects of the show. He had served fifteen solid years in Mixed Feelings and was a founder member of the band. He was also an accomplished guitarist and personal friend. He said,

> I enjoyed playing my guitar-synth rig but all that changed when John Maul came to the band as he played absolutely *everything*. He was a brilliant musician but not a band player. He played my guitar parts as well. What with Barry getting regularly pissed

at gigs and Terry being just as bad and speeding up songs, this made me decide to leave. I had had enough.

He had also found himself a lady friend. I was gutted. Ralph couldn't possibly leave! How could I replace him? It had been bad enough with singers fucking me about. I resigned myself to another stressful search. This time for a guitarist. I needed to find a 'straightforward' guitarist only. No special effects, no synths, we had all the effects with John Maul.

At this point and with due respect to any current or future bandleader reading this, I feel I should mention *finance*. Ralph had generously put a lot of money into the band in the form of PA gear. He was a single man with a good day job. If he left he would require paying off. Benevolent friends are rare.

One must always put money aside from every gig to pay for any extras. Situations like someone leaving the band required money too, as I always paid them a 'leaving' fee, (usually four gigs). Linda said I was stupid. Once the gigs were coming in, I had this covered. I never hesitated to spend money although I was lucky as the Met Police fed my family and paid the mortgage. The band money was for a decent car, beer and holidays, when I found the time to enjoy them.

It was also nice to be able to spend money on guitars. I spent a great day in Denmark Street, less wife, and treated myself to a nice Taylor acoustic guitar, in Andy's Music Store. I soon acquired a few more, desirable bass guitars. I even bought a John Entwistle 'Buzzard' bass at a bargain price, which I spotted in a Glasgow junk shop.

In January 2000 my dear Mum died from cancer. She was 83. She was placed with Dad in the little Deanshanger churchyard. She was much loved and we 'saw her off' properly. She had left my brother and I a couple of grand each. Not a lot, but her and Dad never had any money or owned a house. She had saved it up 'for her boys'. Best of all, she left us gifts of loyalty, respect and love.

I spent most of that two grand on a Status bass, once owned by Mark King. I invested the rest in malt whisky. It was a sheer joy to play and made of graphite. I had always wanted one. It always stayed in tune but it simply didn't look right. It was headless and had no sex appeal.

The Fender Jazz bass was really the best. It had a fantastic tone range, which was easy to adjust on stage and I always went back to it. I bought three Fender Jazz basses over the years and two Precision basses. How I dreamed about those lovely instruments when I was a boy. It's a good thing Fender don't make motorbikes. Yamaha make excellent pianos, guitars, saxophones, drums and probably bagpipes. They also make lawn mowers and fucking noisy motorbikes.

Never be afraid to ask your bank manager for a loan. I borrowed two lots of £30,000 from Barclays Bank and never had a problem with repaying it within 24 months. I opened a business account with Barclays Bank and they have always looked after me.

I spent thirty grand on a PA system. My ex-National Ballroom, bouncer pal, Graham Logue of Shure UK, will testify to that. He did us proud with generous discounts and we had the best QSC PA any band could wish for. Up until he worked for QSC, Graham got us a sponsorship with JAMO, a Danish PA company. We were given an unlimited array of 2 x 15 cabs and assorted top 15" cabs with radial horns. It was solid stuff but the speakers were hopeless. We used the newly designed cabs on two gigs and blew the lot. It was good hi-fi but simply not up to Rock n' Roll.

I had been a fan and customer of Sherman Audio, which was good British made PA gear, but it did my back in humping it around. It would take four of us to carry one 2 x 18 bass bin up a flight of stairs. Ken Hughes, the owner of the company, was most ungracious towards me after I had spent a small fortune with him and then switched to QSC.

Graham Logue introduced me to many contacts in the business, including the boss of Allen & Heath sound mixers, of which we bought two. The excellent and reliable, 16-channel Wizard which we used for most eight-piece gigs and the superb, A380 32-channel mixer for the larger concerts. Superb stuff.

BASS AMPS

As far as bass amplification went for me - and you will notice that I complain about it a lot in this book — I must have been unlucky. Bass players will maybe understand me.

I was now earning the money to buy the best but was unhappy with most. I tried them all, Ashdown, Hartke, Vox, Marshall, Hi-Watt, McGregor, Hughes & Kettner and Galleon-Kruger. None were right for me and most were too complicated to set up.

After spending much money and losing it on messing with bass amps, we must fast-forward a few years to the disaster that was Trace Elliot. I spent £1800 on this British-made gear that let me down several times on stage. It would just stop working in the middle of a set. I wrote a strong letter of complaint to Trace Elliot and was actually invited down to the factory in Brentwood. I took the gear back.

The fault was in the separate amp top. In all fairness to them they were most apologetic and seemed to take a perverse pride in the caustic letter I had written, which they had pinned to the factory notice board. After all, I was an unknown bass player in a non-chart band. If they thought me a wanker, they never showed it. I was treated with respect and given a choice of new speakers and new amp top, all free of charge. I took them home with me, one 15" wedge cabinet and a two x 10" wedges with a replacement solid-state, 500 watt top.

One thing I learned from the early stages of running a band. *Always* carry a spare amp with you. From the early days we would carry a spare 100watt HH top. At the time of Trace Elliot, I had a spare 6-channel 200watt Sound City top, which lived in the roof compartment of the van. This was just in case the main PA amp went down, which it sometimes did. Never did it come in more handy than at the first gig where I used the brand new replacement Trace Elliot rig.

We had been on stage just twenty minutes at The Dorchester. It was the wonderful 'Make a Wish' Ball. The dance floor was packed. It was right in the middle of 'It's Raining Men' when that mean, green-faced bitch decided to stop working.

The crowd must have thought I was doing a Pete Townsend, when I unplugged the Jazz bass, put it down and then picked up the Trace Elliot top and threw the bastard across the stage, narrowly missing sax player Jez Guest's, head.

Fortunately Jamie Hardwick, by then our established keyboard virtuoso and much accustomed to me stopping in the middle of numbers, immediately picked up the bass line.

I connected the little Sound City amp and finished the show without a hitch. Trace Elliot again replaced the sick amp and sent me a brand new unit. I refused to drive there again. Two weeks later I sold it in *Loot*, together with the speakers. I never used Trace Elliott again, unless it was hired in for me.

I was amiss as to what gear to get next. I had always wanted to try the legendary American-made, Ampeg, so I purchased a basic BA115 combo. This turned out to be a cracking piece of kit. It did not fart or rattle and had a healthy tone range although it was heavy and I was not getting any younger. It served me without fail for several years.

More recently, I was at home and decided to go for a morning stroll with the intention of arriving at The Steam Coach at about 1pm. I wandered through Hemel Old Town and stopped at the window of Fretz the local music shop. I ventured inside for a chat with Barry Garvin, the bass-playing proprietor. It was a well-stocked and well-run shop. I spied a small black and yellow bass combo. It was priced at almost £1000 and named after my brother: MARK. I walked out with it.

The next night I used it at the Grosvenor House Hotel. It was the first time that I ever carried my guitar into the ballroom, with my bass rig in my other hand, it was that light. I set it up on stage and it played like a dream. The wide tone range was simple and easy to set. No confusing and unnecessary graphic equalizer. All I needed was a treble, middle and bass control. The rest is bollocks. You should be able to control your overall tone with the tone controls on your bass. Especially the simple Fender Jazz bass. I have still got that super little MARK combo with its single 15" speaker. No tweeters needed. It never let me down.

STAGE LIGHTING

It would be appropriate at this point to briefly mention the importance of not only sounding good through a good PA system but looking good too!

Right from the birth of Mixed Feelings I was intent on providing a good 'light show' and the first one I constructed myself, by making four small open fronted wooden boxes painted black and each containing six 100wt domestic spotlight bulbs of different colours. Red, green, blue and yellow. There was no proper controller, just a wooden panel of four foot-switches made by Ralph.

I quickly found that the best colour combination was red and blue. Our next step was to be given, free of charge some dusty old 'Peanut' spotlights from the Rolls Royce Social club at Garston. These 300watt lanterns were mounted on home-made stands and got very hot. Next, we progressed to professional 1,000watt aluminium 'cans' of which we mounted 24 on trussing surrounding the band. The lamps or lightbulbs for these cans were very expensive, the cheapest being £40. They got intensely hot too.

The invention of the cool LED (Light Emitting Diode) changed things and although expensive at first, are now the mainstay of the entertainment lighting industry. I invested in these fabulous multi-colour stage lights in 2008 and now Mixed Feelings have an incredible lighting show including LED 'intelligent' lighting and a stage backdrop, 'Chameleon Star Cloth.' It is funny to remember that our first star cloth was 14' x 10' and made in 1990 by Terry's Mum and Dad in the lounge of their home, using lengths of black cloth, several strings of Christmas tree lights and a lot of sewing. It worked too! Subsequently, we were the first band to possess a Star cloth. The word soon spread.

STAGEWEAR

Always look after your band clothes-wise, but never buy them white suits. I learned the hard way when I spent £2000 on ten white suits, which were quickly ruined by red wine, beer and gravy. Musicians are incapable of looking after their stage clothes, especially when supplied for free. They will usually sling them in the car boot until the next gig.

During the 1990s Mixed Feelings was the smartest band on the circuit. I spent a lot of money on modern clothes. A day out at Carnaby Street would set me back £1600, but the band looked like the crew of The Starship Enterprise. All this paid off handsomely but disgruntled others.

Event supplier, Gerry Bamfield commented;

> Johnny Howard told me he was pissed off, because Mixed
> Feelings were getting all the good gigs. He asked me, 'why was
> that?' I told him straight. It's because they are not static like you
> lot. They dress modern, are not boring to look at and move
> around on stage!

Eventually, we acquired a van that was rugged enough to carry a huge amount of gear and crew, without going into the realm of 7.5 trucks. I decided to lease a brand new 3.5 Iveco, long wheel base van, which could be parked on a West End meter bay. These reliable Spanish-built vehicles were perfect for a working band like Mixed Feelings. It also gave a good tax-saving and real peace of mind when driving to Amsterdam, Edinburgh or Paris. Stormont Trucks of Dunstable fitted out the van to my requirements. All wood-panelled inside, with a three-seat crew compartment behind the driver, protected by a solid bulkhead.

Fully kitted out with the best gear, we now entered a very busy period in the life of the band, whereby we were doing lots of gigs, but much of my time was taken up in the search for the ideal guitarist. I had sleepless nights over it. This guitarist would have to be able to play all styles and not feel it beneath him to perform the Masonic Grace, The Hatikva, The National Anthem and Abba songs.

I had already heard about brilliant local guitarist, Pete West, from Terry, who had 'depped' on drums in Pete's band, Don't Panic. Pete wanted the job in Mixed Feelings too. When I approached Pete to join, I was disappointed to find he had dislocated a finger and was unable to perform for several weeks. So Ralph thankfully held on until Pete was 'match fit' and Ralph finally left Mixed Feelings on 20th November 1991. He did the occasional 'dep' gig for us but then stopped performing altogether. We remain good friends.

Pete West's first gig was at The Needham School, Ely. This was in a school hall with a large stage. Pete drove himself there and I wondered why he needed a Mercedes van, which was actually bigger than ours. I was petrified to see him lug onto the stage, via a sack barrow, a huge Mesa Boogie rig. The band backline now resembled that of the Grateful Dead. This was no 'clean' guitarist.

Pete recalls, (for the benefit of guitar bores)

> I have always been fascinated by guitar amplifiers. Nothing shifts air like them. I was one of very few guitarists who owned a Mesa Boogie amp in the late '80s, the undisputed Rolls Royce of guitar amplification back then. I parted with £3000 buying a Mesa Boogie Quad Preamp and Simulclass 295 Power amp plus a further £1800 a steal, for the brand new Mesa 2x12 and 1x12 speaker cabinets. My Mixed Feelings guitar rig now competed in size to Allan Holdsworth's and Steve Lukather's of Toto.

I happened to notice, at some of the larger gigs, Pete putting leaflets on dining tables and leaving them on the bar. At first I thought this a joke but soon realised that Pete was deadly serious. Pete says,

> At large venues I would often distribute leaflets before the band played, disclaiming any liability for hearing loss, nausea, headache, tinnitus and any future mental incapacity. There was one instance in Bury St. Edmunds however, where I recall my large Supersonic Boogie rig came into its own, delivering astounding sound pressure levels of pain to a most unpleasant individual, who was full of his own self – importance and who wanted to spoil the party for five hundred people by storming onto the stage and pulling the plugs out. He was promptly thrown off the stage by Jon - who claimed that this was also the occasion - when my guitar volume had loosened his fillings!

Pete West was, without doubt, the loudest and scariest guitarist that ever graced the Mixed Feelings stage. I hated to tell him to 'turn down the volume.' Simply because *all* guitarists, without exception, get 'offended' if you ask them to do that.

Pete's formidable array of speakers put the fear of Jehovah into many clients. Especially at a Jewish wedding, when I tried to explain to Pete that he didn't need to play the 'Hatikvah' like Eddie Van Halen. On one occasion at the Royal Majestic, a tidy little Jewish venue, he had shamelessly put in his 'small' rig of four Mesa Boogie cabs with four Mesa Boogie amps. When he played the classic guitar solo on the Commodores' 'Easy' many dancers covered their ears and grimaced. I saw Tommy Murray, the amiable Irish Banqueting Manager, sink to his knees and clap his hands over his ears. Unfortunately, I could lip read. 'For fuck's sake.' After the gig Tommy said to me, 'Where did you get that noisy fucker from?'

Pete also liked real ale and was a valuable 'extra' roadie. He would often help Terry and me to break down the gear and wrap leads at the end of the gig, which was always a tiring time when the rest of the band had long departed for the journey home. Pete regarded this as exercise to help solve his weight problem and a chance to laugh at some of Terry's hilarious wanking tales which flowed freely while he was wrapping leads. From November 1991 to June 1992 he performed over 90 gigs with the band. He left with WT and like all of them, regretted it. I swear he was the cause of my partial deafness today. Pete remembers,

> I have wonderful memories of my time with Mixed Feelings a professional band on many levels: What a killer line-up: Kathy Edge, (an amazing singer with a fiery temperament – very Whitney) Barry Elliott, John Maul, Terry Wilson and yourself. You always looked after us, obtaining hot meals and drinks after travel. Also, we were very well paid and often paid on the night, unprecedented. You were a fine bandleader, something that has never been repeated by others. Sadly I left the band due to 'woman trouble.' Which was my then girlfriend, telling me I wasn't twenty anymore and I should 'grow up' and settle down. To think, I could have continued playing in Mixed Feelings and having a whale of a time.

His guitar was a left-handed, 1984 black Tokai Stratocaster, with Seymour-Duncan pickups and he played much in the style of his hero, Joe Satriani. He also played a beautiful Gibson Les Paul sunburst.

So Pete left and I temporarily stopped putting cotton wool in my ears. On Terry's next recommendation we took on another local man, Dave Williams, an amiable and interesting guy from Watford. He turned up for his first gig, carrying *all* his gear in both hands, quite the opposite of Pete West.

Dave ambled into Woburn Golf Club carrying his amp, leads and guitar in one hit. When he set up his little rig, I was concerned that he would not be loud enough. He also declined to be 'miked up' through the PA. 'Don't need it,' he said. His guitar was a beautiful, red Fender Stratocaster and his amp was a tiny Music Man 1x12 50 watt combo. It looked so small but bloody hell, could he make that thing sing! It was as loud as hell and the tones he got from his Stratocaster were amazing. I put the cotton wool back.

Dave would use his fingers to pluck and he also used a 'steel' bottleneck. He was a brilliant blues guitarist, much in the vein of Ry Cooder. So, dinner music at some wedding events was adapted to suit Dave Williams' unique style of 'Swamp' music, including the haunting theme to 'Southern Comfort', on which Dave used a 'steel' and which surprisingly, made people put down their knives and forks and applaud.

Dave Williams was also very laid back and would do anything for a quiet life. At this time in the life of the band, we had not yet advanced to using a proper sound engineer. My son Greg was still only 15 years old and straining at the leash to leave school and work full time for me. He would later develop into a fine sound engineer. The main requirement needed for this relatively modern skill is not a university degree but a good pair of ears. This he had. But for the time being, I was doing the job myself, with the vocal mixer on stage next to me.

We were performing at the Park Lane Piccadilly Hotel, whereby, Kathy Edge and Dave Howard were singing the opening song, 'Up Where We Belong.' Kathy was so loud that I noticed some of the ancient dancers at this posh Jewish wedding were putting their hands over their ears at a certain point in the duet. Why is it that *old* people always dance so close to the PA speakers?

On stage and nearest to our little 12.2 Roland vocal mixer was Dave Williams, happily strumming away. I gave him a nudge on the elbow and said, 'Dave, can you turn down the number two slider please Mate?' Dave, new to the band and keen to assist, immediately yanked down the 'slider' controlling Kathy's mic and Kathy within a second, turns to Dave and me and yells, 'Right! which one of you fuckers turned me down?' I keep a straight face and point to Dave. 'He did.'

An infuriated Kathy, storms over to the mixer and pushes her slider back up, even higher than before. At the same time, she turns down Dave Howard. Who then promptly walks over and turns himself back up and turns Kathy back down. She then, thunder-faced, goes straight back and turns her self up again and Dave down. 'For fuck's sake, leave the mixer alone,' was my term of expression, although I was shaking with laughter.

We got through the first quarter of the evening with lots of applause, in spite of some old parrots stuffing napkins in their ears. At half time, Kathy was ferociously lecturing a sheepish Dave Williams and wagging a finger in his red face. 'Don't you ever fucking turn me down! You've only been in this band two minutes and you fucking turned me down!'

Poor Dave Williams. After his roasting, he turns to me says, 'Sir! Sir! I've been suckered!' Another lesson learned. *Always* keep your vocal mixer out of the reach of the bloody singers. In fact, get yourself a proper sound engineer. I led the chastised guitarist to the bar for a large Glen Morange.

Dave Williams lasted just over three months with the band and saw us through the summer of 1992. I liked Dave very much but I don't think he liked our music or Sergeant Major Edge. *I never saw him again.*

In fact most blues guitarists would probably vomit to our choice of music. I really needed a guitarist who could play all styles and *wanted to.* The stuff that Dave didn't like, was the stuff that I liked playing and sold the band. I simply loved music in all its varieties, apart from Jazz. That's why Mixed Feelings was so popular. In spite of the kindly advice given to me at Bushey Police Club, by the Chief Superintendent's wife, I continued to 'self indulge' with certain songs and instrumentals. After all, it was my band.

I deliberately avoided – unless requested – the dreary guitar-orientated songs, which most other bands featured, such as 'All Right Now', 'Bad Moon Rising' and that boring, 'I Shot The Sheriff'. There were however some crappy songs you just had to play, because they were crowd pleasers, like 'Mustang Sally'.

For Kathy Edge, two 'production' numbers which always brought her a huge ovation were from the brilliant musical, *Les Miserables.* She sang, 'On My Own' and 'I Dreamed A Dream' better than any female singer on the circuit at the time. This is why Mixed Feelings were in demand.

Very few bands attempted some of the songs we did; 'Toccata,' (Sky) 'Music' (John Miles), *The War of the Worlds, The Phantom of the Opera* and then, *'Les Mis.'* We were constantly accused of playing along to backing tracks. Something we have never done.

The next guitarist I found was Bishop's son, Pete Callard, who did his first gig in the band on the 3rd of October 1992, at the Firs Hall, Edmonton. Pete, who we called 'Rev' was a gentle soul who played in a brilliantly, 'swinging' guitar style. Every solo, cum Rock or Blues, was played in a 'Jazz' flair with a myriad of notes flowing from Pete's speedy fingertips. Pete was easy to get on with and was intelligent company. He loved cricket but had an irritating habit of saying 'cool' whenever something was pointed out to him. Kathy Edge soon sorted him out. 'Saying *cool* is the most *uncool* fucking thing you can say.'

Roadies again

At this point in the narrative I think it appropriate to again refer to the often unsung heroes of a band, the 'roadies'. I was lucky in so far as the band had sufficient well-paid work to enable me to employ a full-time driver and 'road manager', (a nicer term).

When one thinks of a roadie, there springs to mind visions of beer-gutted cave-dwellers and living proof that interbreeding does not work. Most are exceptionally strong, about five feet tall and the same width. We met many of these mainly antipodean humpers in the West End when working with event companies. Most wore shorts when temperatures were below zero.

Rarely were they clean cut and smart, but with Mixed Feelings they simply had to be, such was the amount of 'posh' gigs we were doing. I made them dress in smart black suits too, once the humping had been done. We did have the misfortune to employ one spaghetti-hoop eating idiot, who shaved his head totally and looked the epitome of a prison camp guard. He was the unemployed son of a friend and as a favour I gave him work, but he had an IQ lower than his shoe size. Toastmaster Howard Robbins remarked that I should be commended for employing handicapped people.

Never employ sons, or daughters of friends. The difficulty comes when you have to sack them. This one's brooding presence was not a good advert for the band. Another London toastmaster commented, 'It's hard to believe he beat 100 million other sperm.'

When I told him to grow his hair a little, his mother complained of 'Bullying in the workplace.' I asked him one night, to 'gently persuade' people to leave the stage and he replied, 'Yus, but Jonifun, I won't be held responsible if I break their fucking jaw.' So 'Endus Bellus' had to go.

I soon replaced him with Martin Carew, a fellow 'Gooner' who went to school with Greg. He worked superbly for the band for several years. He turned out to be an excellent roadie, driver and timekeeper. (Grade 1) He could also work the mixing desk.

Lessons were learned especially when roadies were driving your van, which in our case had magnetic, Mixed Feelings ads on the side. It is not good practice for your roadie to spit out of the window. One London cabbie pulled up alongside the van in Park Lane and said, 'You have just gobbed on my cab and I booked you lot for my daughter's wedding!'

It is always possible to find a weekend roadie. There are plenty of strong lads out there looking for some extra beer money at the weekends. Plus it's good for their cred to be a 'roadie'. These are 'Grade 3' roadies, who are simply, 'humpers'. Then there are roadies who can set up a PA system and a light show. These are 'Grade 2.' Then there are the

'Grade I' roadies who are low maintenance and can drive the van. They can also reliably park the van in the West End, without bothering the bandleader for money for meters.

My brother in law, Paul Singleton, soon made 'Grade 1 roadie'. He had just been made redundant at his long-time workplace, The Deanshanger Oxide Works, and so grabbed the opportunity to work with me. He soon adapted to the job and did it full-time. He was dependable and resourceful. He was also a fully qualified electrician, which was handy when wiring in 60 amp powered lighting rigs, a risky procedure for the untrained man. How Dave Howard never blew the band up is a mystery.

According to Paul, we almost set fire to the London Hilton,

> One of my jobs was to wire up the 'Le Maitre' stage
> pyrotechnics which would be detonated when the show
> opened. I wired them up accordingly, with a 'gerb' stage left
> and right. These things would fire a sparkling silver firework
> fountain about 12 feet into the air. Jon had told me to inform
> the hotel security which I did and they assured me they would
> turn off the fire alarms. No one did. When the band started,
> the fireworks went off and so did the fire alarms! The room
> was full of smoke and the whole London Hilton Hotel had to
> be evacuated. People were moved out of their rooms and into
> the street in bath robes. The London Fire Brigade turned up
> in force and cleared the ballroom. We were banned from using
> fireworks from then on!

Paul quickly learned to set up the PA, lighting rigs, and mixing desks. He found us dressing rooms and more importantly, located real ale. He was excellent but the late nights took their toll on his family life and he left with suspected WT after two years of solid service. During that time he had acquired a taste for Abbot Ale and always maintained that working with Mixed Feelings was the 'best job I ever had.'

My 'big' little brother Mark was also out of work, after serving years at the same defunct Deanshanger Oxide Works and took over from Paul. Another Grade I roadie too. Once again he was reliable, quick to learn and with a lunatic sense of humour. He left no-one in doubt as to who could fart the loudest. He could set off car alarms two blocks away.

Mark was also a useful, 'procurer,' finding anything, which could be of use. He could locate dressing rooms and was gently 'diplomatic' with clients maintaining that 'diplomacy' was not my best asset. For all the laughter we shared, the long hours involved and the travel to and from Deanshanger, eventually caught up with him too. Mark and Paul were no longer young men neither had their wives been used to their men staying out all night at weekends. Mark eventually found a job as a sales rep for Ann Summers.

'Sensible' roadies were hard to come by. One mistake was a Chelsea FC 'Shed boy' who was big, friendly and as strong as an oak tree but purely gormless. This became apparent when we were working at the London Hilton Ballroom and the event company was Bedfordshire based, Roland Miller, which had decked out the room in 'star cloth' and the competent but loud, boss of the company had seen the star cloth wobbling, as our roadie was behind it stacking flight cases. 'Jon, can you get your 'oaf' off my star cloth?' was not the cleverest thing for Andy Miller to say, as our 'oaf,' with eyes glazed in fury, emerged from behind the star cloth in true Stamford Bridge style, fists at the ready, 'Who fackin' called me a 'Hoaf?' I'll kill his fackin' 'ead.' In spite of the dire threat of his head being terminated, Andy Miller kept his and there was no fight. He liked our band, even more so after Dumbo had been fired and gave us some quality gigs, many of them in the West End of London or at the Birmingham NEC Hilton, with a couple of events in Dublin too. We would also perform at his wedding in August 2006.

One of our best (Grade 2) roadies was local lad, Bob Wise, a twig of a youth and every bit the Peter Pan who looked eleven years old. He was continually refused service when trying to purchase beer at the Pub even though he was 19 years old and still believed in Father Christmas. He also liked to smoke a bit of 'Ganja.'

I had long left the Police at the time he joined the band but had my personal views on the use of cannabis as a recreational drug or medicine. I certainly did not want my band to use it on gigs. Consequently, we never gained a reputation for 'doing drugs' as some bands did. It certainly clouded judgement and on the one occasion that Terry ate a cannabis cake that Bob had made for his birthday, we opened the show with 'Love Shack' and he stopped after just sixteen bars, thinking the song had finished.

I did however allow Bob to light up an occasional 'spliff' on the way home from gigs, when all was done and dusted. It was a 'relaxer' and re-booted the laughter in the van, keeping us daftly awake on the long journey home. We could not stop laughing at the canine tales of 'Buster Wilson' whose tricks with his tongue were so embellished by Terry that if true, Terry would be transported for life.

Bob Wise remembers;

> I first started working for the band in 1997, when I was 19 and it completely changed my life! Learned about electrics, PA's and stage lighting. I also loved going to work with a family of lovely friends. They were like brothers and sisters and the happiest days of my life. I was taught how to wrap XLR leads properly. Never around the shoulder and elbow, but in careful loops and with a flick of the wrist take out any kinks. It seemed we were always at the Prince Regent Hotel in Woodford Green and another of my jobs was to go to the bar and get a round of 'Jewish Cokes' and the lady behind the bar said, 'How do you guys manage to drink so much and keep on playing?'

Another occasional 'Grade 3' roadie, was actor and comedian, Steve Coogan. He was friendly with one of our girl singers and would turn up early in the evening and carry small items of gear in. (Mainly her stage clothes). He liked the band and came to see us on several gigs in the West End, making notes at the dressing room antics of certain members of the band, especially, 'acrotwat' Terry, who would do half-naked handstands in the dressing room. Sumo wrestling also took place, with certain persons pulling their underpants up the crack of their arse. Some of Steve's comical TV characters were based on the rock n' roll frolics of the lunatics in Mixed Feelings.

Schools Out!
L-R Pete Callard, Helen York, Jamie Hardwick,
Dave Howard, Jon Nicholls, Sue Acteson, Terry Wilson

Blaze of Glory! - The Young Guns that sold the band *Photo Keith Collman*

'Where did you get that noisy fucker from?'
Pete West (2019) with his 1992 'mini'rig

Dave Price
'Played Guitar exactly how I wanted'

'If ever a bandleader fell on his feet it was then'
Luton Hoo 1996. L-R Dave Price, Ian Manser, Jamie Hardwick, Helen York,
Jon Nicholls, Sue Acteson, Dave Howard, Terry Wilson

Park Lane Hotel 2002 L-R Terry Wilson, Gary Priestley, JN, Jamie Hardwick,
Johnny Amobe, Dave Price. Sitting Sue Acteson, Helen York

Left. Mike Mason
'Tremendous Front-Man'

Right, Gary Priestley
'Longest serving singer
in Mixed Feelings'

*Photos
Glenn Stanley &
Keith Davidson*

Tony Moriah
'Had the richest and most accurate of voices that had every fronted our band'

Lynsey Shaw& Suzi Jari

Same Bass, Same Face, 33 years later. The Bass has been given a Facelift..
Note. MARK Bass Combo is excellent for 20,000 fans at the Salisbury Festival 2012

Jamie Hardwick. 'The wittiest person I have
ever met. He soon introduced the COM award'

Regular Winner

Salisbury Festival 2012   *Photo. Glenn Stanley*

COM in Dublin 2007

COM sets himself on fire in Switzerland 1998 Nick Foister on left

With Alexander O' Neal in Oman 2008
who cannot hear a 'mutha-fucking thing' (Nominated 'guest' COM)

The 'hard work' performing is the setting up and taking down. Note. QSC PA system,
Allen & Heath 'Wizard' mixing desk and freshly painted black and white dance floor

Berlin 2007. The morning after.
Greg Nicholls, Terry Wilson & Jon Nicholls

Austria 2002 on the Piste with Terry Wilson,
Gerry Bamfield & Greg Nicholls

'Keeping the dance floor packed all night'

Salisbury Festival 2012. A dynamic front line. *Photo Glenn Stanley*
L-R Lyndsey Cleary, Gary Priestley, Suzi Jari, Chris Madin, Marina Berry

Photo Terry Wilson
Jamie Hardwick Tenerife 2004

Photo Terry Wilson
Tony Moriah Tenerife 2004

Deanbeats (1964) Reunited (2010)
L-R Jon, Tates, Nick

Mixed Feelings (1983) Reunited (2018
L-R Ralph, Dick, Jon, Vaughan

Lyndsey, Suzi & Linda
at Lee Reboul's Wedding 2015

Brad, Lee & Jon
at the Dorchester Hotel 2017

Mixed Feelings at the Dorchester Hotel 2008
Standing L-R Jamie Hardwick, Jez Guest, Lynsey Shaw, Dave Price, Jon Nicholls,
Suzi Jari, Nick Batt, Dave Peers. Sitting L-R Tony Morial, Terry Wilson, Gary Priestley

Mixed Feelings at the Dorchester Hotel 2018
L-R Mark Rideout, Andy Hardwick, Jonathan Bremner, Ralph Millington, Lee Reboul, Brad,
(Behind Brad) Lyne Birbeck, Marina Berry, Dave Price, Lorena Dale

PART III

9

HANKY SPANKY

I retired from the Metropolitan Police on 1st January 1995. I had enjoyed all 27 years of my Police career and would always be proud to have served my country in such a great organization. I had been called to see the CMO of the Metropolitan Police. I was wearing a NHS neck brace and must have looked a proper twat. I had three fused vertebrae in my neck. A legacy of rugby football.

The CMO was a kindly Welshman and must have been in a good mood that day because he let me go without fuss. He shook my hand and I walked away from the Metropolitan Police. I lost the neck-brace. I had left 'The Job' but never the Met 'Family'. I was about to embark on the next part of my life. That of a professional musician and bandleader.

The only times I got despondent in my new career, was when someone who I liked left the band. There were few reasons why a person should want to leave a good band like Mixed Feelings. It was a secure job that paid their mortgage and usually provided them with a hot meal and drinks at gigs. I clothed them too. All they had to do was turn up, perform and go home. Plus, they *always* got paid on time. Yet still some whinged.

The *main reason*, I discovered over the years, as to why the majority of male performers left, was because of 'WT'. What woman wants her man out until 4am in the morning *four* nights a week even though he was bringing home good money? It is a *good woman* that puts up with living with a musician. Bringing up a young family always adds to the problem, when Daddy is not there at weekends. More than one regretful 'leaver' said to me, 'She doesn't like me doing this.' Plus, 'She thinks I shouldn't come to work to drink beer and enjoy myself.' Most regretted leaving Mixed Feelings and have since told me so.

Some left the band because they didn't like being told what to do by me. One called me a 'bully' for the manner in which I spoke to him. 'You look like a bag of laundry tied up with string. Any chance of running an iron over those fucking trousers?' I never intended to hurt anyone's feelings. I simply thought a small minority of musicians were undisciplined wankers as they proved to be.

I rarely had 'trouble' with my musicians, although one constantly whingeing trumpet player left because I wouldn't pay him the same rate as the singers. So I told him that he could fuck off. He was so professional he fucked off *before* the gig, thereby losing himself a night's pay and leaving me as he thought, without a trumpet player. Within an hour, his better replacement arrived and gratefully took his job.

After leaving 'The Job', I intended to take the band to the top of the event ladder. To accomplish this I needed to speak to the top agents and one of the biggest was Norman Phillips, who was based at Sutton Coldfield, near Birmingham. I wanted to see him personally, to convince him that I was now a professional bandleader and no longer a Police officer. I could at last, be taken seriously (or so I thought!) I telephoned him and he kindly gave me an appointment to meet him one morning in January 1995.

Wearing my best Top Man suit and reeking of Givenchy Gentleman, I drove up the M1 to his big house near Birmingham where I entered his office complex and saw busy secretaries tapping away on typewriters and answering telephones.

I found Norman a forthright man. He invited me to his office and offered me a coffee. He asked me about the band and what I expected to achieve. He had himself, been a professional bandleader and musician. These were the best type of agents. They knew all the pitfalls of running a band. He was very frank about what I should do.

'Are you VAT registered?' I answered in the negative. 'Get yourself VAT registered. A band that is not VAT registered has no credibility whatsoever in the corporate market.' This was good advice.

I acted on it next day and I was surprised how easy it was to register for the dreaded VAT. I attended just one local VAT seminar and met the Customs and Excise people who were youthful, trendy and helpful. Norman's advice was, 'If you never want a visit from the VAT inspectors then submit your returns every quarter before the due date and pay promptly. They will leave you alone.' They did.

His next piece of advice was even more important and went like this: 'Always pay your musicians on time. If you delay payment, when the money is in your bank, then you will gain a reputation as a bad payer and they won't want to work for you.' I wrote all this valuable advice down in my old Police notebook.

'Who is the most important member of your band?' Was his next question. 'The guitarist?' I mumbled. 'No! It's your male singer. It is *he* who will sell your band, so if you've got a good one, pay him well. He's your centre forward and main entertainer. He should always earn more than the fullback.' Norman spoke clearly and sincerely,

Next, find a good keyboard player and look after him too. They are hard to come by, and tend to go where the money is, so pay them well. Your bass player and drummer is the rhythm section of the band, so pay them the going rates. Drummers are two a penny and usually mad as hatters. There are loads of them out there. Every kid wants to be a drummer. You should never have problems replacing a guitarist but find one who *looks good* and can play *all styles*. Female singers are a pain in the backside. They can be temperamental and prima donnas. But they are essential to making a good show band. Two females and one male singer is ideal. Go and see my band 'Red Sun' they are good. Don't pay your female singers too much. Once again they are two a penny. Loads of 'em out there. Spend money on their costumes. It is rare you get a gorgeous woman who can really sing. They are *Stars*. So keep them looking sexy and dress them nice. Brass players are cheap but usually cheerful. There are loads of them about.

I have never forgotten that man's advice. He was a wise owl. It was the one and only time I ever met him. He gave us some good work. I went and saw his band, Red Sun, too and they were good.

The West End was dominated by the brilliant and sophisticated Johnny Howard Band, which often went out on a Saturday night as multiple 'Johnny Howard Bands' and would perform at the top venues: Grosvenor House, London Hilton and the Dorchester Hotels. It was not unusual to see the JH band at three different events on a Saturday night. Johnny himself would turn up at all three venues and be on stage at some point with the band.

Johnny was a handsome and charming man. His hugely successful band played all over England, gaining a residency on the BBC Radio show *Easy Beat*. Johnny used many well-known session players, like Vic Flick and Alan Parker.

I needed to go into the West End, to see for myself exactly what this band was about. I needed to see if I could possibly compete with my little band of five or six musicians. I donned my black bow tie and suit and simply walked into the Great Room of the Grosvenor House Hotel, where a large company party was happening. Security men stood on the door but no one stopped me. The black tie in the West End was a passport to most events, second only to the Met Police warrant card.

When you see the Great Room at this famous hotel for the first time it is breath-taking. It was the largest banqueting suite in Europe and I was told it was once an ice rink. There were probably upwards of a thousand people on the dance floor and surrounding dinner tables. I stood on the spacious balcony that encircles the whole ballroom and waited, as the formally dressed Johnny Howard Band sauntered on to the stage, loudly announced by Bryn Williams, the well- known London toastmaster.

The PA system was a surprisingly small and simple set up for this huge venue and consisted of a single pair of Bose 802 speakers, which did the trick. At least you could clearly hear the vocals when the band kicked off with 'I Just Called To Say I Love You', the top-selling song by Stevie Wonder. It was sung beautifully by a tall good-looking blonde lad, Gary James. He looked about 17 years old.

I noted, 'How can I compete with that?' There were fourteen of them. I watched the band as they turned over the pages of their 'Dave

Tanner' music scores, which all the West End Bands used and went into more contemporary but gentle songs; 'You're Just Too Good To Be True' followed by a waltz, 'Moon River', then 'Fly Me To The Moon.' I made more notes.

The backing band were professional, music-reading musicians and some were quite elderly, i.e. in their fifties. Some of them – including the bass player, who was playing an unusual but ugly black Steinberger headless bass. They also had stacks of music in front of them. Johnny was flitting amongst the musicians like a mother hen, turning the pages of their music to the next song.

There were two female singers supporting Gary. They were established pie detectives. One in a glittery, navy blue ball gown, the other in a brown satin, three quarter length dress. Brown dresses never look good under lighting. There was no sexy dancing from these singers. They just stood there, waving their arms out of sync. Good singers mind. Already my mind was buzzing. Could I afford *two* girls in Mixed Feelings? *Two* girls who could both sing lead vocals, harmonise and dance?

The next band I would go and view would be Alpha Connection. They had already broken into the West End and were starting to cause huge waves of dissent among function bandleaders. They were taking all the good jobs and they only had one male singer! No girls.

I needed to learn from this prominent young band. They were fast getting a respectable reputation in the business and they were certainly in big demand, working six nights a week. I first saw them when I went to the Four Seasons Hotel at the invitation of band musicians and founders (now successful agents) Steve Cook and Russ Brewster, both ex-Royal Marines and nice guys. A breath of fresh air in a jealously guarded world of cut-throat prices and huge mark-ups. It was just what the band business needed. They were friendly, approachable and extremely professional.

The eight-piece band was an unusual line-up and consisted of keyboards, bass and drums, plus a dynamic four-piece brass section. They were fronted by a stocky, northern singer, Greg Valentine. He was also an ex-royal Marine and a real bundle of energy. The music was totally live with a great sound but what made this band so different from all the other bands, was the *choreography*. The robotic and mesmerising

'Horn' section dominated centre stage, moving in well- rehearsed, precise dance moves. It was great to watch. They also changed costume several times during the show.

It was around October '95 that Linda had been diagnosed with breast cancer and it came as great shock to us both and brought lots of tears. So, leaving the Police had come at the right time. With a tidy sum of money, known as 'commutation of pension', I bought her a brand new MGF sports car to add some cheer to her life, which she doubtless feared would soon be over.

We took a pleasant day trip in the little sports car to Hull the following summer, to see Alpha Connection perform at the Mecca Bingo club, which featured a live band from 6pm-7pm. This was a fun gig and a mid-week 'diary filler'. Thanks to Russ and Steve, we would soon be on the same, 'Bingo' circuit. We both thought Alpha Connection great and I had an idea in my head that I could create a similar act - a visually brilliant show band - but with two sexy girl singers and dancers, that changed costume.

Our 'Little Miss Dynamite', Kathy Edge, had left the band as she was fed up with Dave Howard, who she referred to as 'Mungo'. But she really wanted to do other things, like go 'solo'. Consequently, Alison Cooper, a London session singer, had stepped into the breech to get us by. She had a superb Barbara Streisand voice but was not exactly the eye candy I was looking for. She was a magnificent singer and sang, 'Don't Know Much' with Dave Howard as good as Linda Ronstadt. She was also built like a butcher's daughter. Terry quickly named her 'Moped' – 'fun to ride but you wouldn't want your mates to know.'

Reverting to my search for girl singers and following the usual ad in The Stage, auditions were held in the basement studio at Wootton Drive in September 1994. Fortunately, we have always been blessed with good neighbours who have never complained about the succession of cars coming and going. (Or for that matter, the arrival of the returning van at 3am in the morning!) At 10.20pm I had switched the lights out. I was pissed off as nothing of real quality had materialised.

The last farmer's daughter had gone home. We had seen around twenty girls. I was a bit despondent but knew I would continue the search. Trouble is we had Baywatch babes turn up that couldn't sing and look-a-likes for On the Buses 'Olive', who could.

My doorbell rang at 10.45pm. I had just poured myself a large Talisker. The last girl had gone home at 10.15pm, so my immediate reaction was, 'I'll take a quick look at her and if she's fugly, I'll tell her auditions have finished.'

I whipped open the front door and there stood an answer to a prayer. Two gorgeous Miss Worlds. Lancashire blonde, Helen York and Susan Acteson, an Essex brunette. 'Sorry we are late, we got lost. We only work together too, so it's both of us or nothing,' said Helen nonchalantly. I uttered another quick prayer upwards. 'Please God, let them be able to sing.'

We went down the wooden stairs into the basement and I put the lights back on, switched on the cassette deck and put two SM58 mics on stands. Greg was with me, 'Lets hope they can both sing!' He whispered to me. Helen gave me the cassette backing tracks. Both were wearing black mini-skirts and matching black tops. High patent heels and black tights clad their shapely legs. The backing track clicked into 'Love Shack' by the B52's.

'Fucking hell!' Were the two most commonly used words in my extensive vocabulary of filthy language. They were uttered in amazement there and then, as Sue and Helen launched into that raunchy 'evergreen' song that every party band should do. The vocals were strong and accurate and the choreography just hypnotic and sexy. They wiggled their hips, breasts and bums in sync with each other. It was a well-rehearsed and sexy dance routine. They then did, 'Dancing In The Street'. I could have watched them all night.

I had found what I had been searching for. Not only were they sexy, they were classy and pretty girls. I asked them when they could start and they were available immediately. That was great news. They had been doing session singing with one of my favourite songwriters, Russ Ballard, and there had been a flirtation with Brotherhood of Man but according to Sue, this semi-famous band didn't have much work and they were owed money. I showed them our band date sheet. That was it. They were in.

If ever a bandleader fell on his feet, it was then. It was a massive turning point and changed the band forever, taking us upwards into the West End and beyond. Everyone wanted Mixed Feelings. These two girls, were the best looking, top singers and sexiest dancers in the business. They both had their own transport and were baggage free. None of the other bands had 'crumpet' like it. They revolutionised the show and of course we featured 'Love Shack', which is a definite floor filler. They brought with them a good selection of rehearsed songs and never used written lyrics on stage. Soon the word was spreading and our new show was being noticed.

As Paul Fifer, a happy client wrote,

> Thank you for the fabulous party last Sunday at Pinewood Studios. Your group do not just play and sing the music, they give a Performance, superbly choreographed and lit. *That is what separates Mixed Feelings from the others on the circuit.* Your re-vamping of the Group has added a new dimension of professionalism and glamour and your girls not only look good but sing superbly. This is not just our opinion. One of our guests, who is casting director at one of the leading firms of West End Theatre producers, has told me that.

I gave the trustworthy and funny Sue Acteson money to buy new costumes. She purchased basques and black patent thigh boots. White Abba costumes and white boots too. Her modern dress sense was excellent and she possessed a laugh dirtier than a coal miner's hankie. She could also harmonise superbly with Helen. She was probably the best harmony singer we ever had in the band.

The phenomena of these two sexy girls would never look right behind the massive piles of music of the conservative, Johnny Howard Band, or the 'so macho' Alpha Connection. About a week later, I got a telephone call from a ranting Barry Upton, of Brotherhood of Man, who threatened to 'punch my lights out,' for 'nicking' his girls. 'Never heard of you,' was my retort.

But it didn't end there. My phone never stopped ringing. It rang unceasingly, sometimes, thirty times a day. Linda, a trained secretary, kept a good record of all the calls and sold the band easily. She was quite brilliant on the telephone. However, she remembered a phone call from another well-known London bandleader, Denny Wise. I had personally never spoken to him before. He was mighty pissed off that Mixed Feelings were now taking the West End by storm. I never realised there was such a level of animosity. As Linda recollects,

A few months after Sue and Helen joined the band we were sitting in the garden enjoying a glass of wine in the sunshine, when Jon put his phone on loudspeaker. The call was from an angry bandleader called Denny Wise. He called Jon a 'See-you-en-tee' and accused him of losing him work, nicking all the top gigs and bringing the industry into disrepute, by bringing two 'effing slags' into the band.

I was disappointed with Denny. He had a good band, although like Johnny Howard, he shared his music-reading musicians with other similar bands. He had even changed his surname to a Jewish one in order to net more Jewish gigs. He failed because he never had 'a pair of fucking slags.'

Another call I got was from Peter Richardson. A successful entertainment agent, who asked me why an ex-Police officer should want to run a band? He told me I should 'leave it to the professionals' like Johnny Howard and Ray McVay. He also implied the name of the band was 'rubbish'. Nevertheless, in spite of Pete's characteristic prickliness, he and his business partner, Paul Baxter, gave us even more superb, West-End work. The nicest call I got was from Johnny Howard himself, who congratulated me on my success with the band and asked me what the 'secret' was. I told him, 'A pair of fucking slags.'

Soon afterwards Johnny Howard joined hands with the aforementioned Peter and Paul and so Fanfare 3000 was born. The agency then became the sole management of The Johnny Howard Band. They decided they wanted a piece of Mixed Feelings' action. If you can't beat 'em, join 'em. The venerated Johnny Howard Band disappeared forever into London dance band legend. The name and image was changed and the fairground attraction of Rollacoaster created.

In spite of Denny Wise's crude assessment that my new girls were 'fucking slags', they sold the band every time and it was just a few months after Sue and Helen arrived that there began a long association with the Aberdeen Oil Company. The first gig we did for them was a two-nighter, held at Gleneagles Hotel Perthshire. On the Friday 'cabaret' night we successfully completed the first part of the gig and I gained the impression that the clients were more than happy with the band.

We were due to perform on the Saturday night for the Grand Gala Ball, which was for the same people in the same marquee. Here I must say, we were having a wonderful time and had spent a glorious Saturday enjoying the Gleneagles hospitality, walking the golf course, admiring the breath-taking scenery, enjoying a grilled steak lunch, swimming, cycling and tennis. Not to mention a free bar in the hotel, given to us by the generous AOGA committee. 'Just put it on our room.'

We had all met in the bar at 5pm and the event was due to start at 7pm. The band had been given a table for dinner among the 600 diners. 'I would like this gig back next year guys, so let's give them a night to remember,' I told the band. I then took a quick shower and changed into my stage suit. There was a knock at my door. It was a hotel messenger who said, 'The Committee would like a meeting with you in the main bar.'

'What's all this about?' I wondered. 'Did we drink too much the night before? I was also aware that Dave Howard had got pissed and been sick up the back of the tent. I apprehensively made my way to the classy main bar of this famous old hotel. Standing in the big bay window, were six smartly dressed gentlemen, all suited and booted for the evening event and drinking champagne. 'Ah Jon,' said one. 'Thanks for coming. Can we have a word?'

I joined them and shook hands with all six, smiling men. 'We had a great day's golf today and are hoping you are going to give us another great night, tonight! We loved your show last night and were just discussing whether to have you back next year. We *never* have the same band two years running.'

Just then, in the golden evening sunshine, walking along the gravel path outside the bay window, came my two attractive girl singers, wearing their new red ball gowns, split high up the front to show their shapely legs. They saw me in the window with the 'committee' and waved. As they walked past they stopped and hitched up their dresses, bent over and 'mooned' their beautiful arses. It was pure choreography. 'Bloody hell!' and 'Fuck me rigid!' were just two of the comments from our astounded gentlemen. The third comment was, 'Jon, you have definitely got the gig back next year!'

Many bandleaders turned up to view our new show. We were spied upon and even videoed by one prick, who tried to copy the show song for song but failed, purely because he had Cinderella's sisters fronting his band. As Michael Black advised, 'Whatever you do son, be sure some bastard will try and fuck you up.' How right he was. Rumours were now put about that Mixed Feelings were 'hell raisers' at which I took a perverse pride.

In all reality I had gone past the 'standard' function band norm with Mixed Feelings. The first thing we did was a fully harmonic ABBA medley, which in the mid-nineties was very popular. ABBA tunes had some brilliant bass lines which I enjoyed playing. We also maintained our Kool & the Gang medley but I pushed it to the limit when I brought in the totally outrageous Alice Cooper, 'School's Out' set. This consisted of Dave Howard, who had managed to get himself a school gown and mortarboard cap, from a Dunstable junk shop, plus a swishy, crooked handled cane. The girls were well up for it and I dressed them in pleated school gym skirts and stockings, with straw boaters, collars, and ties. They even carried hockey sticks onto the stage. It was, 'Ann Summers goes to St Trinians'.

Madonna's 'Hanky Panky' brought the house down with the simulated spanking on stage. Especially when volunteer 'spankers' and 'spankees' were called for. According to one toastmaster, there was a queue to the back of the room. It was one of the funniest things I have ever seen and I laughed until I split my trousers. The girls never ever thought it demeaning or sexist and regarded it as wonderful 'Wacko' fun. It was raucous musical theatre and Dave Howard really thought he was Jimmy Edwards.

Did it sell the band? Yes! Did we do it at Barmitzvahs? Yes! Especially for the Essex contingent, who demanded it. I even had publicity photos printed on the strength of it. The further addition of *The Full Monty*, and 'You Can Leave Your Hat On' had men stripping off, on stage. Was it tacky? Yes! But audiences had seen nothing like it.

We did it at the Met Police Club Bushey, for the Kentish Town Police annual dance. A riot of appreciation followed. We were booked back on the strength of it, for the following year. Then I was told on the night, by champion dwarf chucker and social secretary Jan Leloch, 'That the (female) Chief Superintendent, 'Mam, fucking fun spoiler,' is gonna 'fuck off if you do that spanking song.'

It was a stonking gig and just before the interval, I announced that due to 'complaints last year' there would be no 'Hanky Spanky' in the second half. This was met with a barrage of booing. So we did it.

There was tumultuous applause as the girls bending over on stage got another simulated arse whacking from the headmaster. Chief Superintendent 'Funspoiler', OBE (offended by everything) duly fucked off and we never got booked back. I believe Jan was promptly sacked from the social club committee and we were banned from performing our, 'Hanky Spanky set' at Bushey Police Club, as it lowered Police professional standards. What wonderful headlines it would have made in the newspapers: 'Met Police Spanking Den in rural Hertfordshire'.

We had hit the international scene. Many bands advertised themselves in the music press, websites and media as 'International' show bands, simply because they had performed at a wedding in Glasgow. As new keyboard player Jamie Hardwick said,

> We certainly went places. From Christmas Eve in Bahrain...
> to the Gleneagles Hotel, The Silver Whisper Cruises, Ireland
> to Seville, Marrakech to Amsterdam, Switzerland to Austria,
> Oman to Tenerife, Abu Dhabi to St Petersburg, Estonia to
> Monte Carlo, Barcelona to Seville, etc. We forget how far and
> wide the band took us!

It is at this point of the narrative that I can no longer bore the reader with the time and exact date when, 'so and so' joined the band.

Jamie Hardwick came in on keyboards after John Maul decided to leave under friendly terms but suffering from WT. Jamie had answered an ad I had placed in *The Stage* and I was auditioning individual keyboard players at my studio at Wootton Drive. He arrived at my door and used the Roland set-up lent by John. He was only 21 years old and nervous.

> I remember answering an ad in *The Stage* and turning up at
> your house where you gave me the music to 'Love Lift Us Up
> Where We Belong' then being given cassettes of the set which I
> took home to learn. I turned up to the gig the following Friday
> fully rehearsed. The band was Dave Howard, Kathy Edge, Pete
> West and Terry Wilson. First thoughts were, 'Blimey, they
> have a drink before the gig!' They also had a great PA system.
> I always used Roland keyboards. They worked easy for me.
> When I joined I was using Roland RD250 Piano, Rhodes
> Synth 760 and a DX7. But for all the joking and stories, Mixed
> Feelings played for the *audience* and not for themselves – I

thought the band was very experienced at doing a show and it was the first time I felt it that I was playing with a *real* band and not a group of reading musicians. Something that I have always thought throughout my 22 years with the band.

So there in Jamie's words, hinged one of the reasons for our success. *No reading musicians on stage.* What Jamie, with his great humour, really meant was, 'How can you possibly ogle the women's arses on the dance floor, when your head is stuck in a music pad?' Jamie was a native of Solihull, Birmingham and at the time was living in Guildford. He had no fear of driving up and down the motorway. I remember him driving to Monte Carlo and back *overnight* to do a gig for the BBC Youth Orchestra and get back for the Mixed Feelings gig next day. He was a real 'super trouper'. Jamie eventually moved back to Solihull from Harrow due to WT. This didn't bother him for long. He soon found himself 'a good un'.

In short, Jamie Hardwick was a fine musician, keyboard player and great company. He was also the wittiest person I had ever met. He soon instigated the COM award. Terry was proud to be the recipient of this prestigious award many times in spite of the fact that not only was he a good drummer but he was also extremely useful as the band 'Mr Fixit' and could mend anything from a snapped brassiere strap to an often-broken star cloth. As Jamie says of Terry,

> My first thoughts on Terry? I remember him being very friendly and he welcomed me to the band. He took his drumming seriously. Gradually things unfolded over the weeks that it was apparent he was the band clown! I remember realising his talents, when we played at the Royal Mint and they wanted an international theme and Terry sang 'Viva Espanã' in 4 different languages! I also remember first thing after coming back from that summer gig in Monte Carlo and Terry saying, 'ere, come and look at this fucker,' and taking me into the toilets to show me that his cock had been pierced and an earring put in place. I also remember him 'resigning' after every gig. He would of course, drink anything, including the jar of seafood cocktail vinegar and oil and throwing up in the van all the way home.

This COM award (Cunt of the Month) was quite the funniest thing at the time and lasted until 2015 when Jamie, Terry and myself finally left the band. The recipient of this exalted honour was usually announced to much merriment in the local pub, where musicians customarily gathered prior to the gig. Regular winners were Terry, myself and all male singers but Kathy Edge won it once when she had been given a slip of paper to announce over the mic, 'There is a Taxi for Mike Hunt.' When she found out she had been 'set up' she created merry hell.

Pete Callard had been with the band for two years and eventually became fed up with our very commercial music. He was a fabulous player but was always hankering after playing more Jazz which is not what high paying clients wanted.

In September 1994 we were invited to perform at what was known as a showcase event, at the British Aerospace Club, Hatfield. The agent had given us a lot of good work so I agreed to do it.

When you run a band, you never ring musicians and singers and beg them to do a showcase free of charge. You simply, *tell them* they are doing it. It's the same with any gigs that come in. I kept everyone informed by a weekly date sheet. We had plenty of work, so to 'showcase' meant they would never be out of pocket as it would result in more gigs. Plus, as Michael Black would constantly remind me, 'Would you rather sit at home on a Tuesday night and watch fucking EastEnders, or do a gig?' During the early, 'hungry years', we did several showcase events and they usually paid off.

Just before the interval, a band called After Dark was announced. I couldn't see the band, as I was in the bar nursing a pint of Green King with Terry and Pete Callard. We were on last as the main act and I had sent the singers to get changed. After Dark were performing the Crusader's song 'Street Life' and it was a very passable version. Then I heard the guitar solo. Terry and I looked at each and carried our beers into the main arena. Pete didn't bother coming.

On stage left was a plainly dressed female singer with a 'folky' voice. She would have been better placed in Steeleye Span. Fronting the band was a blonde headed, baby-faced guitarist who looked about 14 years old. He was planted like a band mascot in pride of place, right in front of the drummer.

The band then launched into that lovely Carpenter's song, 'Goodbye To Love'. I couldn't wait for the guitar solo and sure enough, the boy guitarist played it note for note. The sustained sound was amazing. He was using a Mesa-boogie mark 111 combo and playing a PRS EG4 guitar. The final part of this brilliant song features an even greater, Tony Peluso guitar solo and this guitarist was right on the button. It was just like the record. 'Nice band!' I said to the grinning guitarist Dave Price. I gave him my card and he called me a few days later.

Pete buggered off on a holiday to New York for a month, on a tour of the Jazz clubs. There was an old saying, 'If you want to lose your job go on holiday.' I had to rely on Pete West and Dave Williams to help the band out. When Pete returned, I had replaced him. It was hard telling him that he had lost his job but I knew what I had to do. He was a real gentleman and had served us well. He took the news bravely and left without a fuss. He even gave me a bottle of Jack Daniels as a departure present. He later rose to great heights as the editor of *Guitarist* magazine and became the guitarist in the Shirley Bassey and Lionel Ritchie bands. I am proud to think he was once our guitarist.

Dave Price did his first gig on Thursday 26th January 1995, at the Stakis Hotel, Northampton. He was solid, dependable and played guitar exactly how I wanted. *Aggressively.* He was a brilliant and hard-hitting soloist and is still the guitarist and musical director of Mixed Feelings as I write these lines, in March 2020.

We have been lucky in the continuing excellent quality of male singers we had in Mixed Feelings. Some were good front men but average singers. Some were good singers but average front men.

Some fool had told Dave Howard he was so brilliant he would 'make it to the top' if he went solo, so he left with stars in his eyes. He would not be the last. He disappeared into pub-land obscurity. *I never saw him again.*

I had already decided to take the band another step forward, by adding a further male singer. This would hopefully ensure that I would *always* have a male singer fronting the band.

Terry introduced me to Ian Manser, who was a young Hemel Hempstead lad with an accurate and warm voice. Unfortunately he would never be a 'professional' singer as long as he had a hole in his arse. He played the fool continually but he did make us laugh. He did almost two hundred gigs with the band, including an overseas trip to Abu Dhabi. His first major gig was at Gleneagles Hotel when he fell straight off the front of the stage into the audience, who thought it hilarious. I thought him an absolute twat and was going to get rid of him the next day but he told he was almost blind and never saw the edge of the stage. So I looked after him purely because he had a lovely voice. Good male singers are hard to find and he certainly had that rich, George Michael tone. In the end I found his lunatic behaviour exasperated me too much, so he had to go.

Then there was Nick Foister (1997-1999) I spotted him when he was singing in the Hemel Hempstead Marlowes, with a holiday camp company. Nick was a good front man, a perfect 'announcer' and possessed a massive soul voice. He had a great sense of humour but was wholly, irresponsible with money and accepted that he would always be a 'skint' Geordie, not unlike Barry Elliot. He would always spend all his weekend's pay on videos, clothes and beer. Then he had no money for food and to pay his speeding fines. He lodged with me for some time and also rented Terry's flat in Hemel Hempstead. He made over three hundred appearances for the band.

Mike Mason (1999-2002) came to the band when Nick Foister left. He was keen to join and came from the same holiday camp stable as Nick. Mike Mason was straight from the set of *Confessions Of A Window Cleaner* and a tremendous front man. His presentations were electric and women fell at his feet. He says:

> Being part of Mixed Feelings was the most fantastic time for me. You just can't beat the sound, the vibe and the feel of live music. It just makes the hairs on the back of your neck stand up. I was certainly not unaccustomed to performing on large stages in front of huge crowds. From the first note played, to the last lyric sang, the entire performance was electric and some of the fondest memories of my life. To stand in front of a crowd of thousands and shout "Scream" and this huge wall of sound screamed back at you is a moment I will never forget and will cherish forever.

Mike soon found love with Ellen Sleutjes, a stunning looking, leggy Dutch blonde who Linda had 'headhunted' from Luton band, Deja Vu. She had replaced Helen York who had left to go into a West

End Musical. They quickly became an item and moved in together. Mike with his new-found extra cash had treated himself to a tidy Fiat Barchetta sports car and would turn up at gigs with the roof down, so that everyone could see him and her. He looked the 'rock star' part and paraded around like a lord. 'Not a lord but a count,' remarked Terry.

Mike loved that car which leads us onto the subject of *parking* in the West End of London, which is always a trial. No more so, when Mike got himself clamped, just off Park Lane and copped a huge £200 fine.

Two nights later, the band was again in Park Lane at the Four Seasons Hotel and I decided to get one over on Mike. I had made up a fictitious parking ticket for a £200 fine for 'Parking in Resident's bay'. We also kept in the van, a quality wheel clamp, which we used to secure the van when it had to be left out overnight in an unfamiliar location.

Bob Wise was our roadie that weekend,

> We had set up the gear as usual and gone to the pub and Jon noticed that Mike Mason had parked his car outside the Hard Rock Café in Old Park Lane. He told me to get the wheel clamp out of the van, after the band had started and clamp Mike's car. He also gave me a false parking ticket to put on the windscreen. After the gig, Mike got changed, said his farewells and was back within minutes. He was swearing at Jon and calling the Police a bunch of mother fucking arseholes and worse. Jon was trying to keep a straight face and pacify Mike. 'How much is the ticket for?' he asked Mike. 'Fucking, two hundred fucking pounds,' was Mike's answer. Jon had also put Jamie's phone number on the ticket and when Mike had phoned it, Jamie answered in the room next door and Mike became suspicious. In the meantime, I had slipped out to take the clamp off, as I had the key. I had just got the clamp off his car when Mike saw me and realized he had been set up. I was terrified, as he started shouting and swearing at me, calling me a cunt and chased me down Piccadilly, totally intent on murdering me.

Mike Mason and Ellen Sleutjes loved the high life. I could not afford them. They both left the band after yet another row about money in 2002. They had served the band well.

We lost a brilliant front man but gained a powerful, black singer in Johnny Amobe (2002-2003). Of Nigerian stock and a big guy, Johnny was our first black singer but none of Mike Mason's clothes would fit him so I had to buy all new stuff. He was a great stage performer, worked hard and sweated profusely. He was always soaking wet after the first song. Terry blames Johnny for splashing his expensive, Zildjian cymbals with sweat which permanently discoloured them. Unfortunately, Johnny was a 'barrack-room lawyer' and left after demanding more money as like some others, he was under the delusion that he was worth a lot more than he was getting. Before he left the band, he did the best thing ever when he introduced me to his pal and fellow singer, Tony Moriah.

I cannot speak too highly about this talented man. Of Guyanese heritage, well-mannered and kind, he supported The Arsenal, lived near the Emirates Stadium and became the regular vocalist and frontman of Mixed Feelings from 2003-2009. He had the 'richest' and most accurate voice of any of the singers that had fronted our band. He made more than eight hundred appearances, mesmerising audiences with his wonderful voice, a cross between Luther Vandross and Lionel Ritchie. He would often turn up at the gig with a box of 'Krispy Kreme' doughnuts. He had become hooked on them since we had performed at the confectionary maker's 50th birthday party.

Tony was great company and never happier than when travelling abroad with the band to such lovely places as Crete, Tenerife, Muscat & Oman, France, Switzerland, Germany, Austria, Italy, Spain, including Seville, Barcelona and Valencia and in June 2009 aboard the luxury yacht, Silver Whisper, to Monte Carlo. The only thing was, he didn't drink alcohol – but that didn't make him a bad person - *and* I trusted him. The band loved him. We had landed on our feet again.

At the time of the Millennium there were many offers for the band to take our show overseas for New Year's Eve 1999, but I made it plain that this was a once in a lifetime event and I wanted it to be an occasion when our families could come. It was the Oxford Rover Club which finally booked the band for this huge night of celebration. The booker was ex-Arsenal and Oxford United footballer, Rodney Smithson. He loved the band.

I recorded in my diary;

> Friday 31st December 1999. Performed at the Oxford Rover Club last night. The band was paid £10,000 plus VAT. The BAND consisted of Jamie Hardwick, Dave Price, Terry Wilson, Jon Nicholls. SINGERS were; Mike Mason, Gary Priestley, Sue Acteson and Ellen Sleutjes. Road crew were, Greg Nicholls & Hannah Slack. All band members were paid £1000 each. Greg got £500 and Hannah £300.

Yes. We had a *female* roadie. A robust Sheffield lass named Hannah Slack, who was Greg's girlfriend. She could down a pint of beer faster than any of us. She was also technically good and soon learned how to wire up a PA system and lighting rig. She was 'Grade 2' and did many gigs with the band. Greg took a perverse delight however, in winding her up and she would burst into tears and come running to me when Greg called her a 'Yorkshire Pudding' or a 'Northern Chippopotomus'. We lost a good roadie when he dumped her.

So here I had the solid, four-piece band that would be the backbone of Mixed Feelings until 2015. Terry, Dave, Jamie and myself. It was rare that one of the 'formidable four' dropped out of a gig and it was the best combination that any bandleader could ask for. Great company and a joy to play with and I was privileged to call them my friends. None of them over-played, all were brilliant, dependable musicians and none of them ever let me down (except Terry, when he fell off the drums pissed at the Harrods Ball).

It was this combination that saw the band perform at over two thousand gigs and over forty major international events in the next ten years, including two cruises on the Silver Whisper.

I was however, getting the usual persistent problems with singers. I was recommended to audition Gary Priestley (1997-2014) by Red Sun bandleader, John Kerton, from Birmingham. 'He'll be fine for you Buddy!' he assured me.

John had met Gary while they were both working at Butlins and had told him how good Mixed Feelings were. He advised Gary to travel to Hemel Hempstead Pavilion to audition. John told me he would be perfect for us. He was right and Gary would become the longest serving singer in the band. As I write this, he is still doing the occasional 'dep' gig for Mixed Feelings.

Chris Madin, a Doncaster singer, stepped into the breach left by the passing of Tony Moriah in 2009. He was with the band for three years and was a talented, all-round musician and powerful singer but left to do his own thing including making a few appearances in the *Strictly Come Dancing* band. He married our singer, Suzi Jari before they both moved to Yorkshire.

Lee Reboul, a handsome young singer, with a great voice and personality, replaced Gary in 2014 when he left to pursue a solo career. His story is outside the scope of this book but I will say he ticked all the boxes. He was loyal and dependable in every way and a terrific vocal 'impressionist' who could impersonate most singers. Another 'diamond' was the dynamic Jonathan Bremner, who joined the band at the same time as Lee. Both are still singing (covid 19 permitting) with the band at the time of writing in 2020.

I liked Gary Priestley's cheerful personality. In his early gigs with the band, he struggled to hit the high notes but he got there in the end. His voice strengthened due to the many gigs we were doing, which as Gary said himself, 'Would make or break my voice.' Gary recollects,

> This band had a real vibrant personality. It was never a boring band, like many around at the time. Always great fun and I will never be part of another band like it. It was so enjoyable and the pay was good too. I will never forget the first gig I did at the fabulous, Gleneagles Hotel, Scotland and we stayed in a small pub in the nearby village of Auchterarder. The landlord kept the pub open for us, until we got back after our gig at 3am. Terry stood on the bar in his underpants and set fire to his chest hair, much to the amusement of the locals. Greg got thrown out for running around the pub naked. I thought, 'What have I let myself in for here?'

Gary Priestley was also a good dancer when the majority of male singers, who came before or after had flat feet. Probably down to his Butlins experience. He almost made a perfect 'Ricky Martin' and took him off brilliantly in the new 'Supanova Latino' sets, which sold the band. He also looked good in his expensive and personally tailored, stage suits. I was pleased to see he cared for his clothes too. He would get his stuff dry-cleaned and not demand payment off me.

On the girl singer front, the lovely Sue Acteson stayed with the band for thirteen years before leaving to marry Terry Wogan's son Mark. Helen York left after ten years to work in a West End Show and then set up her own successful band. Those two magnificent girls took the band to the top of the tree. True professionals they were and 'effing slags' they weren't. Helen recently said to me via text,

> I hope you write the whole bloody lot! I am not ashamed of any
> of it, some of the best days of my singing career!! They were
> great memories Jon. I thank you for that always.

Debbie Harris and Tara Macdonald worked in the band for a short time but left to pursue solo careers. I was then extremely lucky to find two superb girls, in Lynsey Shaw who joined the band from 'Girls@play' and Suzi Jari. These two superb singers, saw the band through many top events, including some big outdoor festivals. We later found two other beautiful gems in Lyndsey Cleary and Marina Berry. Both were head turners, strikingly beautiful and absolute band sellers.

Suzi Jari, was the daughter of a Metropolitan Police officer and another bubbly Essex girl. My friend and fellow ex-cop, John 'Dick' West who I had worked with in my early days at Paddington Green Police Station, spotted her while she was singing solo at Bushey Police Club. I remember his phone call, 'I have found you a super girl singer and she is just perfect for Mixed Feelings.' How right he was.

Suzi was the 'right stuff'. An attractive, sexy girl who could sing any song asked of her. Suzi and Lynsey Shaw were tall, wholesome girls and alongside Gary and Tony I had a stunning front line in height, looks and vocals.

It would be appropriate here for Dick West to comment;

> I was fortunate enough to be invited to attend a number of
> auditions for the group. These were, invariably, held at Bushey
> Police Club and I never ceased to be amazed at the numbers
> of hopefuls who arrived, anxious to become part of this band.
> Both men and women travelled from far and wide, leaving no
> doubts as to how well known, and how popular Mixed Feelings
> were. The standard of singing varied but very few seemed to
> meet the high standards set by Jon.

While I am writing about singers, I must finish this chapter with a little tale taken from my diary concerning a male singer and regular COM. We had flown up to Scotland for a weekend in Turnberry Golf resort, which is owned by Donald Trump, situated in a beautiful location in South Ayrshire.

We were engaged to do an event in the Hotel Ballroom, for Sir Peter Vardy's Charity Foundation Group. We got to know the kindly Sir Peter, who had made a fortune in the car trade. After being allocated our rooms we gathered in the hotel bar at 4pm, where Sir Peter and his wife Margaret joined us. We had been briefed, by our nervous agent, Howard T'Loosty that on *no condition* were we to 'swear' or was Terry to tell 'Those filthy tales of dirty dog, Buster' in the presence of Sir Peter or his wife, as they were devout Christians.

Howard was always good company, although regarded by musicians as a 'flapper'. He would give us many quality gigs and usually attended the event, which indicated - like Michael Black - that he was on a substantial mark-up. On the football banter side, I didn't trust him to lie straight in bed. He was a Spurs supporter.

Sir Peter shook hands with every member of the band and welcomed us to Turnberry. Being a friendly and generous man, he authorises a 'free bar' for the band. Bad mistake. One of our male singers promptly orders cigarettes on the account and Dave and Jamie immediately switch from beer to Jewish Coke. They are usually sensible if we have a gig later. But Dave's raucous laugh soon requires ear defenders. We successfully manage to keep Terry under control and the expressions, 'Blow me down,' 'Did it thump?' and 'I'll go to the foot of our stairs,' are predominant in the merry chatter.

We are fed handsomely in the main restaurant. The popular choice is Aberdeen Angus fillet steak washed down with a nice, Corbières red. Everything is running late and the cabaret, Brian Conley, is also late on stage. He dies a death. This crowd just want to dance. The band finally get on stage at 11pm and storm it.

One of our male singers on this event is Damien Flood who did an eighteen-month term with the band. He had been recommended to me, by Helen who had been working with him, in the West End Musical, *Rent*. Damien was a strikingly handsome guy, with a smooth accurate voice. He was a very good lounge pianist too.

The small problem with Damien was that he suffered from LMF. (Bomber command historians will understand). He would often turn up late for gigs which continually pissed off the other musicians and never apologise for his tardiness and often misplace items of stage wear, which had cost me money. He simply didn't like to be managed or be told what to do. He didn't give a shit, which made him unpopular with the other musicians in the band. As Dave Price said, after waiting around for hours to give him a lift to gigs, 'You can always rely on Damien to be unreliable.'

The gig finishes at 1am and the party continues in the main bar. Damien is on the grand piano surrounded by squiffy dames whose husbands have abandoned them to gulp whisky. Good idea. I retire to my bed with a large 'Lagavulin'.

At breakfast next morning most of the bleary eyed musicians are there for 9am. The girl singers are absent and never usually appear much before 11am. Sir Peter and his wife join us at the table and we chat about the gig. Sir Peter tells us how much he enjoyed the band. We also talk football. Respectfully observing the 'no swearing' rule, 'Blimey' is the collective expression, as we tuck into a superb Scottish breakfast of porridge, then scrambled eggs and smoked salmon. 'Where has Damien got to?' asks Howard cheerfully. Damien suddenly appears, bleary eyed and sits at the table. 'Morning,' he says gruffly and nods at Sir Peter and Lady Margaret. Damien is wearing a subtle T-Shirt and emblazoned on the chest in huge letters is 'WHO THE FUCK IS PRADA?'

You can always rely on Damien, *'Semel cunnus semper cunnus'*.

10

DJS AND DIPSTICKS.

I have to mention a much-maligned section of the entertainment industry, especially amongst musicians. You will find little mention of 'Disc Jockeys' at events, unless they are of celebrity status, but their contribution towards the success of an event is immeasurable. Always make a friend of your DJ.

Sometime back in the '70s the Musician's Union launched a yellow sticker with the words 'Keep Music Live' thereon. The sticker would appear on dressing room walls, particularly in working men's clubs. It was anti-DJ. Some bandleaders and musicians were openly hostile to the lone DJ often booked to appear with them. The general feeling was, 'We are musicians and you are the talentless bastard who will simply play records.' First mistake.

I always looked upon the DJ as a valuable co-worker who could be manipulated to your advantage, particularly when the band was on its fifth gig on the trot and you were all knackered. I befriended many DJs and most were very good at their job and extremely professional. Some were incompetent and some arrogant but invariably they could be your best ally.

It is always a smart move to buy them a beer and lend them your roadie, to help them set their gear up. Then you would ask nicely, 'Do you mind playing the last hour?' The DJ invariably says, 'Would love to mate!' Providing your client didn't object, this was great news as the musicians could get away early, leaving the crew only to take down gear, when the show was over. It was always a wise idea to give the DJ a copy of your playlist too. There is nothing worse than 'Dancing Queen,' being done twice.

I have happy memories of working with DJs. I remember with affection, the always friendly Rodney Prout, the very professional David Whale, and 'Pete's Pink Elephant', plus the brilliant Stan Lee King and many others who were at the top of their game and who we regularly worked with.

It was always nice to offer the DJ the use of your PA system too, as nothing looked worse to the client than an array of assorted and usually tatty Peavey DJ speakers at the side of the stage. Yes, the crew had to wait but nothing looks worse to a client than the band breaking down before the gig has finished. Especially when he is paying five grand for a one-hour set.

Some DJs we worked with were quite famous in the '60s and most were nice. We worked several times with David Hamilton and Kid Jenson but I thought the best 'old school' DJ was Tony Blackburn, who was always amusing and would have a beer with us.

One of the best out of town DJs was David Whale, who had set up Orange Discotheques in Reading in the early seventies and had done very well out it. He drove a new Porsche 911 and employed many people. He liked our band and gave us lots of quality work, mainly in the West Country and The Cotswolds.

So successful was Orange, that they held an annual dinner party to which about two hundred guests would be invited including many friends, family and fellow DJs. This quite lavish, black-tie event was to be held on a Sunday afternoon at Newbury Racecourse in the large banqueting suite. David had booked my band and asked me to find him a 'cabaret comedian'. Further to that, he didn't wish to spend more than £100. He would rather spend it on champagne. I knew of one man that might help at that price, so I rang Dennis Beards, a Wolverhampton comedian I had met on the club circuit some years previously. He had also performed at some Police 'smoking concerts'. We had become friends and so he immediately agreed to do the gig for £90 cash. 'I won't let you down son.'

He was, without doubt, the funniest comic I ever had the pleasure of working with. It was *my* sort of humour, to which Jethro has since come close. The nationally famous but grossly overpaid and unfunny, Michael McIntyre, who we worked with on several occasions, was never in the same league as Dennis Beards. Likewise, Jimmy Carr, with his bad-taste jokes and Muppet features was the same. I knew all of their crap jokes when I was at school. I was always amazed at what obscene sums of money naive clients were paying for these charlatans, who were often top of the bill at the firm's Christmas party. £30,000 for a half hour spot was the norm.

So I could get Dennis Beards for £90. His crazy act was never 'politically correct' and although long gone and forgotten, I loved the man. He performed in the manic style of Tommy Cooper, with all his tricks and stunts going wrong, coupled with the ripest of language. Dennis even wore a maroon fez with big ears attached and designed to fall off. Always the same old act but each time, a side splitter.

Being interested in military history and an enthusiast of RAF Bomber Command, I liked Dennis, especially as he had been a Halifax Bomber pilot during the dark days of WW2 and I believe he won the DFC. Bravest of the brave and he was afraid of no one, let alone a difficult audience. This funny little guy possessed an outlandish Black Country accent.

The band were set and seated in the main ballroom, with the rest of the guests. David provided us with a good dinner with unlimited wine. He came over, 'Has your man arrived yet?' I told him I would go and check the dressing room. 'When he gets here, give him a drink and ask him a favour from me.' I looked at David, 'What's the favour?' He said, 'No blue or racist jokes as there are kids here.'

I go down to the car park and a clapped out Volvo Estate rolls up. Out gets Dennis, with his case and table. He always carried a small folding table to put his tricks on and during the act, would get a member of the audience to help him carry it to the stage. The leg would suddenly drop off, as part of the act and Dennis would exclaim, 'Be careful ya silly fucker! Now look what you've done. You've broken me fucking table!'

This always got laughs, providing it wasn't a party for the Women's Institute. We go to the dressing room. I fetch Dennis a large Famous Grouse. I ask him not to swear during his act tonight and definitely, 'no blue or racist jokes' as the client has his family there. 'Alroight son, don't you worry, leave it to me. I won't let you down.'

The time arrives and Dennis doesn't require playing on by the band. He limps on to the dance floor looking every bit as knackered as he is. He is wearing his fez with the big ears and an ill-fitting suit with a huge bow tie. The table is in place. I introduce him to a ripple of applause. I pass him the microphone and go back to my table.

The audience goes quiet in anticipation. Dennis turns to face them. 'Good evening everybody. This West-Indian gentlemen enters a masturbation contest and comes first, third and fifth!' I roll off my chair and hide under the table. Furthermore, he then says, 'For those who don't masturbate, you're all wankers!'

A red-faced Dave storms over, 'Jon, can you pull him off?' I say to Dave 'Not in front of the kids!' Plus, 'They love him!' Dave says, 'Yes but he is using disgraceful language and people are walking out!'

Dennis is getting loads of laughs but I have to cut his act short. I fire the band up, 'We are on now.' Dennis is halfway into his hilarious, 'Catching the bullet with his teeth, trick.' What can possibly go wrong here? It's not rude. I hear the loud report of the .44 blank firing Webley pistol and an ear flies off his Fez. Dennis then shouts at the bespectacled shooter, 'Shoot straight ya blind fucker!' and further adds, 'Now look what you've done to me fucking 'at!'

I already have his money, so I get him another large Grouse and pay him in the changing room. I thank him sincerely and my sides are aching. 'So I'll fuck off then,' is his parting shot. God bless you, Dennis Beards. You were the best.

One harmless, but grossly irritating, DJ we had the amusing misfortune to work with was the part-resident DJ at Mere Golf Club, near Manchester. Let's just call him Chris. A broad Coronation Street accent did not help to change our unanimous view that he represented England in Dennis Beard's wanking contest. His repetitive and grossly exaggerated bragging as to where he had recently performed got on our wick. 'I were in New York last week, I were. Working in Billy Joel's Gay Piano Bar, I were. Oh yes! Next week I'm in Berlin at the Diamond

Cutter. Then I'm off to the Monte Carlo Sporting Club, I'm the main DJ there, Oh yes! Never been so busy!'

After gigging with him a few times we wished he would stay in bloody Monte Carlo. He was reasonably efficient at his job, although having been given our play list he would still play most of our songs. The best thing about him was that he would willingly do the last hour. Having set the gear up on the huge stage late afternoon, we were relaxing with a pint of Boddington's Best, at a table in the corner of the lounge bar.

Mere Golf Club, I believe, was owned by the proprietor of Kitchens Direct and Moben Kitchens. A lovely club too, at which we performed many times, courtesy of Russ and Steve of Alpha Connection Agency. The crew consisted of Terry, Greg, Martin and myself. Gary Priestley had arrived early too. So the atmosphere was somewhat lively as Terry had already drank six bottles of Fullers' London Pride on the motorway, matched by me, whereby we had put into practice his new 'invention'.

This was a large plastic funnel, attached to a short length of rubber hosepipe. It was Terry's idea to get this patented as a 'Pissaroo' for bands, lorry drivers, police and other 'unfortunate fuckers' who were stuck in motorway traffic and needed to piss urgently. The big funnel, according to Terry, would also allow females, 'to get their arses on it too.' Quite simply, the hose was poked through a gap in the corner of the ill-fitting side door, a fault common to Iveco vans. So this gadget was very useful, especially when stuck in a jam on the M6. Previously, one had to kneel down and 'reedle' through the gap.

We were discussing the benefits of the 'Pissaroo' when DJ Chris came and sat down with his pint of Fosters. 'Ow are we doing lads? I'm so busy I am. I were in Aberdeen last night, doing the Angus Whisky awards. Monday I fly off to Hollywood for the Oscars and when I get back, I'm doing a private party for my best mate, David Beckham.'

Picking up Chris's car keys, which were laying on the table, Terry stuck the whole bunch down the front of his jeans into his underpants, stood up and unzipped his flies and retrieved them. He then stuck the car key in Chris's beer and stirred it, tinkling the glass in the process. 'Now shut the fuck up!' Terry shouted. Chris quietly drank his beer.

Terry Wilson was a legend at Mere Golf Club. Was he not the lunatic drummer of Mixed Feelings who could perform incredible feats with his dick? At Christmas 1998, Mixed Feelings performed at the club staff party and a brilliant event it was too. Plenty of booze was laid on for the band and after the show the crowd had spilled out into the bar where rumours had circulated that 'Terry the Drummer is going to pick up a six-pack of Boddington's Bitter with his dick.'

Terry had long been proud about the fact that he had a gold ring through his todger. He had performed the delicate operation himself. He did not consider himself 'abnormal' in anyway. He was just a typical drummer.

Greg was his 'second'. A wire coat hanger was procured and twisted into a double hook and a six-pack of Boddington's Bitter was placed on the snooker table. Terry was cheered into the room like a Roman gladiator, wearing a white bath towel, toga-like.

There were about forty revellers left, who were worse the wear for drink. Greg assisted Terry to climb onto the snooker table, who then raises his arms in triumph. The room goes quiet as he faces the crowd and connects one hook of the coat hanger to the nylon ties of the six-pack. He then turns his back on the crowd to make the final connection to his dick. He turns to face the crowd.

He is loudly announced by Greg, 'Ladies and gentlemen, Mr Terry Wilson will now attempt to lift a six pack of beer with his cock.' Cue for women to scream, then countdown and lift off! Unfortunately, Terry squatting like a constipated sumo wrestler does not budge the six pack. Red in the face he yells, 'Take one off, take one off!' Crowd begins to mutter. Greg unclips a beer and a heroic attempt to lift a five-pack also fails. Crowd booing. 'Take one off, take one off,' Terry yells. Another failure. Eventually, the crestfallen drummer is down to *one* can and the hissing crowd throw peanuts at him. Nevertheless we have lift off! A single can of Boddy's bitter is swinging like a plumb bob between his legs. There are whistles and shouts of 'Wanker!' and 'We want our money back!'

On the way home, we drink a full bottle of Johnny Walker Black Label whisky and finish the Boddington's Bitter before we turn to the bottle of 1970 Warres Vintage Port, won in the raffle. The 'Pissaroo' is put to good use. Terry then disconnects the hose and places the end of the funnel in his mouth, and blows the Post Horn Gallop. He remarked, 'This fucking funnel tastes salty!'

While we are on the subject of staff parties: They are *never* what you would hope them to be. The majority of hotel staff are poorly paid and have little money to blow on a binge. They rely on the hotel owner's goodwill, to provide for them. If your band has performed at a venue many times during the year and are popular with the staff, you may be 'invited' to perform at the staff Christmas party. This is usually held on an 'unfashionable' day, such as two nights before New Year's Eve, when everyone is sick to death of Christmas. It is a false assumption that you will get more gigs at the hotel by doing the staff party as it is rarely the hotel who 'book' the band, but the client. Having now smashed the West End of London by crazy demand, we performed at Christmas staff parties for the Dorchester, London Hilton Hotel, Claridge's and many other top hotels. I always charged a fee to cover the band and crew for £100 expenses per person and I expected a meal and free booze.

It's the same with charity events. I found that if they can pay wages to executives of over two hundred grand a year, then they can afford to pay your top fee. They want the best party band on the circuit, so would book Mixed Feelings. If they charge £100 per ticket then punters expect a top band, not a Jazz quartet. We were lucky (and privileged) to do the Prince's Trust, the Make A Wish foundation, Sparkles, Phillip Green, Dreamflight, Help for Heroes and many other top charities and we always got paid well.

The only time I did a registered charity for free was at our regular venue, Bushey Police Club and it was in aid of the Metropolitan Police Widows and Orphans fund. I still have that letter of thanks. I had told the band that we were doing a 'freebie' as a favour to the special club that hosted so many of our gigs. I also got in an extra four-man crew to hump the gear up the steep backstairs. If I was doing this for free I was going to have a bloody good drink.

On the night, our ten-piece band plus crew were given a free bar by the club and promptly went on 'Jewish Cokes'. Needless to say, the bar bill for the band was about £300 and although I offered to pay it, we were banned from the club! As Dick West remembers,

> I wanted to book 'Mixed Feelings' for my own event and was
> told by club manager Graham Mann that the band was banned
> for six months for drinking the bar dry at a recent charity
> event. I told him that I had sold my event out, because people

had bought tickets just to see Mixed Feelings. Common sense prevailed and I soon got them re-instated. However I did book them for my son's wedding soon after and Duncan paid for them to have a meal and drinks at the Italian restaurant next door to the London venue. 'Have whatever you want' was a dangerous invitation to this lot. The bill for this was almost more than the total I paid for the band! Apparently they all ate fillet steaks, drank 48 bottles of Peroni and nine bottles of Chianti and then did a storming performance!

Some of the greatest gigs we have ever played were charity events. Our country holds some wonderful, well deserving charities, with fine people who work hard to raise money. For 25 years the band has performed at the 'Make A Wish' children's charity, always held at the Dorchester Hotel and organized by a wonderful fund-raiser, Leslie Rose OBE. Leslie is a great man and sticks to the trusted formula of Bradley Walsh as compere, Lord Jeffrey Archer as auctioneer and Mixed Feelings. He also books a top 'cabaret' act.

Through this classy event, we have been lucky enough to work with Brian May, Madness, Boyzone, Sophie Ellis Bexter and many more top acts. At midnight, the cast of a West End Show will usually perform on the dance floor. This way, we have seen some great singing from the live cast of *Les Miserables* and *We Will Rock You*. These are fantastic parties, often with half a million pounds or more raised.

Bradley Walsh would hilariously introduce the band, usually insulting us before joining us on stage to sing! It was just like old times but his voice had got better. He would also annoy Lord Archer, by introducing him as 'Jeffers'. Leslie Rose was the brains behind it all and always laid on a quality selection of drinks in the dressing room together with a super dinner. I wished every gig were as good.

Many more gigs were taken from performing at charity events and after a gig at the salubrious Wentworth Club, we were booked for the Prince's Trust and Dreamflight events, not to mention Russ Abbot's son's wedding and Tony Adams' Sporting Chance charity, which gave me the opportunity to meet my Arsenal heroes.

Some of the lesser known but worthy charities laid on events at top London venues and one such was the Joshua Gilbert Rhabdomyosarcoma

Appeal, on Saturday 7th February 2004. I recorded in my digital diary at the time;

'The band are booked for the second year running to perform at the Shining Light (JGRA) Children's Charity Ball.' This prestigious event is at the classy Landmark Hotel, in the main ballroom. The organizer, Robert Berg has asked me to try to obtain the services of 'Jim Davidson' as cabaret. I have contacted his manager Laurie Mansfield and booked Jim for this event although I have my reservations and tell the organizer.

Having worked many times with Jim Davidson, I suspect that his forthright style of blue and sexist humour would not be suitable for this predominately Jewish audience. I try to persuade them to book the dafter and cheaper Bobby Davro, but no. They want Jim.

It is a bright winter's afternoon when we arrive at the hotel and park outside the front door opposite the iconic Marylebone Station. There is a real ale bar on the concourse of the station and I know that Terry will be itching to get in there. The station pub could not be more conveniently situated for musicians working at The Landmark, where beer is half the price of the hotel.

We soon unload the van and hump the gear the short distance, through the front, which is often easier than the side window doors. We set up a small but good, self-powered QSC PA consisting of a pair of one by 12" top cabs and a pair of 1x15" Bass bins. Because we have Jim to supply PA for, Greg organizes another pair of 1x12's along the back wall so he can be heard all around the room.

Professional as always, Jim arrives for his sound check at 4pm. Greg, Jez Guest and myself are standing in the foyer and the ballroom doors are closed, prior to the punters arriving.

Jim is looking very smart as usual, with a white shirt and tie, nice suit and beautifully crafted wool overcoat. He gives us a friendly greeting. On his arm is a gorgeous brunette. Jim spies Greg and asks, 'Hi Greg, have I got a monitor on the floor? I will probably work the floor here.' He then says, 'Can you get me a drink please mate? A large brandy and lemonade and a glass of champagne.'

I send Martin to the downstairs bar, with fifty quid in cash. There is little change. 'Lets go and look at the room Greg.' Says Jim, who seems to be in a slightly belligerent mood. The beauty does not leave his arm.

Then I hear Jim shout, 'Who the fuck has put all these fucking balloons on the tables? I don't do fucking balloons!'

He comes over to me, 'Those fucking balloons will have to go!' I take a look. There are around twenty tables of ten, all fully laid for dinner. Each table has a mass of balloons tethered to a centre weight. The room looks like a silver forest. There are even giant balloons tied to the PA speakers. Must have cost a small fortune. 'Who the fuck is in charge here?' Shouts Jim.

Two of the glamorous lady organizers enter the foyer and walk towards us. They are wearing their expensive ball gowns and crown jewels. They are 'prepared to party'. Jim repeats himself, 'Who's in charge of this event?'

'Good afternoon Mr Davidson,' one of the ladies says. Jim mimics her and says, 'Don't you, "good afternoon Mr Davidson me." There are fucking balloons on the tables and I don't do balloons!' The ladies look shocked. This is Jim Davidson OBE. Star of TV. I am also surprised at Jim's foul language towards the ladies but I keep my trap shut.

One of the ladies asks the wrong question, 'Are the balloons the wrong colour, Mr Davidson?' It is Jim who has gone the wrong colour. 'Look! I don't do fucking balloons, because people won't fucking see me.' The ladies are getting visibly upset but I keep quiet. 'We will take them down.' One of the ladies says meekly. 'You fucking better!' yells Jim.

Just at that delicate moment, a little girl in party dress and sparkling tiara, the daughter of one of the ladies, walks out of the ballroom with her young friend. They look all of ten years old. Jim explodes, 'Are there fucking kids here tonight?' 'Only a few,' replies one of our ladies. 'How the fuck can I do my act with kids in the room? I can't fucking swear or tell my best jokes if there are fucking kids in the room. Right. I'm off!' I am astonished at his rudeness and again bite my tongue. He is right of course. He can't do his earthy act in front of children.

Jim produces his mobile phone and phones his manager. 'Laurie? Right I am not doing this fucking gig at the Landmark tonight. Firstly, they've got fucking balloons and secondly there are fucking kids here. Should have booked fucking Zippy and Bungle. Right Laurie, How much was I on? Ten grand, is that all? Fuck me.'

He shuts his phone down and finishes his drink. As Jez Guest commented,

> I was quite shocked and I thought Jon was going to hit him. I had never seen a man speak so rudely to women as that. Jim obviously didn't like female organisers. I think he is a woman hater anyway. If it had been a bloke he was talking too he would have been decked. But he redeemed himself.

Jim calms down, 'Right,' he says. 'I was on ten grand tonight, so you don't have to pay that now. Furthermore,' Jim produces his chequebook and writes out a cheque. 'What's the name of your charity? Right! Here's a cheque for ten grand, a donation from me. So you are now *twenty grand* up, ladies! Not bad for doing fuck-all and furthermore, you can leave your fucking balloons up. I'm off.' And off he rode into the sunset with the brunette still clamped to his arm.

We run to the station bar. Within seconds of taking my first gulpers of Abbot ale, Greg calls me back to the ballroom. I return forthwith. 'What are we going to do for cabaret now?' asks the tearful lady organizer, her mascara smudged. 'Jim Davidson has let us down.'

I tell her not to worry, 'Mixed Feelings will provide the cabaret! It will only cost you a hundred quid extra and it features Gary Priestly as Barry Manilow!'

The crowd are seated and gobbling their smoke salmon starters as Mixed Feelings musicians take the stage and I announce, 'Due to travel problems, Jim Davidson cannot appear tonight but we now have an alternative star turn, "Gary Manilow" Barry's younger brother, all the way from New York.'

Half of this gullible crowd believe me! 'Ooh I say, he does look a bit like him, doesn't he Val?' and 'He is not as slim as his brother' and 'His nose is not so big.' Gary wearing his slick silver-grey suit, kicks off with, 'I Can't Smile Without You' and I whistle the intro. The diners go mad and stand up. Whole tables of ten stand on their chairs and sway with hands interlocked.

I've never seen Jim Davidson get the crowd standing on chairs. Then we go into the beautiful, 'Weekend In New England' which packs the dance floor and Gary sings it superbly. We hit all the 'classic' Manilow songs and frantic toastmaster, Howard Robbins, rounds up the dancers like a sheep dog hustling them back to their tables for the main course. The party has started! Jim who?

We were already familiar with these songs of course. We had done them with Barry Elliot, some 15 years ago. Jamie has all the dots buried in his messy music folder. 'Looks Like We Made It' and 'Even Now' have our audience at Gary's feet. After his super, 45-minute act, I see him sitting at the table and flirting with our lady organisers. He is drinking their champagne. He has saved the day. I give him an extra £25. I am learning from Michael Black.

'Extras' in the form of a stage and dance floor are often required at most Jewish events and it was not unusual to see previously mentioned 'event supplier' Gerry Bamfield, providing the goods. A book could be written about his legendary calamities. Gerry was reliable, eccentric and funny and like Jim Davidson could be extremely rude to clients.

I once made the mistake of hiring Gerry as roadie for a Breast Cancer Charity event at Brocket Hall one winter's night. At the conclusion of the evening, Gerry had inadvertently been locked out by the elderly male organizer. He had merely shut the side door because an icy draft was blowing into the room. When I let Gerry back in, he said, 'Who shut that fucking door?' and the organiser said 'I did, we were all getting cold' and Gerry, wearing his 'Mixed Feelings' crew shirt said, 'don't you fucking lock me out you wanker!' We never got booked back for that one.

How Gerry ever got booked back is beyond me. Yet he got loads of work, in spite of his mishaps. Practically most of his gear was homemade. Why is it that I am attracted to daft people? I just love people that make me laugh. That's why Terry kept his job for so long and he knows it. As for Gerry, we had been mates for years but it was not clever to let him drive your van wearing your crew shirt. As when stationary at Marble Arch, he leaned out of the driver's window and made masturbatory gestures to a terrified motorist who had 'cut him up' and shouted 'You fucking tosser!'

I liked Gerry, a Hemel Hempstead man who suffered from permanent WT. I soon learned never to ask, 'How's your love life?' as I was promptly told 'Don't you fucking start!' He became a fixture at many of our Jewish gigs. His cheery welcome was always 'Hello Twinkle.' He was great value in monetary and laughter stakes and I hired him for many events.

He would supply his homemade stage, which no PA equipment could be safely stacked on. It was known as 'The Trampoline' or 'Bouncy Castle'.

In the summer of 2008, the band was hired to play a birthday event, for the chief accountant of Tesco, on the lawn of his beautiful detached Surrey home, near the Thames. This genial and substantially loaded Irishman had asked me if I could supply a stage and a 'black and white' dance floor. I assured him I could.

I telephoned Gerry, 'Can you supply a black and white dance floor mate?' 'Of course I can,' was the reply, 'For you darling, anything.'

It was 2pm on a hot and cloudless summer's day when we arrived at the drive of the house to shake hands with the client and be shown into the massive rear garden which had good access for the van via a field at the rear. We saw a superb 'hooded' Rock marquee had been erected.

Greg had decided to put in a big PA for the event and used the 20K QSC rig. We were putting in an eleven-piece band and the 38 Channel, Allen & Heath mixing desk would be put up alongside the stage.

The client had told us to, 'Get a cold beer from the bar boys!' and 'Have whatever you want.' A happy band is a good band! We loved gigs like this and they were simply the very best type of gigs you could do. Private family parties, in beautiful surroundings, on a balmy summer's night. Then I noticed the client looking perplexed.

Gerry was on his hands and knees, painting the dance floor black and white. He had done all the white squares and had started the black. There was an over-powering smell of Wick's gloss.

'Hello Twinkle,' says Gerry. 'I thought you had a black and white dance floor?' I said to him. He gives me a broad smile. 'I'll have one in an hour.' I ask, 'Will the paint be dry in time?' He holds up the five-litre tin. 'It says one-hour drying time!' Fucking hell.

Terry is coming over with two pints of cold Fosters. 'Here you go mate, get that fucker down your neck. There's no real ale, so we will have to go to the pub!' Better set up my bass rig then.

I whip the cover off the Ampeg bass combo and plug it in. Job done. Jamie has just arrived and Dave Price. 'Blimey, You can smell that paint at the front of the house,' says Jamie. 'I smelt it when I came off the M25!' says Dave. 'You shut your fucking gob! It'll be dry soon!' shouts Gerry.

Just at that moment, a chubby little lad, aged about six, rides his BMX bike straight across the freshly painted dance floor. This bike has extra fat tyres, which leave great tread patterns across the floor. Gerry is apoplectic. He bellows at the top of his voice, 'Get that fucking bike off my fucking dance floor ya little fucker!' It was only the client's son.

There was no sit-down dinner that night, just pretty girls serving a delicious Oriental finger buffet: sushi, fish cakes, dim sum, chicken legs, prawns on sticks and more. We were on by 8.30pm, which was earlier than usual. Ricky Martin's 'She Bangs' never fails to make people want to dance although most just waved their arms in the air, which is all you can do when the dance floor is like flypaper.

I had related the story to Linda next morning, 'Why do you keep using Gerry?' I replied, 'He makes me laugh!'

I hired Gerry for some 'extras' at a high-end Barmitzvah party, at Claridge's. It was to be a lavish affair. At a meeting at the family home, 'Dad' had had a vision of his son, surprising all the guests, by jumping out of a box. He wanted the box upright on the edge of the stage and the front paper covered, so he could burst through it. OK. We would need a simple, open backed coffin-type box. Probably about six feet high with rice paper on the front which would tear easily. I assured the client I could supply that. He was delighted. He was also a Spurs supporter and wanted the girls to wear Spurs shirts. I had those at home, so no problem. Can I supply the stage too? Of course I can! So I book the ebullient Gerry who assures me he can make an appropriate wooden box.

The big day arrived and we got to Claridge's at 1pm and managed to park outside the front door, behind Gerry's Mercedes Sprinter. This was before the florist, photographer, caterer, videographer and toastmaster had all got there. We had a good get in. I always use two roadies at this venue.

Gerry was on his knees on the dance floor. He was screwing together, with his electric screwdriver, a wooden box exactly 27 inches wide. The width of the wallpaper he had attached to the front. It looked suspiciously like child's bedroom wallpaper too. There were pink and blue elephants on the inside. I said to Gerry, 'I thought you were going to use rice paper, so the lad can jump through it easily?' Gerry shrugged his shoulders and said, 'He'll get through that easy enough. It's only lightweight paper.'

Much to the concern of the Banqueting manager, a large aerosol of black paint is produced and Gerry commences to spray the sides of the box black. The famous Art Deco 1920s ballroom now stinks like a cardent repair shop. The client and family arrive. 'Will that smell of paint be gone before my guests arrive?' I re-assure the client, 'Yes of course.' I see the staff opening windows. The box is placed precariously on the edge of the stage.

At 5pm precisely, Ben the Barmitzvah boy, a tubby lad with a face like a beekeeper's apprentice, takes his place inside the box. He has been instructed to jump straight through the paper and on to the dance floor, a mere drop of 12 inches, when the band play the first chord of 'Eye Of The Tiger'.

On the dance floor, my two glamorous girls, Suzi and Lynsey, wearing silver hot pants and football shirts, are posing like magician's assistants at the side of the box, ready to escort him around the room like Rocky Balboa entering the ring and then to his place at the table. There he will get a kiss on the cheek and a quick goosing. Lucky boy.

Our smoke machine has been set up behind the box. I have been assured the fire alarms have been switched off. It's all set for a spectacular entrance. All simple stuff, we do it every week. But it is *the most important part* of the evening. If it goes tits-up, then there is no second go. No re-run. It's all being filmed too and my heart is beating fast. The boy in the box is looking at me, nervously scratching his balls and awaiting the given signal.

At 5.20pm the guests are asked to remain seated, the band is already on stage and Dave Price is knocking out 'Top Gun'. With a bang of his hammer, Mum, Dad and little Sister, are introduced by smooth Toastmaster, Steve Warwick to the sound of 'We Are Family', as they parade theatrically, hand in hand, around the room to the cheering of the crowd.

Terry gives a drum roll, 'Ladies and Gentlemen and now the moment you have all been waiting for! Please welcome the star of the show - the incredible, the amazing, Ben!' The crowd look towards the stage as Dave hits the first power chord, Greg fires the smoke machine and the box is enveloped in dense white clouds.

Ben dives straight at the paper but it doesn't tear. Like a Fred Dibnah demolition of a chimney in slow motion, the box slowly keels over off the stage and crashes on the dance floor. There are screams from the crowd. Ben is still inside the smoking box and is yanked quickly to his feet by the girls and marched around the room, hands raised aloft and all smiles. We quickly switch from 'Eye Of The Tiger' to 'Glory Glory, Tottenham Hotspur'. There is some booing, but not enough. Gerry is quickly picking up the wreckage of his disintegrated box. 'The fat little fucker never hit the paper hard enough!' shouts Gerry. (It would have helped if he hadn't used *vinyl* wallpaper!)

Here I must mention a popular wedding prop, the 'Confetti Cannon'. These silly gadgets are cardboard tubes stuffed with confetti and can be purchased from party shops for a few quid and are usually fired off by the Toastmaster or band singers when the Bride and Groom make their entrance. Gerry had made his own Confetti Cannon and insisted it would do a perfect job.

We were booked to play a Jewish wedding at the Langham Hilton Hotel, which stands opposite the BBC Building in Langham Place, just off Oxford Street. It was not our favourite venue as the get-in was a pain in the arse, through the rear courtyard and up steep steps. One usually had to double-park the van outside the gate, thereby causing traffic problems. Once inside the narrow ballroom, the only place to perform was the central area. Only a narrow stage could be squeezed in between the pillars. The stage depth was only eight feet.

There was just enough space behind the stage to fire a Confetti Cannon, and Gerry assured me that he would aim the thing at the ceiling above the dance floor and the confetti ball would then break up above the heads of the crowd and 'snow' down on them. I assured the client that we had the best Confetti Cannon on the market and charged them accordingly.

Gerry's cannon looked like an old fashioned blunderbuss. Two bags of confetti had been rammed down the barrel and were to be fired by a CO_2 capsule when the trigger was pulled. Gerry assured me that it 'always worked' and so he prepared to fire the thing in the large gap behind the drums.

At 5.30pm the 'New Mr and Mrs Cohen' are introduced and they skip into the room as we play 'Mazel Tov'. Gerry points the Blunderbuss at the ceiling and pulls the trigger. There is a feeble 'poof' from the gun as a solid, football size lump of confetti flops out of the barrel and hits Terry smack on the back of the head, almost knocking him off the kit. He is covered in pink and white confetti. I find confetti in the band backline for weeks after. None of it reaches the intended dance floor or the Bride and Groom. It's *never* Gerry's fault as he yells, 'Your silly little fucker of a drummer had his head in the way!'

11

THE REAL THING AND WORSE.

At some point in the early nineties I realized that I would need a good 'horn section', consisting of trumpet and sax. I was determined to net even more West End work and to enhance sets such as The Blues Brothers and Kool & The Gang. I was further encouraged after seeing the mesmerising, robotic horn section in Alpha Connection who were easily the best on the circuit.

In the early days we had experimented with single sax players. Many were keen to impress but most of them overplayed on every song. On one memorable occasion we were joined on stage at the DOB Club, Kilburn, by Dick Heckstall-Smith, formerly of John Mayall's Bluesbreakers. 'In The Midnight Hour' never sounded better. Dick would often pop into West Hampstead police station for a chat with me, so I had invited him to the gig. He was brilliant and world famous, but I thought him far too old for my band.

Around 1992 I found a fine female sax player in the young Lisa Grahame, who worked especially well with Jeremy Moore on trumpet. Together they made a great team and were with the band for most of 1992-3. Lisa had a great sense of humour and was good company. She now plays in the Jools Holland Rhythm and Blues Orchestra.

Snooks bar in Hemel Hempstead was an early source of horn players and I experimented with a couple of good players, Dave Savill on trumpet and Bruce McConnach on sax. These were experienced players and excellent musicians. I tried them out on a couple of gigs but to my horror they brought their Jazz Band habits with them, carrying pints of ale with whisky chasers on to the stage and then proceeded to light up their fags.

My longest-serving and most dependable sax player was also spotted in Snooks. I thought Jez Guest was excellent. A young, good-looking, ex-professional footballer who was doing a Sunday lunchtime gig with The Middlemen. This was after I had taken over – at the invitation of manager Mick Jones - the booking of rock bands, which turned Snooks around and quickly saw off the non-spending Jazz fraternity.

Another sax player I first saw there was the excellent Nick Payn who did regular work with us when I expanded the band to the Supanova Dance Orchestra. I also found that a solo sax could easily fit in with the band. If I needed the addition of a trumpet then a sax player would invariably recommend one.

The first opportunity I had of taking a horn section overseas was Christmas 1995 to Bahrain. The band was everything I wanted, but I was still experimenting with horn sections. I took Steve Main on alto sax, Matt Horner on trombone and Jeremy Moore on trumpet. None were older than 21. It was my first young horn section and proved a good one.

The British Airways 747 Christmas flight to Manama City was packed with a mix of British and Arab families going on holiday or home for Christmas. The rear section of economy class was taken over by the Mixed Feelings ten-piece band. 'Screecher' balloons were being inflated by Sue Acteson and launched Zeppelin-like, screaming around the cabin. A demonstration of how she could get her lips completely around the end of one sausage balloon, brought a tremendous round of applause and several offers of marriage.

I had 'bunged' our gay British Airways head steward twenty quid and a continuous mix of vodka, gin and whisky miniatures followed. It was 'party on'. Terry had draped a flight blanket over himself and was doing impressions of the Virgin Mary. It also looked like he was hiding the Eiffel Tower between his legs. I suspected it was a bottle of wine.

We had auditioned for this, the first of many overseas gigs, by hiring the function room at Porters Park Golf Club in Radlett. Where Simon Davis, ex-special forces soldier and now manager of the Bapco Club, Bahrain, was suitably impressed and booked us immediately. It was Sue and Helen who sold the band to him.

He did comment that 'as gorgeous as the girls' legs are' they must wear long ball gowns when entertaining Arabs as they all live on 'Planet Horn' and think British women easy meat.

Simon was waiting for us the other side of the arrivals. I don't think he was that enamoured by Helen hollering 'Whoo hoo! Happy Bloody Christmas Simon!' and 'Get your kit off!' We were sharply told to behave and bussed in silence for the twenty minutes to our hotel, which was on the edge of the club complex.

Simon was visibly angry at our boisterous seasonal greetings and this ex-British Army NCO was determined to impose his authority. I was promptly called to his office and told that we were all pissed. I would have never have guessed. He said 'It might be Christmas but you are not here to piss it up. You are here to work!'

The following night, Christmas Eve, we were due to perform at a Carol Concert for the Petroleum Company staff, the Arab workers and their families. Sure enough, at 5pm, the Arabs began to arrive, about two hundred of them and they promptly scrambled for the front seats which had been laid out on the open-air concourse and snatched up the carol sheets. It was broad daylight and a warm, golden evening.

Simon called me over and said, 'I hope you know all these carols!' Of course I *knew* them! What child who had been raised under an English heaven didn't? I just didn't know how to *play* them.

The band had been set up on a big stage, which had been built in close proximity to the crowd. We were within touching distance. A big Soundcraft mixer was set up stage-right and already the Bedouin sound engineer was fast asleep. Maybe he had been on the whisky too? The carol sheet contained all the well-loved favourites: 'Away In A Manger', 'Once In Royal David's City' and worse, 'We Three Kings Of Orient Are'.

Fortunately, all the words were there, but most of us had never played carols before and there was no music available. They just assumed we knew them. I thought we would just be playing modern music. It was

Jamie Hardwick, our proficient keyboard player, who came to the rescue. 'I know all these. We had to play them at school.' Our trumpet player, Jeremy Moore, as pissed as he was, said he knew them too. He blew them accurately, joined by the full brass section.

We sounded like a Salvation Army band. Dave Howard, Sue, Helen and myself led the carol singing. The Arabs just sat there perplexed and used the carol sheets as fans. 'O Come, All Ye Faithful' was belted out triumphantly, plus 'While Shepherds Watched Their Flocks By Night'. The Arab males were on 'Planet Horn' as predicted by Simon. 'Now I know why they wear those long gowns,' said Terry, 'You can't see them wanking!' (He was to treat himself to a 'Masturbation Marquee', 'Wank Wigwam' or 'Tossing Tent', as he called it, just a few days later). The Arabs were simply mesmerised by the girls. The main thing was, Simon was delighted and all was forgiven.

We were given a free bar, where the girls were both chatted up by the robed Saudi Arabs. One asked Sue, 'What gift can I give you for Christmas? You can have anything you want.' I was hoping she would say 'A Rolex watch!' But she said 'Kent Menthol cigarettes. I can't get them anywhere!' The next morning, 200 'Kent Menthol' had been placed outside her bedroom door.

Dave Howard was in the corner of the bar with his head in the litter bin. He had guzzled far too much Taylors Vintage Port. 'We always have port at Christmas,' he burbled. 'Yes, but not a fucking litre,' replied Jeremy, as Dave threw another mighty 'Hughie!' into the bin. 'That's his Christmas drinking over,' I thought and I was right. He never touched another drop for the rest of the week. We were thousands of miles from home and it was Christmas Eve. It was the first time I had been abroad at Christmas. I phoned home and then decided to explore Manama City. So who is gonna come?

The usual suspects got to their feet and Jamie, Terry and myself were given a complimentary taxi into town on this warm night. First stop was the Souk. We were astounded at the vivid colours and pungent smells of the Arab market. We went back there four days later to buy our 'Arab outfits'.

We had been told by Simon to ignore the 'Beggar Wallahs' who littered the pavement and pestered us for 'dina'. Terry commented that there were probably 'Gobble Wallahs' around too. Sitting beneath a streetlight was a legless and toothless beggar, complete with begging bowl. Jamie gave him a £1 coin. He then miraculously grew legs and stood up, protesting that it was the wrong money! We took refuge in a nearby novelty shop but he followed us inside bellowing, 'Bloody fucking English Barsted! I fuck your mother!'

He was promptly set upon by the smartly-suited little Indian store assistant and forcibly thrown out onto the pavement, where he was dealt a colossal kicking. I thought little Mowgli might kill him but he came back in to the shop with a huge grin on his face. He jumped to attention and threw me a massive military salute, 'I kick his bloody bollocks off Sir.' So we felt obliged to buy a fancy wristwatch. Which was another comical experience. One was a mini drum kit, another a grand piano and the other a bass guitar. We paid over the odds – about £25 each - as we had not yet learned to haggle.

We needed a drink and found that the only pubs were in hotels. Sporting our bizarre wristwatches, we entered the nearest hotel lift where we were joined by a couple of northern Brits who were heavily made-up with eye shadow and rouge. Jamie recollects;

> We were in the lift at the Hilton Hotel, Manama City, when two little guys got in with us. They said that they were the pop duo, Black Lace, and were performing in the hotel bar later and would we like to come and see them? Jon said in his predictable manner, 'Never heard of you!' They were so disappointed that they started singing their hit record 'Agadoo' to us!

Jamie was suitably unimpressed at their singing and promptly decided to demonstrate his gymnastic skills by vaulting himself upside down on the brass rails and kicking the lift ceiling panels in. The debris of which showered us all with plaster, dead insects and dust.

The next Arab lift passengers were not too impressed as we ran into the dimly lit, top-floor bar to hide. Only to hear a voice say 'Hello Terry!' A Hemel Hempstead builder was drinking at the bar. Terry introduced me to his mate Tim. He later said, 'He's "Dim Tim", he drinks in the "Patch". His missus has got massive jugs.' I assumed she was the landlady.

We managed to get a table near the stage and ordered three large Jewish Cokes, although we never used that actual term. Mind you, they were handsome measures of Jack Daniels. I also noticed that some Arabs were drinking from brown paper bags, disguising a glass. When I asked one of them what they were drinking, he replied 'Whisky. Very kind of you!'

It was around midnight that the resident band took the stage and they were a brilliant seven-piece 'Flip' (Filipino) band. They were The Junction Band and gave me wonderful inspiration for Mixed Feelings. They started with the theme from *Top Gun*. The guitarist was brilliant. They had just one young male singer, who could mimic Jon Bon Jovi, Michael Jackson, Tom Jones and Elvis.

Three attractive and scantily clad female singers likewise took off Tina Turner, Janis Joplin, Dusty Springfield, Madonna, Abba and more. That was it! The secret was in the variety. In watching that band I instantly created a new show in my head. In spite of what Peter Richardson had said, 'Mixed Feelings' was the right name.

Seven more nightly shows successfully followed at the Bapco Club, the last one being New Year's Eve. The band went down a storm and Simon was so chuffed he gave us a free bar every night. The relaxing days were filled with walking, talking and drinking around the swimming pool. Why wouldn't the long, curly-haired Dave Howard dive in the pool like the rest of us? A few days later we found out when the singers took a Jeep safari into the desert and his wig blew off.

The following Christmas, the same gig was done by a smaller band called Jamtastic and the bandleader, Mark Rideout, told me; 'Upon our arrival at the Bapco Club, the boss, Simon Davis, said to me, 'We had a brilliant band here last year called Mixed Feelings, but they were total piss artists and drank the place dry.'

As the demand for the band and the quality of gigs improved, I stopped *all* drinks from being taken on to the stage during the show at home and abroad. Bottled water was only allowed for singers, concealed from view by the sound monitors, but even that became a precarious practice after Gary Priestley managed to pour a pint of water into a brand-new monitor, whilst leaning forward mumbling, 'These new monitors are nice Jon!'

The only time I lifted the rule was at Jewish weddings, when the band had the tedious task of providing 'live' dinner music in the form of a 'Jazz Quartet'. So Jamie, Dave, Terry and myself would take up our

Jewish Cokes and place them on top of a guitar or keyboard combo. Bass combos were more precarious as on more than one occasion the bass notes caused the glass to 'wander' and fall off. I could never understand why amp-makers do not provide a beer glass recess on the top of amps. When I suggested this to Jim Marshall at his Christmas party at Wilton Hall, Bletchley, he said he was 'working on it.'

Mixed Feelings quickly gained a reputation as 'The UK's No. 1 Show Band'. With the expansion to the Supanova Dance Orchestra, our status was genuinely boosted, much to the disdain of certain envious bandleaders who labelled us 'a bunch of piss-heads'. We never disguised the fact and usually lived up to our long-term motto: 'Prepare to Party', which meant the band too. We also got to know many of the Capital's top venues and their staff got to know us. 'Mixed Feelings often means *mayhem* but a brilliant show is guaranteed'.

The cost of drinks at London hotels was ludicrous, with a bottle of Carlsberg 'vicar's piss' costing £6.00. So we brought our own booze to gigs. I don't care what anyone says, a beer or two 'kick starts' a band. A whisky or three may fuck you up (as it did with me a few times). In my clothes bag I would often carry a couple of bottles of wine. Terry and Greg would bring a dozen bottles of beer. We would always have a party before and after.

Many funny occasions spring to mind regarding the demon drink, of one Thursday night at The Royal Lancaster Hotel. I recorded this at the time;

'We have four gigs this week. All in the West End and the Band is booked to do this gig via Michael Black and it's the fifth time we have performed at this City computer company party. Michael telephoned me on Sunday morning just four days before and stated that I had not signed the contract. The reason for this is because he had never sent me one.

This is an old ploy of Michael's, whereby he waits until the last minute in order to get a cheap deal and tries to get the band to turn out for as little money as possible. The thing he didn't realize with me was, that the less money the band get, the smaller the band gets. We used to do this gig as a twelve-piece band. Now it's an eight. Every year, instead of the money getting higher, it gets less. When I remonstrate with the wily

Michael, I get the usual bullshit. 'I need your help on this one Son. They don't have a pot to piss in.'

I put in the eight-piece and we arrive at The Royal Lancaster at 5pm as agreed. We have a struggle getting the gear in, as another event company is coming out. There was a party during the afternoon, which is poor practice.

The Nine Kings Suite is set for the arrival of six hundred guests. Tables are even set on the dance floor. In the bar area they have the boring 'casino tables' with roulette wheels. I can never understand why they have that shit. It detracts from the dancing. Bar prices are unfortunately sky-high, nevertheless we love playing here and we always set up our gear as quickly as possible. The four of us do a live sound check to the usual 'Watermelon Man'. Then follows a Disco check. I go out front for a listen.

Terry is standing on the dance floor like a little boy lost, in his new anorak. He is itching to get to The Swan pub next door. This fine pub, now frequented by musicians and tourists, used to be the haunt of 'Hyde Park Rangers' when I was a young PC at Paddington, forty years ago. We now call them 'sex workers'.

By the time Terry gets on his fifth pint, 'Mr Hyde' will have appeared. I will be told to stick the band up my arse and we will get the usual boring diatribe, 'Me and Elaine are fucking off to Cornwall, Hemel is a shithole.'

We are at the bar of The Swan, talking to 'landlord Chris' who has just bought us a round of London Pride. I invite him over to the Nine Kings Suite to watch the band later. The singers and musicians arrive. None have got any money. I buy the drinks. We go over to the hotel at 9pm for something to eat.

We are on stage after Paddy 'Stargazer' Dara O'Briain and it's Terry's birthday again. He has a birthday *every* gig and we have discovered that this crafty ruse often works. The client will send up a bottle of champagne.

Terry's birthday is duly announced when we are into the first set. A ripple of applause goes up from the crowd. We zip through *Grease, Jersey Boys*, Kool & The Gang and some latest chart stuff, for one hour and thirty minutes.

Smiling toastmaster, Robert Persell, brings to the stage two bottles of Veuve Clicquot champagne and dumps them by Dave's amp. He blows us a kiss goodbye and leaves. Terry's eyes light up and the tempo speeds up. The champagne is for him.

The band finishes the first set just after midnight and I tell the girls to change into their Abba outfits, ready for the second set, which will start at 12.30am. We cannot get near the overcrowded bar and I hear Terry say, 'Fuck this! Let's drink the champagne.' We go back to the stage and pop the corks of both bottles, which almost hit the ceiling above the disco dancers. I take some clean wine glasses from a nearby table. The champagne is warm and fizzy but livens us up. I take DJ Greg a glass too.

We are well into the second bottle when Carol the client comes over and says, 'Can you announce the two winners of the casino and present them with the champagne prizes?' 'Where is it?' I ask. She says: 'The Toastmaster put them on the stage.' Terry tells the client, 'We've drunk them fuckers.'

The following morning Michael calls. 'What's this about the band drinking the fucking casino prizes? The client was not happy, Son.'

There is a simple moral to the story. *Never* put booze on a Mixed Feelings stage. It will be drunk. So we never got booked back for that one but it didn't stop us continuing to announce some special celebration or another and the funny thing was a repeat was on the cards at The Portman Hotel when it was announced that 'Dave Price's wife has just given birth to a baby son today but Dave wanted to be here with you tonight.'

With that, a woman heads straight for the stage and Dave Price. She walks to the side and shouts, 'You should be ashamed of yourself, not being with your poor wife tonight!' However, two bottles of Moët and Chandon are placed on the stage next to Dave. We drink them at half time, toasting 'Little Jimmy'. At the end of the gig, the client says to me, 'Did you find the champagne?' I replied, 'Yes and thank you very much!' She then says, 'They are the lucky menu prizes.'

The following morning I got a phone call from Paul Baxter of Fanfare agency. 'What's all this? I hear you drank the client's champagne! She was not happy.'

DIARY ENTRY 3 October 2007. The Battle of Berlin.

Terry, Jamie, Greg and I are flying to Berlin. We meet at Luton

Airport in the bar. We check in at 6am. It's early morning but never too early for a couple of pints of Staropramen and a smoked salmon bagel in the departure lounge. We are booked by event planner, Mike Clynes, to perform at a hotel near the Brandenburg Gate for a special awards event for Johnson & Johnson. We are the advance guard.

We arrive at Berlin at 10am. We go via taxi straight to our billet, the Marriott Courtyard Hotel and check in. We then set out to explore. The rest of the band, including Dave Price, Tony Moriah, Gary Priestley, Suzi Jari and Lynsey Shaw, are coming out tomorrow. Courtesy of Mike Clynes, our task is to meet the crew and gear when it arrives and help to set it up. Which really means a free day of sightseeing in Berlin or it could be a gigantic piss up.

We have a great day wandering around the city. It has been totally rebuilt after being smashed to bits by RAF Bomber Command in World War II. There are grey, high-rise concrete and glass buildings everywhere. We see bits of the Berlin Wall, the Reichstag Building and Holocaust memorial

Then we went to the Brandenburg Gate, where a stage had been set up in the nearby hotel at which we were to perform the following night. All the PA and backline has been hired in and already in place. The friendly British crew tell us to go for a beer. Oh dear.

We enter a large oak-panelled bar and ask big bubbied barmaids for Lowenbrau. We also want to try the fabulous German sausages we have heard so much about. 'Curry Wurst mit chips' is ordered for four. We sit outside in the warm afternoon sunshine. We all decide the sausage was shite and not worth the 14 euros each. It is merely a long pork sausage with curry powder sprinkled on it and a side dish of stringy chips.

We walk back to the hotel at 5pm and get showered before we meet in the hotel bar for a Pilsner before going out on the town. We stop for a litre of Lowenbrau at some shiny new bar, then venture off down the back streets. Eventually we come to a lively area where we see a bar called Druid Absinthe. 'Shall we try it?' asks Greg.

We step inside. It is dark and noisy with music from the Scorpions and Lynyrd Skynyrd. We order four Belgian Leffe Royale beers and are amazed at the varieties of absinthe on show. I have never tasted the stuff but have heard it is dangerous. There is a notice on the bar; 'Flaming Cannabis Absinthe five euros'. 'Go on, let's have one,' says Jamie. It looks like Fairy Liquid. We knock them back in one. It tastes like hot aniseed balls.

We are ravenous and are recommended by the barman to go to The Blockhaus. It looked like a concrete fortification from the Siegfried Line. We have fillet steaks and a couple of bottles of Benchmark red wine, a truly excellent dinner. After midnight many of the 'sensible' bars have closed. So, we ask a taxi driver to take us to a bar where Terry insisted he wanted to see an exhibition with 'Washers put on the Donkey's cock'. The smiling cab driver understands and accordingly takes us to a dubious 'nameless' night club at the corner of a busy main street.

There is a barrel-shaped, bearded bouncer guarding the door. The cabbie takes us inside to collect his commission and hands us over to the scrawny male proprietor who demands 200 euros for the four of us suckers to get in, which included two drinks each. The club was dimly lit and practically empty, so we went and sat on the stools at the bar, where a Bavarian milkmaid complete with pigtails was serving drinks.

As our eyes get accustomed to the darkness, four women wearing basques, suspenders and stockings, zero in on us. They are all 'RAF' quality. As 'Rough As Fuck,' according to Terry. One spoke; 'Hello Englishmen! Vould you like a drink?'

We are entitled to two drinks each, so ordered gin and tonics and in all fairness, they were substantial measures of Gordons. We quickly guzzled those and then started on the next. The women, who are drinking champagne, intermingle with us. 'When is the pole-dancing going to start?' asks Terry. 'When you buy us champagne darling,' was the reply. The place had the atmosphere of a derelict church. I said to the boys, 'Come on lads, drink up and we'll bugger off back to the hotel. We can get free drinks there.'

The ancient big Berthas lose interest and retreat into the gloom. In the absence of any 'Dirty Dancing' or 'Donkey Washers' we drink up and make our way to the exit, closely followed by the creepy little German manager. He had locked us in and he was 'not going to let us out until we paid 260 euros for champagne bought for the girls.'

I tell him we have not bought any champagne and I demand he unlocks the door. He refuses. While I am arguing with him, Terry has discreetly taken the door keys from under the counter and is 'jiggling' the lock. Greg had now emerged from the toilets and I tell him that

'Herman the fucking German' won't let us out. He then promptly whacks him straight on the chin, with a cracking right hook. Down he goes. By which time Terry has managed to get the door open.

We then spill out on to the pavement, only to be confronted by 'Bernard the Bouncer'. He snarls at us, only to catch another haymaker from Greg and down he goes. Then the club owner, who had stupidly got back to his feet, rushes at Greg and is clouted again and falls on the pavement. We now need to scarper and quick. The German police would be here any second and it wouldn't be our story they would believe. We start to walk away pretty sharpish, but 'Bernard' grunts and grabs Greg around the ankle in a forlorn rugby tackle, for which he gets a boot in the chops.

I have the gut feeling that we will soon be inspecting the walls of a police cell. 'Run for it boys!' I shout and the four of us leg it up the main street, not knowing where the hell we are going. 'How long do we have to run for?' asks Jamie, puffing on his fag as we trot up the street.

Suddenly a taxi pulls up alongside us and the driver shouts in English, 'Get in boys.' I am cautious about this because I am concerned the driver might take us back to the club or to the police station, but fortunately he was on our side. He congratulates us for bashing the club owner.

I dare not tell the driver the name of our hotel but asked him to take us to a pub. He then drops us off at a 'Wild West' bar, which I adjudged from a pocket map to be near our hotel. He kindly refused to take payment. There, we have another beer before walking to our hotel. Fortunately, we are not far away and got back about 3.30am. We all have a large Glen Grant before retiring.

We arrive at the gig around 2pm next day and sound check. By which time the singers have arrived at the hotel. A mini bus is sent to collect us for the gig at 7.30pm. We are well looked after, as always, in the event organiser Mike Clynes' generous style. We enjoy a very nice dinner and unlimited wine and champagne.

The event is running late and we finally get on stage and do a two-hour, non-stop set. At one point during the show two German police officers walked across the dance floor. My heart stops as I thought we had been rumbled for the fracas the night before, but it seems they are simply after a beer while they gawp at the girls in the band.

DIARY ENTRY. Saturday 27 June 2004

It is sunny day and yet another juicy gig from the Alpha Connection Agency. This event is at the ICC Birmingham for a national cleaning product supplier and we are in Hall 3. We go through security to the rear of the Hall. It's an easy get in, as the van can be reversed right into the venue.

I note we are working with Liverpool soul band, The Real Thing, who had a big hit in the '70s with 'You To Me Are Everything'. I am looking forward to that. I note we are supplying back line, drums, monitors and mics for them, as part of our contract.

The ICC are supplying lighting and front of house PA. The Real Thing have not yet arrived, so we quickly unload the van in the loading bay and make our way into the hall. I see that a square stage has been set up in the middle of the huge room, which can easily accommodate three thousand guests. It has been decked out entirely in funeral black drape and riggers are up in the Gods, flying moving heads and par cans on to the stage and dance floor. The whole place is buzzing with the usual, friendly staff at this great venue.

Greg is not on this event for some reason, so we are using the excellent in-house sound engineer at the ICC to mix our sound. We quickly set up the back line and microphones and plug them into a multicore stage box.

Martin, our 'Grade 1' roadie, knows exactly what to do and Terry has quickly set up his enormous Yamaha kit in the centre rear of the stage. The real reason for Terry's expedient set up is the call of The Prince of Wales pub outside the back gates. This topping pub sells a magnificent array of local real ales, including the scrumptious Ansell's Mild and is usually frequented by musicians and crewmen. Jamie has arrived, proclaiming that it only took him twenty minutes to get there. He lives locally, so it's right convenient for him.

We are set by 4pm and I have tuned my Jazz bass. The sound engineer from the ICC has been most helpful and has already directly-injected our equipment into their house PA, which is a huge JBL system. We do a quick run-through, with just a trio of bass, keyboards and drums; this time it's the classic Booker T instrumental, 'Green Onions' and Jamie gets a real '60s big Hammond organ sound on his Korg.

I put my bass back in its case and walk over to all four mics and I test each one with the usual 'One, two, one, two' – that'll do for our four singers who, as usual, can't be bothered to turn up for a sound check but will complain about the stage monitors later.

I note that Terry is chatting with the drummer of The Real Thing's backing band, who has just arrived. The bass player has also arrived, he is another nice guy and we shake hands. He is using my Ampeg 115 combo. I note that he produces a beautiful 5-string Music Man bass, which sounds quite lovely.

I carry on with another quick monitor and mic check this time, 'Un deux, trois, un deux, trois.' I am happy with that and happy with life. Righto! Let's get over the POW. Suddenly, in my face, appears a little black guy who is wearing a Nike tracksuit. He is not much taller than Kenny Baker.

'How long are you'se gonna be Pal?' He has a strong Scouse accent. I suspect he could be one of the singers of The Real Thing. I say to him, 'Give me a couple of minutes mate. One of the stage monitors has packed up.' He then says to me antagonistically, 'Well fucking well hurry up Pal, as we need to sound check!'

I reply to him, 'Who are you?' He replies, 'We are The Real Thing, that's who we are, Pal.' 'Never heard of you!' I say. Tiny Tim takes the bait and flips; 'You'se a fucking wanker! *Everyone* knows The Real Thing! I'll knock your fucking head off!' I say to him, 'You'll have to get a box to stand on.'

He is now screaming, 'Outside now! You fucking wanker, I'll fucking sort you out.' I reply, 'I don't fight midgets, mate.' He has now lost it completely and screams, 'Outside now, arsehole!'

I say to him. 'Calm down Pal, I've got news for you. If you're the Pretty Things you ain't using our gear tonight. 'No, we are the fucking Real Thing!' he yells. I continue, 'So go and get your own fucking drum kit and amps.' At this comment there is supportive applause from the riggers above, who are watching the antics of this horrid little gnome.

I then take all the Shure mics down and put them away. Tiny Tim then says, 'Listen you wanker, you have to supply our fucking kit tonight or we don't have a fucking show.' I say, 'Correct Pal. You don't have a show, so best you fuck off back to Everton.' He is now restrained from attacking me by another singer who has appeared.

I say to everyone who is on the stage; 'Due to his attitude problem, none of you are using our gear tonight, so you better get gear ordered in.' Another of the singers from The Real Thing is on the stage. They seem OK guys and apologise for the attitude of little legs. 'You still ain't using our kit.' I tell them.

Then a guy, who says he is manager of The Real Thing, arrives and pleads with me. I refuse to change my mind and leave Martin to guard our gear. After all they are from Liverpool. I am just walking to the pub, when my phone rings. It is our agent, Russ Brewster. He wants to know what's going on. 'They say you won't let them use your gear. They have to. Please Matey.' Then he adds, 'The client won't pay us!' That forces my arm, so I reluctantly go back to Hall 3 and tell The Real Thing they can use our gear. Limp handshakes all around.

'The Real Things' are due on at 10pm but insist on going on at 9.30pm. We let them get on with it. They take the warm-up spot with their average singers - none of whom would be good enough for Mixed Feelings – and die on their arses. They do a 15-minute version of 'You To Me Are Everything', which is actually a good song, but bores the crowd. After twenty minutes, the lady client says 'Can you get them off and get your lot on?'

I look around and notice that no one is dancing. They are all too busy hitting the free bar at the back. When there is a free bar, no-one dances. The Real Thingys are glad to come off and head straight for the M6. Mixed Feelings pack the dance floor until 1am. Dull it isn't.

While we are on the subject of obnoxious bands, I was reminded by Jamie Hardwick to tell the story about the 'horrible Tony Hadley band', when we performed at a birthday party for business man and football director, David Sullivan. This was an extravagant event held in the Music Room of the posh Landmark Hotel.

The agent for this event was Howard T'loosty. As a special surprise for his seventy guests, who had at David's request dressed as gangsters, he had booked Tony Hadley and his band. Also on the bill was our old friend Bobby Davro. The contract stipulated they would use our lighting rig, drums and backline and put in their PA system, which we could all use.

We had become friendly with Spandau Ballet star Tony Hadley, who was a fellow 'gooner' and nice guy. We had previously backed him 'live' on stage for the Help For Heroes Ball at the Birmingham Metropole and also at Wentworth Golf Club for a children's charity. We had learned about twelve of his songs including his big hits 'Gold' and 'True'. He sang Elvis numbers too. The women loved him and always crowded the front of the stage, in spite of the fact that he had developed a substantial 'breadbasket' since Spandau Ballet days. He would usually walk on to the stage carrying a pint of ale.

In my opinion, backing any known singer was fun but a real challenge, as I could not read music but wanted to do it right. I had learned a lesson from the long ago, 'Susan Maughan episode' and Dave Price had carefully written out Tony's songs in simple-to-read, chorded parts. So, I spent an hour or two at home in my studio learning the songs and getting them note perfect by playing away to Spandau Ballet on the Mac. But for now he had his 'own' backing band.

Saturday came and we turned up at The Landmark Hotel at 2pm. A nice early time to set up and then relax over a beer or three in the local Allsop Arms in Gloucester Place, or The Railway Bar opposite. The Music Room is only a small venue at The Landmark. Not to be confused with the magnificent main ballroom, with which we were very familiar, having performed there on many occasions. We had a great relationship with this lovely, old, '5-Star' railway hotel and many of the staff had got to know the band.

A big-arsed, articulated truck was obscenely parked in Harewood Avenue, right outside the only side entrance into the Music Room. One had to negotiate a narrow iron staircase, then through the narrow French windows into the room. We had to park the Iveco on a single yellow line, further down the road.

Martin was driving the van and he stayed with it in case the yellow peril arrived. I was using a crew of three on this gig, as an extra pair of hands was usually required on most West End jobs, so Bob Wise was with us as well as Greg. I might add that not one London hotel has easy ballroom access for modern bands.

In this small room the band crew had set up a colossal Eastern Acoustic Works PA system. Four 1 x 18 bass bins and four mid-range 2 x12" cabs, with an array of horns on top, *either side* of the tiny stage. The room was good for only seventy guests and about the size of the bar at the Allsop Arms. Talk about overkill. A third of the room was totally filled with gear and there were huge flight cases everywhere

The Tony Hadley musicians were busy setting up their own back line and large Ludwig drum kit. The drummer had taken up the whole of the centre stage. There was no cheerful word of greeting. Terry takes up the story,

> I held out my hand to the drummer, who was on his knees
> adjusting his bass drum but he didn't want to shake hands. So
> I says him, 'Hello mate, I am the drummer in Mixed Feelings.
> I thought you were using my drums?' He didn't answer. So I
> said, 'Is it OK to use yours?' His reply was, 'No! *Nobody* touches
> my kit.' I then said, 'You can use my kit if you like'. He says,
> 'What do I wanna use your kit for? Use your own fucking kit.'
> So I carried all my kit in and start to set it up in front of him, as
> it was the only place to go. He says, 'Get that fucking shit out
> of my way. You are not setting up in front of me.' I said to him
> 'Where can I go then?' he says, You can set up *after* our set, as
> we are going on first.' I thought, 'What a nasty little bastard.'

I watched this palaver and just assumed that the prick had 'little man syndrome', which was a shame, as I generally found most musicians to be friendly souls. We always helped each other out if we could share gear. This band certainly had The Real Thing 'attitude' but even worse. It was 'Cuntitude'.

Remembering Michael Black's cheerful advice, 'It's nice to be nice,' I kept out of it and trusted Terry to sort it out. Greg was talking to the sound engineer on the huge Allen & Heath 60 channel mixing desk. The hairy little sound engineer, a 'Bill Oddie lookalike', had a white gauze bandage patch tied around his head, which loosely fitted over a very black eye. I naturally assumed someone had previously thumped him. Greg says,

> I asked him if it was OK as per contract, to use their PA system.
> He replied 'Not according to my contract. This PA is for the
> Tony Hadley band only.' I said to him 'OK we will set up our
> own mixer, can we just sub into your system to save humping
> in our PA speakers? He said, 'No.' So I go out to Martin and
> tell him we have got to put in our own PA and we hump in
> a pair of 2x15 bass bins and a pair of 1x15 tops which is our
> *medium* Sherman PA rig and quite sufficient for the Music
> Room. I then set up two wedge monitors on stage and the

sound guy says, 'You're not putting them there and get *all* your fucking gear off our stage.'

It's all very well being 'nice' but there are times when you have to be nasty too. I said to him, 'I'm not surprised you've got a black eye, you nasty little wanker. You'll have another one in a minute!' He says mournfully, 'It's not a black eye. I have just had an operation on a brain tumour.'

I've put my big foot in it again. I apologise, 'I am sorry to hear that mate but are you sure they didn't give you a lobotomy by mistake?' With that, the drummer and bass player advance menacingly towards me. 'Who you calling a wanker you fucking wanker?' I am standing next to Greg and Martin and Snow White's boyfriends think better of it.

I am now steaming and I assert bellicosely, that *I* am running this show; 'By the way, we *are* setting up on this stage so you wankers had better move your kit now! Before we do it for you. Furthermore, you are not using our lighting rig.' Roadie Bob Wise remembered:

> I was horrified and thought there was going to be a fight, so I hid behind the PA stacks. I am no fighter! The Tony Hadley Band thought they were something special and had a severe attitude problem. They were just horrible people. To be honest, I thought there would be total mayhem. Fortunately, it didn't come to that as they were told in no uncertain terms by Jon, that they were to make room on the stage or we would move the gear for them. Later that night, we were having dinner and I was pleased to see everyone getting along. I don't think Tony knew about it, or that his band had been complete and utter arseholes.

Wearing his new Marks & Spencer suit, our agent, Howard T'loosty, arrives and starts asking questions, 'Jon, why do they want such a big PA? You don't have to be loud to be good!' I reply, 'Yes I know, Howard but they are being bloody difficult. They won't let us use their PA. So they are not using our lights!'

Howard flaps at my tit-for-tat pettiness. Waving his arms up and down as if he were about to fly. 'It's in the contract! It's in the contract in black and white that you are using their PA.' Just at that moment, a smiling David Sullivan walks into the room with another gangster. Both are wearing pinstripe suits, Fedora hats and carrying violin cases. They are off the set of Bugsy Malone. Then Tony Hadley blusters into the room with a cheery greeting.

We finish setting up and Tony does a thunderous sound check. Glasses rattle on the ornately laid tables. 'Does it have to be that loud?' implores Howard. 'Tell the retard on the mixing desk.' I say to him. To my delight, Howard goes over and bothers the pond life, who is getting agitated and pointing fingers at me.

Howard comes back. 'He says your band threatened to beat his band up!' I said, 'We don't fight fuckwits. And they are still not using our lighting rig.'

Howard begs me to relent. I relent. Howard is good at pouring oil on troubled water. Talking of trouble, the irrepressible Bobby Davro bounds into the room. He greets us with his usual 'Whoop, whoop!' and smile, and we are laughing already. He is genuinely happy to see us. Bobby is a big-hearted guy and wonderfully funny company. Over the years we have worked with him many times. He is easy to get along with and will usually use our PA system. His faithful sound engineer, Billy, will operate his sound.

We are all set. 'The Dependables', in the form of Jamie and Dave, had arrived and hid in the corner until the row had passed. They managed to set up their gear in the tiny space given. Jamie said, 'That Tony Hadley Band are a horrible lot aren't they? The keyboard player won't budge an inch.' Terry has squeezed in a small version of his huge Yamaha Maple Custom kit, alongside the malicious dwarf 'Alberich', who on sure risk of a severe bollock-kicking has begrudgingly given him space.

On the small stage, about 4 metres x 3 metres are: two drum kits, two bass combos, two Fender guitar amps with effects pedals, two massive stacks of Roland, Korg and Yamaha keyboards with monitors either side of the stage, plus *ten* assorted scruffy and oversize, wedge monitors. Not to mention two Allen & Heath mixing desks, a lighting desk, two massive amp racks and two effects racks, alongside the stage.

There is hardly room to stand on stage. Greg wisely decides to put the singers on the floor, in front of the stage. We re-arrange monitors accordingly. The horn section of Jez Guest and Dave Peers will also play on the floor alongside the stage. The singers will moan but manage.

Greg stays behind to set Bobby up while the rest of us run to The Alsop. Terry is still muttering, 'What a bunch of arseholes. I hope their fucking PA blows up.'

We get back to The Landmark after three pints of London Pride and two ESB. Terry has now undergone the usual metamorphosis and Mr Hyde appears. 'If that little fucker has moved my drums, I will knock him into next week.'

Tony Hadley is in the room next door, which has been designated a Green Room for changing and feeding performers. He is chatting to Suzi and Lindsey. Everything has calmed down. I get the impression he doesn't much like his new backing band and would have rather used us. They are sitting separately in a corner and, by their hand gestures, discussing the best method of masturbation or could it be Hari-kari?

The guests are eating. Tony has to go on early, as he has another party to go to. They are serving coffee to the guests as The Tony Hadley Band take the stage to a massive applause and launch into 'Gold'.

Terry's ardent wish comes true. The PA blows up. All the lights go out and guests are thankful for the table candles. The hotel electrician is sent for and trip switches are reset. The band restarts. Again, it blows. Howard pleads, 'Can they use your PA, Jon?' 'Of course they can!' I jubilantly reply. Greg is quickly on the case as Terry mutters, 'Serve them arseholes right!'

During the 2000s, Mixed Feelings performed for seven consecutive New Year's Eve parties at the Birmingham Hilton Metropole Hotel. This huge venue was the best conference hotel in Birmingham and was conveniently situated next to the NEC. It had three huge ballrooms and was close to the airport and railway.

Contrary to the belief that New Year's Eve was always a gargantuan piss-up for the band, it was never the case. I cannot recollect ever enjoying a New Year's Eve, wherever in the world we were. For fifty years, I was never at home on New Year's Eve. As a cop I would be in Trafalgar Square. As a bandleader, there was an immense weight of responsibility on your shoulders to ensure that the guests enjoyed the music and the dance floor remained packed all night.

The best thing about NYE was the money, when it eventually arrived, which was sometimes as long as three months after the event. A band should always charge at least double the normal fee for New Year's

Eve. This was simply because the musicians required being paid double their normal wages, as in most jobs. It was usually a long night too. Not to mention getting to the venue at 1pm to set up and build the PA and light show. The band would hit the stage around 10pm and play non-stop until 2am.

Just before midnight the 'cavalcade of crap' would commence and one had to make sure the time was accurate as there was always some supercilious twat who would stand in front of the band, looking at you and pointing to his wristwatch. All musicians working on NYE have seen this twat.

The aforementioned 'cavalcade' consisted of the last song of the old year just before midnight, usually the Liverpool dirge, 'You'll Never Walk Alone', then the 'countdown' and I would press a button on the nearby tape player for Big Ben to 'bong'. You could never rely on receiving it 'live' on the radio. Invariably, it would drift off the frequency or be interrupted by adverts. Then, as the New Year began, the cavalcade of crap would continue.

If I never hear that dreadful tune, 'Auld Lang Syne', again in my life, I will be happy, but it gets worse when we play 'Knees Up Mother Brown', 'The Hokey-Cokey', 'Congratulations', 'My Way', 'New York' and other diabolical tunes. The crowd of happy drunks always love it as they kiss their wives for the first (and probably last) time that year.

A NYE gig was always made easier by having a dedicated DJ working with you. Not just music played over an iPod, which many bands call 'Including Disco'. We were fortunate as we usually had my son Greg as DJ, which lifted much of the weight from my shoulders and gave us a couple of welcome beer breaks.

The Birmingham Hilton staff were generally benevolent towards the band and I managed to obtain a small discount on the overnight rooms for the band members and their families.

New Year's Eve at the BHM was booked through a Birmingham-based agency, run by my good friend, John Kerton, who gave the band some choice gigs throughout the years. Like many of the event companies of the time, they simply 'faded away' or in less kinder terms, went 'tits up'.

A new agency took over the New Year's Eve event in 2008 and our next performance at the BHM was generated through this inexperienced company, the managing director of which, was an ex-Birmingham cop who I judged to be an oddball. He was a teetotaller and not at all sociable. When I met him at the Hilton Bar for a business meeting to discuss possible gigs, he drank pints of hot water infused with slices of lemon. He was a man of few words and probably the most boring person I had ever met in my career as a bandleader. I would not have trusted him to sit the right way round on the toilet. I travelled up on 'the rattler' from Hemel Hempstead to meet him, looking to enjoy a jolly yarn and scotch or two with a fellow retired cop, but found him dismal company. He would not have lasted two minutes in the Met Police. I later heard he became an undertaker.

Nevertheless, he booked us into the Hilton Hotel for the next New Year's Eve Ball, which came and went, but it took six months to get our fee out of him. I knew then that this new agency was in financial trouble even though the hotel had paid them *before* the event, so why couldn't the agency pay the band? I eventually got the Musicians' Union on to the case and we got paid in June.

The hotel wanted us back the following New Year's Eve and the amiable Jewish manager approached me direct, which was perfectly legal as the previous booker had gone into liquidation. I booked in the band at the same price we got 'net' the previous NYE and the manager was delighted as he was paying substantially less money since no agency fee was added. The hotel paid us direct for the gig within four weeks.

Eighteen months later I received a letter from a Birmingham-based firm of auditors who claimed to represent the now defunct 'New Event Company', requesting £2000 plus VAT in *commission* for the NYE gig, which we had done direct. I thought it was a liberty and binned the letter. Six weeks later I received a brown envelope by recorded post, demanding that payment be made immediately or County Court proceedings would follow.

I obviously needed proper legal advice. Should I call the Musicians' Union? Should I consult a solicitor? I called Michael Black.

He always sounded pleased to hear from me. 'Hello Son! How are you?' I explained my predicament and he asked me the name of the man who had signed the threatening letter. 'Geoffrey Williams', I told him. Michael advised me;

'Don't worry about it Son! What you do is this. You phone the firm and ask to speak to Geoffrey Williams. When he comes on the phone, you tell him who you are and that you are in receipt of his threatening letter which has "upset your wife". You then say, GO FUCK YOURSELF.'

It worked.

12

WEDDINGS AND PLANNERS.

Goodwood House, near Chichester, is the stately home of the Duke of Richmond. It is also an expensive wedding venue. Mixed Feelings performed there several times. I wrote in my diary after one such gig, 'We were plagued by bloody wedding planners.'

Wedding planners are a sign of the times. I regarded, when getting married, that booking your caterer, music, bar, church, flowers and the rest, was great fun but now it seems fashionable to employ a 'wedding planner', thereby paying through the nose for services that a bride and groom could book themselves.

Most wedding planners are divorced women or rich girls with nothing to do. This form of self-employment requires no formal training. The only tool required is a telephone, a list of suppliers and 'the gift of the gab'. A little bit of common sense helps, but some of these people seem deficient in that department.

Men practise in this fashion too, referring to themselves as 'event suppliers' Once again, no qualifications are required, just some stage or DJ experience. One pleasant thing about event and wedding planners is that they often give nice gigs to Mixed Feelings.

On this particular occasion we had been booked direct by the bride and groom. As soon as we arrived at Goodwood House at 2pm we saw that the room where we usually gigged was decked out in black 'star-cloth'. As we started to lug our gear in we were met by a po-faced, mantis-like young woman dressed in the standard wedding planner's attire of a navy blue pinstripe trouser suit and carrying a clipboard. She introduces herself as 'Siobhan' and says, 'I am running this wedding.'

She sternly delivers a lecture about priceless paintings by Van Dyck, Canaletto and George Stubbs some of which are located behind the star cloth. Then we get, 'Are you using a smoke machine? If so, you can't.'

Five minutes later up pops another young lady in a pinstripe trouser suit. 'I am Virginia and I am the banqueting manager. We can't allow smoke as we have priceless Van Dycks here.'

I now have my diplomatic hat on when I say, 'Hi Virginia! Virgin for short but not for long eh?' Her face has now gone dark. She is without humour. 'I'll pretend I didn't hear that.' She continues. 'Also, you cannot sound check at all, because the band is a surprise for the guests. I hear Terry mutter, 'I'd give her some Van Dick.'

This is now getting quite amusing as a cheerful, blonde, pinstriped bimbo strides in and predictably gets in the way as we try to set up. 'Hello Gents, I am Wonky the wedding planner.' I guessed that Ronke had a slight speech impediment. I say 'Hi Wonky. Are you in charge then?' 'Absolutely.' she replies. 'By the way, my name is 'Wonke' not 'Wonky.' Also, do you know about the pwiceless Van Dycks behind the star cloth?' 'Are there?' I say in mock disbelief, 'any Rembrandts?'

'I would have thought someone would have alweddy explained things. You must not use smoke because there are some weally amazing Van Dycks and Stubbs behind the curtain but I don't think there are any 'Wembwandts'. (Yelps from Greg) She is not finished. 'You must not wehearse as the band must not be heard by the guests in the next woom.' She adds, 'And furthermore, I need to see your wisk assessment (loud guffaws) and public liability insurance.'

I quake with repressed laughter as I get these essential certificates from my clothes bag. Fellow bandleaders will agree that it's funny how we never have to show these insurances at proper venues. She read the risk assessment and takes ages. 'Are there any animals used in this act?' 'Only the drummer.' I reply.

Another pinstriped female arrives who looks about twelve. 'This is my assistant Webecca, ('shut it!' is the look I give Greg) who will tell you where you are eating. One other thing, soft dwinks only for the band tonight.' At this, as I am standing on a Bulldog flight case, plugging XLR leads into LED par cans, I reach total exasperation point. 'Ronke! A band needs beer! God invented beer so that ugly women could get shagged occasionally!'

The girls disappear in a hurry after Terry says, 'Don't worry girls, you'll be safe!' 'How wude!' is her parting shot, as I am finally left in peace to set up until half an hour later Terry taps his snare drum and tinkles his cymbals. It is the irritating ritual that all drummers must perform, to see if they still work.

Into the room rush our four women, clipboards at the ready and fingers over lips, 'Shooosh!' I apologise. 'It's that bloody drummer again. You are fired!' I say to Terry. The bossy women smirk to each other, *'That told that bloody band!'*

We go to the nearest pub for a few pints of Harveys' Sussex Bitter and get back in good time to find that the rest of the band have arrived. I speak to the happy bride and groom who are delighted that we are performing for them. The gig goes brilliantly and the clients are happy. A dozen bottles of cold Budweiser and two bottles of Cloudy Bay are sent to the dressing room by the bridegroom.

On the way back home at 3am, Terry (drinking Beaujolais from the bottle) is keeping Martin awake and regaling us with tales of bizarre places he has masturbated. 'I've wanked on the train, the swimming pool and the top deck of the bus.' I said to him 'and when did you wank on the bus?' He said 'last week.' I realised there was absolutely no hope.

I said, 'So, what do you reckon to the wedding planners of Goodwood?' He replied, 'I'd give that Wonky, a 'good wood' anytime.'

On the subject of weddings, another 'fussy' venue is Pennyhill Park, a stylish hotel where we have performed many times. It classes itself as an 'exclusive hotel' and is situated near Bagshot. I don't like the place as a band venue, as the function rooms are too small. Great for briefing the England Rugby team but not for ten-piece show bands. You need extra hands to get your gear in and out too. As usual, myself and Terry were there to lend a hand to Greg and Craig. So it's minimal gear here. No bass bins.

The easiest way of getting into the main suite is to use the outside stone stairs, which I guess were built during the English Civil War and are narrow and unlit at night. There is a lift, but it is for the use of guests. It is virtually impossible to get your van in close proximity to the steps, due to the 'dirty-weekenders' carelessly parking their Ferraris and McLarens. We are careful not to drop a bongo on the bonnet of a Bentley.

People love to pay a small fortune to get married here. There is money everywhere and it is not unusual to see 'Orcs' from *The Lord of the Rings* languishing in the bar and masquerading as English rugby players.

I opened a letter from Peter Richardson of Fanfare 3000 to learn that we had received a 'serious complaint' from Pennyhill Park, concerning the wedding we had performed at two weeks before. The letter made an allegation that our stage manager, (Greg), had sworn and threatened the night manager with 'extreme violence'.

I replied to Peter to the effect that I considered the event a great success and that we had worked hard to please the client, a wealthy Kent-based haulier, Jim Dodd, whose daughter's wedding it was.

The event was due to finish at midnight and at midnight precisely, with eighty people dancing the 'last lager waltz', 'Big Jim' approached me and requested one more song. So, we did one more song, 'Can You Feel The Love Tonight?' Jim had kept us supplied with beer all night and who were we to argue with him? He was big enough not look out of place in the England rugby squad.

The event finished at 12.03am precisely. Just three minutes over the time. The ballroom lights had already been switched on. From what I could see there were two suited guys standing at the mixing desk, waving their arms in dramatic fashion as they remonstrated with Greg. Investigating the complaint in the letter I asked Greg if he had 'sworn' at them and I can only commend him on his wonderful diplomacy. He eloquently commented,

> They were South Africans. One was a lanky streak of piss who
> told me to cut the sound immediately. I told him I would, at
> the end of this final song that our client had requested. He then
> got nasty and said he was going to pull the bloody plug out if I
> didn't stop this second. I told him that would damage our gear.
> He again told me he was going to pull the plug out. So I told

him 'Listen you fucking Rock Spider. You touch that plug and I'll throw you down the fucking stairs.'

We were banned from that venue. I also realised that Greg would never get a job at the Foreign Office. I also accept that it is a residential hotel. If Dan Cole the England prop, seen propping up the bar earlier, cannot get any sleep then it's tough. I was just happy not to see him appear in his nightdress.

The ironical thing was Peter Richardson received a glowing letter from Jim Dodd, praising that 'fantastic band'. Three weeks later, we were gigging back at Penny Hill Park under the name of 'Supanova'. Fortunately, there were no rock spiders on duty.

In situations like these the only person who matters is your *client*. It is he who is paying you, not the hotel. When your client asks for 'one more song', you do it. Venues should be flexible and employ security managers with common sense. There have been many times when the event ends at midnight and at 11.50pm the ballroom lights are turned full on. This practice is bad form and virtually says to the client, who has paid the venue thousands of pounds, 'It's time for you to fuck off.' We saw it over and over again and usually at 'second division' venues.

While we are still on the subject of weddings, it is a total waste of time and money advertising your band in expensive magazines, like *Bride*. I tried it once for a year and did not get one single enquiry, although it had cost three grand. Most wedding gigs come through recommendation. The best promotions were free, like *The Stage* newspaper which said, 'If you want to keep your dance floor packed all night, then this is the band.' And *Harpers and Queen* magazine which said, 'Generating amazing energy, Mixed Feelings is the best of the UK showbands.'

All bands have, at some time, done weddings although some won't admit it. But not all bands have done *Jewish* weddings, which can be rewarding in more ways than one. Mixed Feelings were and still are, in big demand for Jewish events.

I liked dealing with Jewish clients who can be most charming and kind or sometimes downright rude. (Michael Black was all three). Either way they make me smile. I love their wit and it is built into their DNA for them to negotiate a good deal. They are discerning clients and want to party. As old friend and toastmaster, Bryn Williams wrote,

There is no other section of society that has been more influential, prolific or lucrative and I am deeply grateful to them. Their flare for celebrating is second to none, their eagerness to hold a party, a banquet or ball is phenomenal and they need no excuse to 'have an affair', their words for a *Simcha* or celebration. And bless their generous hearts. They almost always use the services of a toastmaster.

From my own observation, they certainly don't need to drink six pints of lager before they step onto the dance floor which is usually packed from the word go. One of the traditional parts of the Jewish dance routines is to lift the bride and groom up high on dining chairs so they 'connect' with a handkerchief. Now this usually requires the assistance of strong men, particularly if the bride or groom, reside near 'Piebury Corner'.

I have laughed until I cried at many Jewish events, both weddings and Barmitzvah parties. I remember one wedding at the Royal Majestic, where the roly-poly bride was hoisted up on a chair by four struggling volunteers who then promptly dropped her, or rather her 18-stone frame slid off the chair like a spoilt pancake and landed with a huge crash on to the dance floor. The band got the blame. Terry as usual, after four large JCs, had played 'The Hora' at 'Joe Brown' speed and we were frowned upon for laughing. 'It's not funny,' we were told by the bride's father, who angrily reacted to the loudest 'guffaw' in the band courtesy of guitarist, Dave Price who recollected;

> One of the funniest things I ever saw at a Jewish wedding was the guys trying to hoist the bride up on the chair. She looked like Dawn French, only fatter! Up she went and down she came with a massive crash!

The traditional day for a Jewish wedding is Sunday. Although many astute 'fathers of the bride' would persuade their offspring to have a midweek wedding. It always worked out cheaper. Caterers, bands, toastmasters and venues, all offered discount for midweek gigs.

Sunday weddings are often stressful, not because of difficult people but because the band is usually knackered. The gig was probably the fourth or fifth event on the trot that week. Sometimes it would be at a top London venue like the Dorchester, Claridge's or the Savoy. Occasionally, we had to make the weary journey up to Manchester or Leeds, when a fresh driver would be utilized to get us there and back. It required the last reserves of stamina to get the job done. The next day I was a walking zombie. I just wanted to go to the pub at lunchtime, then go home and crash out on the sofa. As a result, we formed the 'Monday Club' and the whole band would sometimes turn up at the pub for a 'debrief' and vote for Terry as COM.

We really began to appreciate the smaller venues, like The Royal Majestic in Willesden Lane. Who the hell gave it the 'Royal' title? It was a small, but spotless, banqueting suite which could comfortably seat 150 people, with dancing room on the polished sprung dance floor and a carpeted stage in a recess, which was designed to hold a six-piece band at the most.

However, we regularly put a ten or eleven-piece band on to the RM stage. It fast became our favourite venue. The main reason for that was the kindness of the proprietors, Richard and Helen Goide, who we first met in the early 'eighties. They always welcomed us and 'Mr' Goide would always insist on his side door being closed as we were trying to load gear in. In summer it let the cold air out. In winter it let the cold air in. 'Shut that door' was the byword.

They were kind and homely people and the Kosher food was always delicious. Real home-cooked roast dinners and the best chicken soup I have ever tasted. Good Israeli wine too. We could also park easily. The Royal Majestic has now sadly closed its doors forever and Mixed Feelings were privileged to be asked to perform at 'The Majestic Final Party'. It was loved for many reasons. Here was one of mine.

It served magnificent 'Jewish Cokes'. The name given to the tipple which revitalised many a knackered brain on a Sunday afternoon. Jack Daniels, (or any whisky for that matter) and a 'fat' Coke and ice. Behind the bar at The Majestic were local Irish ladies, who got to know our band well as we were there so often. They were generous with the whisky measures and the incorrigible Terry would make them scream with laughter with tales of the trapeze he had rigged up in his bedroom.

A big amiable Irishman, Tommy Murray, also added much colour to the Royal Majestic in his position as manager and caretaker. Together with his lovely wife, Marion, they made a great team and always offered us a warm welcome and at the end of the night, when everyone had gone home, Tommy would break out cold bottles of Budweiser with a 'Get that down your fucking neck!'

A memorable Barmitzvah party at The Royal Majestic on a Tuesday in June 2004, is worth a mention. It's a hot day and Richard Goide is moaning that his door was opened. How the hell are we supposed to get the gear in? I have already met our client, a Mrs Bloom, who is the boy's Mum; 'Call me Jan.' She is wearing a baby pink tracksuit, with matching pink Nike trainers. Her hair is a beehive and she is a six-foot tall, 35 year-old, brunette with a computer designed body. Terry, both hands in trouser pockets, turns to me and says, 'Cor, look at the lovely arse on that.'

It was difficult to concentrate on setting up the gear as I believe she deliberately tried to distract us by bending over backs of chairs to adjust name labels on the tables. Her bum was a peach. She knew it and knew we were gawping at her. This was *her* night, although it is the Barmitzvah party of her eldest boy. Her husband, a London cabbie, is with his two sons in the doorway and posing for photos.

She comes over to me and says, 'I want you guys to be part of Josh's party so have what you want from the bar.' (I am liking this already). Josh has introduced himself to me. A smart, well-mannered lad. He has a little brother of about six years old who is already slithering around the polished floor on his arse. 'Get up off that bloody floor!' shouts Mum. 'Don't you dare split them new trousers.' She turns to me, 'Jon, do you mind if I use the dressing room first?'

Like all venues, The Royal Majestic has minor downsides. One is that the dressing room is tiny and there is only room for two people at a time. People needing the dressing room would be the client(s), the toastmaster, the band and, when it's a wedding, the bride and groom.

It's just gone four o'clock and the guests are due to arrive. Mrs Bloom appears in a tight-fitting, Ferrari red, cocktail dress. Matching red high-heel patent shoes too. I hear Terry murmur, 'Fucking hell, I'd get her to keep them shoes on.'

We have done a sound check. Dave and Jamie are here too. If we get changed quickly, we can grab a JC at the bar. Terry and myself go first and run to the dressing room, which is situated halfway up the stairs.

The room smells of 'Clinique Elixir'. Neatly folded on the dressing room counter is a baby pink tracksuit. We unzip our travel bags and take out our black suits, satin dress shirts and black patent shoes. We both change quickly and place our clothes bags under the counter. Greg and Martin will use the dressing room next, then Jamie and Dave. I wash my hands in the little sink and run a brush through my hair. I also splash on some of Terry's Jean-Paul Gaultier EDT, which he assures me is a sure 'knicker-dropper'.

I *knew* it would happen. Terry the grubby little devil cannot resist it. He is investigating Mrs Bloom's pink tracksuit. He lifts the bottoms aside and there is a bit of flimsy lace, could it be? 'No!' says Terry, 'Fuck me! She has left her Alan Whickers here! I bet she ain't got any on under that dress!'

He has a pair of flimsy white satin and lace knickers in his hands. 'Cor, Marks and Sparks. I just got to have a little sniff,' and he drapes her finery over his head, making the perfect facemask. If only I had a camera to hand.

Just then - and so predictable - the door opens and Mrs Bloom steps into the dressing room. 'Have you boys got enough room in here? Just put my knickers on your head if they are in your way!' We retreat to the bar where Terry reminds me that it's not the first time he's been caught. When working with girl band, The Flirtations, he was caught with *three* pairs of knickers on his head.

Later that night the band perform 'Lady In Red' at her husband's request. The 'knicker-sniffer' and new COM is looking very sheepish as the couple shuffle past. His guilt is alleviated by the sexy wink of her eye.

TOASTMASTERS

I have mentioned 'toastmasters' a couple of times. The higher you progress as a band, the more you will come across these fine species of British manhood.

Having said that, we did work with three *women* toastmasters during my tenure as bandleader of Mixed Feelings. The only one who was any good was Christine Akehurst, who had made a guest appearance on *What's My Line* many years ago. She was a fine woman and a publican at one time. The other two we had the misfortune to work with were nice ladies, but hopelessly incompetent. Toastmasters need to carry some sensible level of authority. These did not. They only seemed to be interested in eating. It was fatal when caterer Maureen Sharpstone produced her delicious sticky-toffee pudding buffet, as their arse-beams only proved the point. Never use a toast *mistress*. It's a man's job.

Some toastmasters could be pompous, arrogant and openly hostile towards a young band. Thankfully these were rare. Many of the old school, such as Bryn Williams - a massive fan of The Johnny Howard Band - did not like the type of music we played and never spoke to me for months after we broke on to the circuit and took the best jobs off the big dance bands, the music of which he loved. He openly said;

> One of the real downsides of my work currently is the horrendous noise that the bands are now required to play. I will not dignify it by calling it music, as it isn't. It is a cacophony of coarse, garish over-amplified sound, which is deafeningly hideous. When the band strikes up its mindless, tuneless roar, people skulk on to the floor, stop on one spot, frequently with a fag or lager bottle in their hands and simply wiggle or gyrate their bodies in grotesque movements or jump up and down. It really is quite horrible. Fortunately, at many functions I now do, I leave when the formalities have ended, so do not have to endure this horror.

He had to accept that the day of the big bands had gone forever. Destroyed by the 'horror' of Mixed Feelings. He did eventually give me some respect and we became friends, especially when he found out I was a fellow author and we swapped books.

I am pleased to say that the majority of toastmasters I worked with, especially the London toastmasters, were competent, friendly and helpful. We quickly made friends with several young toastmasters that liked our music and the sexy girls that fronted our band. Whenever I had a meeting with a wedding client I would ask who the toastmaster was. Sometimes they would say, 'We don't need one,' or 'My brother is going to do it.' I would then do my utmost to persuade them that a trained toastmaster is *essential* for their event. 'Your brother will fuck it up,' I told one young couple who laughed at my forthright prediction. A toastmaster will ensure the event runs smoothly and everything runs on time, caterers permitting.

Such was Howard Robbins, a top man, friend and mentor when we were 'new boys', on the Jewish circuit. He used Brylcreem in those days and sold curtains, before turning professional toastmaster, thereby following in the footsteps of his father, himself an established London toastmaster.

London toastmasters are the best in the UK. Outside of town, they were largely amateurs and daytime taxi drivers, bicycle repairers and retired cops. Most were clueless and one Cambridge toastmaster had a stutter, which to my perverted sense of humour, was the funniest thing I had heard for years. 'Ladies and Gentlemen would you per per, *please* take your per per, *places* for dinner.'

Most of the out of town toastmasters also had the annoying habit of buggering off as soon as the wedding speeches were finished. Leaving the bandleader to carry the can. The bandleader would also have to close the evening and announce the farewell speeches from the client, bride and groom.

Howard Robbins, who always stayed until the very end, quickly took a shine to our band;

> Without doubt, Mixed Feelings was the most dynamic band
> on the circuit. Playing exactly what people wanted. They were
> very entertaining, fun to work with and always had brilliant
> singers. I loved Barry's voice. No one could sing 'I Should Have
> Known Better', better than Barry. Not even Jim Diamond!
> No one could sing Barry Manilow better than Barry! Then
> when you got those beautiful girls, Sue and Helen, you were
> unstoppable. Everybody wanted you!

We would usually work with a toastmaster at Jewish events and the London toastmasters were often Jewish themselves. Many were amusing characters, who we soon got to know well. Musicians had nicknames for some. There was 'old spoon-face', (look at your face in the back of a tablespoon), who would also flutter his eyebrows like a humming bird's wings.

Then there was 'Flash Gordon of Planet Panic' who would hang closely around the band when setting up, getting in the way and incessantly asking 'Jon, how long do you think you will be?' 'About three hours,' I would cynically 'wind' him up. He would ask the usual question, 'Have you got a mic for me?' Then, suddenly on the arrival of the clients, shout 'The client is here! The client is here! Don't panic, don't panic!' He would then nervously dance a hop, skip and jump, before rushing to the door.

Then there was our 'umble servant, 'Uriah Heep', a tall guy, who thought himself good-looking, who would continually gawp at himself in the ballroom mirrors at The Royal Majestic, flick his quiff and adjust his collar, while pouting his lips. He had an annoying habit of banging his 'gavel' down on the table, so close to the mic that it almost blew the speakers and frightened the guests out of their wits. He would then use the word 'respectfully', continually when addressing the crowd, which irritated everyone. As Greg remembers,

> One night we were at the Millennium Hotel, Grosvenor Square and I decided to count, (for want of nothing else to do while sitting at the mixing desk) how many 'respectfullys' we got from Uriah Heep. It was 32 in the first hour then I gave up. It went, "Ladies and gentlemen, I *respectfully* ask you for your attention. Quiet please, shoooooosh! Ladies and gentlemen! I *respectfully*, ask you to remain *respectfully*, silent. I now *respectfully* introduce the best man. I now *respectfully* ask you to charge your glasses.

Contemporary fellow musicians will know whom I am referring to. Cooler dudes, were undoubtedly David Collins, Steve Warwick, Melvin Zeff, Neil Hunt and Brian Greenan. We loved working with these calm guys and David Collins was a mine of funny jokes at every gig. He also had the astonishing knack of persuading the clients to finish early, much to our delight. Midnight finish gigs would be wound up at 11pm as 'People are getting knackered from dancing and leaving. Best we stop now.' Or, 'It's going to snow.'

One young toastmaster was Simon Green, who was always a 'barrel of laughs' although he had a short fuse at times. Simon was a big sturdy lad who wore a huge pair of trousers. He reminded me of one of the 'fat orphans' from Blackadder.   It actually turned pear-shaped when we were booked for a Barmitzvah party at The Hendon Hall Hotel. We were engaged in playing dinner music and I asked Simon if he could move some noisy children from off the front of the stage.

Simon possessed a very loud voice and everyone heard him remonstrate with the kids.

The next thing, there was a furious row with one Dad who accused Simon of telling his son to 'Fuck off.' Consequently, an argument ensued whereby they both went outside to 'sort it out'. About a minute later, they both came back into the room showing signs of a struggle. Dad, with a torn shirt collar and Simon with a crimson face, spectacles hanging off one ear. The band was in cahoots of laughter. Simon then got on to the stage, taking the microphone while mopping his brow and apologized to the eating guests, for his use of the Anglo-Saxon vernacular. On the back of his long, red-tailed jacket and over the arse was a huge muddy footprint.

Diary entry.

On Sunday we were at Claridge's Hotel and another classy Jewish wedding. It's mid-afternoon and we are sound checking with Gary Priestley who tests all the front mics and we run quickly through his opening song 'Amazed' by Lonestar.

Gary's warm voice pleases my ears but I cut him short. We need a JC. Terry has already abandoned his drum kit and is leading the charge to the pub. Standing in front of the stage is a scrawny female aged about eighty. She has her hands on her hips and is glaring at me. Her face looks like it has been decorated by Coco's make-up artist. 'Can I help you?' I meekly ask. She bawls back, 'I am the bride's aunt! You had better not play that loud or else I shall call the police.' I smile and walk away.

Our Kosher caterer today is the excellent, but arrogant, Tony Page. Him and I are now mates, since an altercation at the Carlton Tower Hotel some months previously, which he lost. Apparently, I was not the only bandleader to fall out with him. He now calls me 'Darling' and his catering company now give us some lovely jobs. Our toastmaster is Steve Warwick. We have a good team.

I am changed and ready and go into the reception. I meet the happy couple, bridegroom Nick is a City financier and 'Gooner'. He literally orders me to get a drink. Nick says, 'Listen up Jon! If her bloody Aunt Ida comes over and tells you to turn it down, just tell her to fuck off!' I say, 'She already has spoken to me and says she will call the police if we play loud.' The laughing bride nods in agreement, 'Then please promise me you will tell her to fuck right off!'

The band are all on stage when Steve Warwick announces the entrance of the bride and groom and we launch straight into traditional 'Simcha' dancing. The dance floor is packed. Standing in front of me is Aunt Ida. Her face is like a bulldog licking piss off a thistle and her fingers are jammed in her ears. She screams, 'Turn it down!' As sax player Jez Guest recollects,

> This little old lady is complaining to Jon about the volume.
> She is shouting at him. She comes over to the side of the stage
> and tells him to turn down the volume. I could not believe my
> own ears. 'Fuck off,' he says. She said, 'Did you tell me to fuck
> off?' Jon says, 'Yes I did, now do as you're told and fuck off!'
> Funniest thing ever! How *did* we manage to get so much work?

Another weird, but enormously funny wedding took place in Surrey in July 1994, when we were booked to perform in a small marquee in the field adjacent to the bridegroom's isolated cottage.

The couple, 'Joe and Kate', had both been previously married and were openly friendly to us. Three months previously they had viewed the band at The Dorchester Hotel and Joe, who bore a remarkable resemblance to Steve McQueen, had sent the band a bottle of Veuve Clicquot before climbing on to the stage and kissing us all.

It was a glorious summer's day and we were told to help ourselves to the 'Pol Roger' champagne, of which about a hundred bottles were stacked in big plastic industrial bins, with blocks of ice at the back of the marquee bar. I smiled when I saw the four male bar staff, all six-foot muscular Rambos, with shaved heads and bandanas. It was all very camp and comic.

We were fully set by 3pm, when the wedding party and guests returned from the church in a fleet of vintage cars. Like many weddings the band has to be there early, as we are often called to the stage for 6pm-7pm. There was just the seven of us and Dave Howard was on lead vocals, with Sue and Helen providing the eye candy. We were directed to the couple's bedroom to change.

My son Greg was just 16 years old and was now a fledgling sound engineer, and he remembers,

We went up the creaky, narrow stairs and into the little bedroom to change into our stage clothes. I'll never forget it. On the double bed was a yellow pair of satin knickers. There was a matching suspender belt, bra and stockings on the floor. There was a big black rubber cock on the dressing table. I didn't know what the table tennis bat was for.

'Bridegroom Joe', came up to the bedroom just as I saw Terry contemplating a quick sniff of the grundies. 'Don't mind the knickers, they are mine!' Joe said. I didn't doubt him. He then asked me if the 'cabaret' could use our PA system. 'Cabaret? At a wedding?' Joe told me he had booked a drag queen, to go on stage before the band and warm the crowd up. 'She is wonderful,' he assured me.

It was a glamorous London drag artist not unlike Lily Savage and sporting a massive blonde beehive wig. 'She' was at the rear of the tent waiting to go on. 'Hi Boys! Thank you for letting me use your PA,' she says. 'Greg can you play my first track when I come on please dear? It's 'Lucky Lips' by Cliff Richard.'

I went into the tent via the stage. The speeches had finished and there was a row of some twenty kids sitting cross-legged on the dance floor. At the tables sat the usual wedding guests, mums and dads, aunts and uncles. It was a typical family turnout, all anticipating the 'cabaret'.

It was down to me to introduce the act, as there was no toastmaster. I announced, 'Joe and Kate, Ladies and Gentlemen, boys and girls. Please welcome your surprise cabaret this evening. All the way from Piccadilly, Miss Jane Adoree!'

Into the tent swept the six-foot, drag artist. High heels, bulging biceps and a red satin ball gown, split up the middle. The crowd applauds and the kids shriek and whistle as the backing track 'Lucky Lips' is played.

Jane takes the mic and announces, 'My name is Jane and I like it again and again!' She sings the first verse and chorus as per Cliff, 'Lucky lips are made for kissing,' That's alright then. Next verse takes a downward turn with a filthy lyric ending in, 'Cos you've got a great big Dick!' *Chorus..* 'Great big dicks are made for sucking, Great big dicks are made to lick.. Sing along everyone!'

Pandemonium ensues with bewildered children yanked to their feet by shocked parents and dragged out, wheelchairs are being pushed out of the marquee. One Dad remonstrates with 'Jane'. 'You are a disgusting woman! There are children here.' Jane announces over the mic for all to hear, 'Lover boy, if you are not careful, I will sit on your face and make you lick my ring!' I have never seen a venue empty so fast. 'If I have offended you, then bollocks!' was the final riposte to an empty tent.

We had a serious problem getting the guests back in the marquee. Half of the 120 strong guests had gone home. The bride and groom opened the dancing with 'YMCA' and the camp Village People medley. The party finally ended at midnight with twenty people present.

'Help yourself to a bottle or two of champagne for the journey home.' was a joy to hear from a cheerful Joe. We left the venue for the one-hour ride to Hemel, armed with thirty bottles of Pol Roger, given to us by the 'soldier boys'.

The next morning, I found a pair of yellow satin knickers hanging off the van wing mirror.

13

SUPANOVA.

'Never change the name of your band.' That was the advice I had been given by other bandleaders. Some agents thought 'Mixed Feelings' an inappropriate name and told me so. I could think of plenty of bands around at the time with worse names. Mixed Feelings was intended to portray a variety of emotions though our diverse music. That was why we were so successful.

There did come a point when I was forced to change the name. As agent and bandleader, Kevin Hall never fails to remind me, 'Reinventing yourselves as The Supanova Dance Orchestra was a master stroke and it netted you a sack full of lucrative gigs.' But there was reason behind it and I have to thank the security staff at the Grosvenor House Hotel for that.

By the mid-nineties and mainly due to the sexy, choreographed dance routines and brilliant harmonies of Sue and Helen, we were performing in all of the top London hotels. We had cracked it, with over twenty gigs a year at the prestigious Grosvenor House Hotel, where I first saw The Johnny Howard Band.

At one of our Grosvenor House gigs, I saw a notice on the lift wall which stated that equipment could not be taken out of the hotel after

10pm due to noise restrictions. I chose to ignore it. We had a gig in Manchester next day and I was not coming into London in the rush hour to load equipment into the van then hack up to Manchester. The event had finished at 12pm midnight so we hurriedly packed our gear into the lift and took it to street level. Our long wheelbase Iveco van was parked directly outside and the crew had quickly and quietly loaded the gear away. As we shut the back doors of the van, two smartly dressed hotel security men appeared and asked who was in charge. I told them I was.

One of them said 'How did you get your gear out?' I replied, 'In the lift' I was then told, 'You are not supposed to be using this lift after 10pm. Put all the equipment back in the ballroom.' 'What?' I had never been told to do anything so daft since I was in the Met. 'You are kidding me.' I replied. He looked at me and said, 'If you don't put the equipment back, we'll call the police.' 'Call the police.' was my answer. We drove off.

A few days later, I received a letter from the Grosvenor House Hotel, which informed me that due to my 'flouting of hotel regulations', the band known as 'Mixed Feelings' was banned from playing there.

We had a big event at the Grosvenor House the very next night. We turned up as normal and set up. Nobody wore a crew shirt. The problem was, the name was on the bass drum. Jamie and Dave turned up and we did the usual sound check, when suddenly the stage was surrounded by at least eight 'suited and booted', security men. I suspect they had been waiting to ambush us. 'What time are you lot due back in Burton's window?' I asked of the scowling faces.

A sweating 'senior' member of the team came up to me and nervously announced himself as 'Ex-Chief Superintendent John Evans of Dyfed Powys Police, now Head of Security, Grosvenor House Hotel.' He directed us to, 'Pack up your gear and leave the hotel immediately.' I could not resist it. I held out my hand, 'Jon Nicholls, Ex-Assistant Commissioner, Metropolitan Police. How was Noddy and Big Ears this morning?'

He declined to shake hands. He had done his homework and found out I was ex-Met. He exploded with the force of Krakatoa and he again ordered the band to leave 'his' hotel forthwith. Or else we would be 'physically removed'. I told him, 'Listen Mate. It isn't me the client's gonna sue. We've been paid and if you throw us out then you are fucked.'

That night the band were intimidated and followed everywhere by glowering security men. They were itching for a fight. In the meantime, we went to the Shepherd's Tavern. Five pints of Courage Best later, Mr Hyde said, 'Them wankers can't make me leave my drums here tonight. They are the tools of my trade. I'll kick their fucking heads in!'

When we finally got on stage to do our first set, we found ourselves surrounded by the KGB and some of them sounded like it, with thick Russian accents. One was not impressed when I asked him what submarine he had served on.

We played a blinder but I obeyed the new rules and came back the next morning to collect the gear. Terry's drums were safe, I assured him. Two days later I received another recorded delivery letter from the Grosvenor House Hotel. 'Mixed Feelings is *permanently* banned from performing, or even entering, the Grosvenor House Hotel.'

So, I simply changed the name to The Supanova Dance Orchestra. I had new publicity printed and a new website designed. I had crew shirts printed with the new name and a new bass drum front skin. I told all agents and clients that whenever we were booked at the Grosvenor House, the name was now Supanova.

It soon went around, ridiculously and hilariously exaggerated by Michael Black, that 'Mixed Feelings have been banned from the Grosvenor House for causing a riot and smashing the place up' and 'they had a massive fight with the security, the police and fire brigade were called. Twenty people were taken to hospital.' and that 'The drummer had thrown the hotel manager down the stairs.' We laughed about it and it didn't deter the suitably amused, Michael from giving us plenty of work. He said he preferred the new name. So, I kept it as an 'alternative' band name and we got busier.

We performed at the hotel just two weeks later as 'The Supanova Dance Orchestra' and although viewed suspiciously, by one or two security men, we got away with it. I never had a problem there again. Some of the security knew who we were alright but common sense prevailed and they turned a blind eye. They even let us hump our gear up the back stairs and on to Park Lane, to save the *bastard inconvenience* of driving back into London next morning.

So, the alternative name of The Supanova Dance Orchestra stuck and we now opened the show with a riotous Ricky Martin medley. I had clad the girls in sexy Brazilian style 'Samba' dresses and the guys in expensive pastel, tailored suits. They learned the new dance routines too. Then we went into a medley of Earth Wind & Fire. It was truly spectacular.

This was the 'heyday' of Mixed Feelings-cum-Supanova. Nothing in our business lasts forever and bands come and go, but fortunately our 'heyday' lasted a good twenty years and we were the talk of the event business. I had expanded The Supanova Dance Orchestra to a fifteen-piece band, with the inclusion of a six-piece brass section, giving trombone players a rare gig. A percussionist was also added. It was a band at the top of its game and we continued to play at the Grosvenor House Hotel without any further problems.

As regards security, and in spite of my brief fall out with the security at the Grosvenor House, I have to say that these guys are *absolutely necessary* and mostly do a good job. With the threat of international terrorism always present, my personal fear, God forbid, was that of a lone wolf killer, walking into a Barmitzvah party and opening fire with an automatic weapon. Even the Royal Majestic employed a security man to watch the door.

Such was my concern, that I brought in my own security guard for some gigs in the shape of old friend Dave Edwards (Ex British Army and Met-Police), a good bloke who was formerly trained in personal protection. No stage invaders or 'knob hounds' got past him.

Security is essential at most gigs, not only to stop gate-crashers but also to deter thieves who may get into the dressing room while we are on stage. Unfortunately, singer Sue had her make-up bag stolen from the dressing room at Claridge's Hotel when we were on stage at a Jewish wedding event. The dressing room, a smaller function room next to the main ballroom, was unfortunately shared with the caterers and many Eastern Europeans were among the serving staff. We never bothered calling the police. From then on, we hid valuables under the stage mixing desk.

Security is invaluable if your stage gets invaded. Providing there actually is security. Over the years our stage was rarely 'invaded' by the audience, but there were some notable occasions when drunks did give us a hard time. Men were easier to handle than women and a quiet word in their ear such as 'it's dangerous up here, Mate,' or 'We'll call you up to sing in five minutes.' Would calm the situation.

We did many gigs at the Intercontinental Hotel, Hyde Park Corner and at one gig, in 2005, we were working for a motor company via Michael Black. The punters had been treated to a sumptuous 4-course dinner, with lashings of wine followed by liqueurs. The cabaret booked for the event was Rose Royce, featuring Gwen Dickie, the brilliant singer of 'Car Wash' and 'Wishing On A Star'.

She was not enamoured by the fact that her backing band had not turned up for their 5pm sound check. They were a band of funky, all-black London musicians who we had worked with more than once. It was a popular combination of two bands and they usually used our kit. The first to arrive was her drummer, who casually ambled into the ballroom, carrying a snare drum and drumsticks, at 5.45pm, he was closely followed by bass player, Clint Williams, (later an excellent, 'dep' bass player in Mixed Feelings). However, on this particular night, Gwen was a very pissed off lady and fired off a salvo of expletives at the late arrivals. Michael Black, standing by the stage in his blue Armani suit with the coat hanger still left in the shoulders, also put his oar in. I was amused to hear him say to one of the late arrivals, 'You are fucking late son! Inexcusable son. Where the fuck have you been?' The answer was, 'I slept in.' Michael said, 'Slept in? Slept in? No wonder you lot have never won a fucking war. Can you just imagine? 'Load the cannon Leroy!'

Rose Royce went on first, doing a storming one-hour set. They are a great band but we followed on well at 11pm and, to keep the dance floor packed, I chose a medley of songs from the same genre. Kool & The Gang with 'Celebration', into the great 'Ladies Night', then 'Get Down On It'. Timeless disco hits, to keep the dance floor full.

We had got just a few bars into our third song, when uninvited guests arrived on stage in the form of two 'Jugglies'. Which according to Terry are 'Ugly birds with big tits.' The stage was seriously creaking under the weight of an extra thirty stone. Both were pissed and carrying glasses of 'tart-fuel' (Bacardi & Coke) I knew what was coming as one said, 'Fuck this shit! Let's have some fuckin' Abba.'

One of them grabbed Tony Moriah's mic. 'Sing Dancing Queen,

Lionel!' Tony quickly grabbed the mic back but she was stronger than him and wouldn't let go. So, they are now wrestling for the mic. She has got Tony in a 'hammerlock' and he releases the mic as he sinks to his knees. The other one has headed straight for Gary Priestley, a look of abject terror on his face. 'Giss us that fucking mike, fat guts!' Gary, open mouthed with fright, *gives her* the mic. How many times have I told singers to *never* give a punter the mic. I learned that lesson when a bloke ran off with the mic at Kempton Park. He managed to call everyone 'Wankers' before we could switch him off.

I tap the biggest lump on the shoulder and gently say, 'Please leave the stage.' She scared me too. Not only was she fat, she possessed a face like a cracked church bell. Not known for a long fuse, I diplomatically say 'Give me that mic, Porky!' I suddenly grab the expensive Shure mic. She was busy addressing the crowd, 'Do you twats want some fucking Abba or what?' I beg her nicely, *'Please* leave the stage.'

There was no sign of the hotel security and with my precious Fender Jazz bass hanging around my neck, I stop playing and gently guide her towards the edge of the stage. She snatches herself away and in the words of Dave Price, who was standing next to me, 'She gave Jon a perfect right hook, straight in the chops.' I saw stars.

I ordered the band to stop playing and led them off the stage. Only the idiot drummer plays on oblivious. Some of the crowd carry on dancing. After about a minute of clattering around the kit his brain finally engages and Wilson discovers he is the only one in the band left on stage with the two old canines, who are playing air guitars and screaming 'Dancing Queen!' down the mics. Although Greg has by now turned off the lights and PA.

The crowd starts booing. They are obviously booing the band and not the Turkeys who are still strutting around the stage Gary Glitter fashion. Greg turns his DJ mic up, 'Can we have security to the stage please!' Where is the hotel security?' This would never happen at the Grosvenor House.

Slow hand claps and boos. Another female climbs on to the stage and speaks to the lumps. Then all three leave the stage. I wonder what she said to them? 'There are free mince pies in the foyer?' Slow handclap continues, which leads to cheers, as I lead the band back on stage. We are heroes after all.

I shout to Jamie, 'Abba.' It's a good call and he immediately launches into the catchy riff for 'Mamma Mia'. The dance floor is instantaneously packed. Next song is 'Dancing Queen'. Bad call. The lumps are back on stage, waving their chip shovels in the air. This time, Sue's mic is grabbed. I immediately snatch back the mic and make a 'Full-time' gesture as used by football referees. I lead the band off stage again.

This time Terry is first off the field. The band bolts and booing starts. Michael Black suddenly appears behind me, 'What's going on Son? Where the fuck is the security.' He then says, 'Greg, be a good boy and go and tell those awful women to fuck off.'

Greg, eager to please Michael, bravely ventures onto the stage and gingerly collects the front mics, arrayed fan-like in his left hand. The lumps are now 'twerking' their gargantuan bummocks at the crowd.

Greg dumps the mics on the Allen & Heath mixing desk and ventures back. I see him talking to the one who looks like the Churchill bulldog. He puts his hand on her shoulder and gingerly guides her to the edge of the stage. Suddenly two huge beer bellies in suits leap on to the stage. 'Could this be security?' I ask myself. Alas no! It's their pissy-arsed husbands and they are spoiling for a fight. 'Take yer 'ands off me fucking missus!' I have sudden visions of Fanhams Hall.

Greg is grabbed by the scruff of his neck and slung off the stage into the crowd. Bloody funny, as he lands on his arse on the dance floor. We now have four of the Adams family on stage. The crowd is booing but no-one leaves the stage. Stage lights are switched off again.

Suddenly, the room lights go up and up steps the hotel security, in the form of a gangly, pale twiglet of a youth. He is wearing his big brother's suit and it looks like a good 'Barclays' would kill him. He is promptly told by the stage tag-team to 'fuck off'. He fucks off.

Crowd booing and whistling. Band laughing. Fortunately, no damage to equipment is done. Our four stage invaders get bored and leave the stage. 'Get the band back on that fucking stage' says Michael. Once again, I lead the band back on to tumultuous cheers.

We go into 'We Are Family' and there is a rumpus at the back of the room. The security adolescent has called the police. The lard-arses are refusing to leave the ballroom. They are promptly frog marched out by the cops. Good old Met.

Another night of 'mayhem'. As Jamie Hardwick comments;

There was a rumour going around, that Mixed Feelings sometimes have fights with the punters. A week later, we were playing at Yates' Wine Lodge in Nottingham, at a special awards party and the place was packed. I had invited my friend, Andy Marriot to see the band. He said 'Can I expect a fight on stage?' He had not been there five minutes, when this little Asian guy comes on to the stage grabs the mic and joins in, singing 'Mustang Sally'. I saw Jon ask him to leave when suddenly, Greg jumps on stage - probably still smarting from what had happed at the Intercontinental – and grabs the guy by the back of his neck and seat of his pants and just launches this guy into space, so far off the stage that he sailed through the air about 15 feet and skittled a group of young ladies with drinks in their hands. Down they all went. Fortunately, no-one was injured. It turned out that the Asian guy was the owner of Yates' Wine Lodge! So we never got booked back there again! Andy Marriott commented, 'I *knew* it was true what they said!'

Michael Black calls me at 8am. 'I have got you a nice Barmitzvah, Son.' 'Oh great!' I say. 'Where is it?' He replies, 'Bagdad!' The usual laugh. 'Seriously now Son, I need your band for an important job tomorrow night. It's top secret and I can't even tell you who the client is.' I say again, 'Where is it?' He says, 'Les Ambassadeurs. At my club.'

Now, this place is a fabulous casino and luxury Members Club at Hamilton Place, Mayfair W1. The annual membership of which is £20,000. Michael has a VIP membership and has booked the band at this prestigious venue for private parties on several occasions, including New Year's Eve.

'So who is the client, Michael?' I ask impatiently. 'Can't say Son. It's for the greatest football team in the world.' I say, 'Arsenal?' 'Don't be fucking stupid, Son!' he replies, 'They won't let that wassname, Arsehole Wenger in there.' So it's a guessing game. 'Liverpool?' I say. 'For fuck's sake, they don't want the cutlery stolen.'

'So it's Manchester United then?' 'How did you guess, Son? Sir Alex Ferguson is a very dear friend of mine and has just phoned me and he personally asked for *your* band. The team are playing Chelsea tomorrow night, then painting the town red with a few sherbets and a knees up at my club.' 'Are you serious?' 'Totally Son, it's definitely on. Now you can't let me down! Now listen Son, I shall need you to help me out on this one! They haven't got any money.'

'What?' I reply flabbergasted. 'That's right son, they don't have any money in the kitty. So I am helping Alex out on this one, I am chipping in myself! I told him what a lovely bloke you were and he is dying to meet you. You will get loads of work from this one son.' He continues, 'The most they will pay is twelve hundred plus the VAT. As a favour to a friend, I told him you would do it.' I laugh out loud. Michael adds this useful advice, 'Just remember Son, a friend in need is a fucking nuisance.'

I make my mind up immediately. We must do it, even though the richest football club in the world have no money. What bollocks Michael comes out with. I know they will be paying at least *triple* that amount. Such are his crafty ways as he constantly reminds me, 'Would your musicians rather be working on a Wednesday night, or watching fucking Emmerdale?'

This would be a glorious feather in our caps and I can put in a seven-piece band at that price. No matter how prestigious the gig, musicians will need paying. Manchester United has just won the Premiership. I will need to get the band together. Michael adds, 'I want your lovely girls on this one! Dressed in red of course!' It's midweek, so everyone should be available.

I call Terry, Jamie and Dave, the dynamos of the band. Thankfully, they are all available and up for it. I phone Gary Priestly. He can't do it. Has got another solo gig at the Women's Institute in Mansfield. Bugger! I phone Damien Flood, who is a massive Manchester United fan. He says he will do it for nothing! I call my two dependable girls, Suzi and Lynsey. They can do it! Game on.

The next day we arrive at 3pm and park outside Les Ambassadeurs. We may get a ticket but that is the risk everyone takes when unloading. We hump the gear down the narrow stairs and into the small 'Red Room', with its red carpets, red wallpaper and gold fittings. Tables are laid for about forty persons, with red serviettes and beautiful crystal wine glasses adorning the tables. Gerry Bamfield has put the bouncy stage in.

Michael is already there and immediately gets in the way. He is immaculately dressed for the evening and his face is tanned the colour of a satsuma. He sports his gold 'Water Rats' badge on the lapel of his Armani dress suit. He has even varnished his fingernails. Greg and I set up the keyboards, small QSC PA, bass and guitar combos and a small lighting rig. We suffer the schoolboy jokes from Michael and Gerry. We are set in an hour and eagerly await events.

Manchester United have been playing Chelsea. The league is already in their pocket. Tonight they have settled for a dreary 0-0 draw. It was a 7pm kick off and at 10pm the Manchester United team coach arrives. Michael tells us in his manic- panic, 'Quick, get on that fucking stage and play Dancing Queen!' Just the glamorous girls are fronting the band.

The doors are opened and first through the door is Wayne Rooney. He runs over to one of the tables and grabs a seat facing the band. Next through the door is Paul Scholes. 'Scholesy! Scholesy! Over here!' Rooney shouts in his thick Liverpool accent. The tall Christiano Ronaldo, who is talking on his phone, ambles over to a table to the left of the band. All the tables are in close proximity to the stage. The suited and booted players and staff of Manchester United FC are all in the room. There is only one female present. She is probably the lady who washes the shirts and hangs them out on the washing line in her back garden, like mum used to.

Sir Alex and the senior management team take a table near the stage. The band is running through 'Dancing Queen' again. All eyes are fixed on the girls, as they leave the stage. Surprisingly, no one says grace. The four-piece band, go through some blues numbers, 'Hill Street Blues' and the classic, 'Top Gun' get a wild reaction from the players who down gobbling-rods to applaud the brilliant guitar playing of Dave Price.

It's probably too loud for Sir Alex, who is facing the band. His face is the same colour as the goldfish-bowl size glass of red wine in front of him. Most of the players are drinking Peroni beer. Ronaldo is still on his mobile phone, while picking at his food, with his fork. He is on the same table as giant goalkeeper, Edwin Van der Sar. Ronaldo stays on his phone throughout the meal. Jamie reckons he is probably on the phone to a cross-dressing chat line. What wonderful company he must make.

The fillet steaks are served and devoured quickly and the girls are back on stage, doubtless being mentally undressed by the whole team, apart from Ronaldo that is, who is still on the phone. The girls know they are being 'ogled' and act up accordingly, sexily wriggling their arses. Both have bright blonde hair and are looking gorgeous in the brilliant split to hip, red dresses with a lurid red lipstick to match. Suzi says sexily, 'Are there any Dancing Queens here tonight?' Immediately, Wayne Rooney hollers, 'Me!' and rushes to the stage and seizes the spare mic. He joins in the singing of 'Dancing Queen' his arms now wrapped around the waists of both girls. He then turns to me and shouts 'Simply The Best!' We go straight into the classic Tina Turner song, by which time most of the players are on their feet.

Rooney surprisingly knows most of the words to the song and succeeds in getting through it, albeit in a different key. He is amusingly, tone-deaf. Everyone by this time is on the dance floor and singing, 'Better than all the rest!' The stage is a foot high. Rooney turns to face the drums and places the spare radio mic back in the stand. He stays facing the band. With a mischievous glint in his eye, he suddenly throws up his arms and does a complete backwards somersault, right off the stage and lands perfectly on his feet. The man is a superb gymnast too. Sir Alex buries his face in his hands. Fifty million quid's worth of player could have broken his neck.

Next on stage is blonde-haired Alan Smith. 'Do Blues Brothers,' he says to Damien. Terry goes straight into 'Everybody' and Alan sings the classic duet with Damien. The place is rocking and everyone is on the dance floor including Sir Alex.

Tonight we are a 'Karaoke' band. Surprisingly, 'Smithy' is a good singer and he asks for 'Mustang Sally' and we go straight into it, which he belts out admirably. The party is cracking along and we play the party catch songs, with Suzy singing a fantastic version of Connie Francis' 'Lipstick On Your Collar' and 'Stupid Cupid' whilst pointing an accusing finger at a guilty looking Wayne Rooney.

The whole team form a circle on the dance floor, about twenty of the squad, and we do 'Saturday Night Fever' and 'Staying Alive'. Each of the players take their turn to dance in the centre of the circle and each one is enthusiastically applauded. Rooney is on his arse with a hilarious break-dance, kicking and flipping his legs in the air. He is a natural entertainer.

The best dancer of all is the handsome Ryan Giggs, who does a Michael Jackson 'moonwalk' into the centre circle, sexily swinging his hips. Lynsey announces the result of the dance competition, which she and Suzi have judged. 'And the winner is, Ryan Giggs!' Loads of boos.

Sir Alex has told me 'no photographs' and we respect his wishes. I have never liked Sir Alex Ferguson, for the sole reason he was the manager of Arsenal's most hated rivals. However, on that night my opinion changed and I now think he is a great man. This has nothing to do with the magnum of Moët & Chandon champagne he gave me.

I go to the small scullery which doubles as the dressing room. Alan Smith and Rio Ferdinand are chatting up the girls. They invite them to 'come up to Manchester to be wined and dined.' Damien is like a kid in a sweetshop. He has the autographs of the whole squad. Contrary to Sir Alex's wishes, he is taking loads of photos. He wins COM again.

I hear singing at the bar and re-join the party. All the players are singing an anti-Liverpool song to the tune of 'My Darling Clementine': 'Build a bonfire, build a bonfire, put the Scousers on the top, put the City in the middle and then burn the fucking lot.' Ronaldo is still on his phone. Just after 1am, the team coach arrives and the players leave up the backstairs, all shaking hands and thanking us as they leave. The girls get plenty of kisses. The paparazzi are already there.

This was just one of the fabulous Premiership footballing events we performed at. I have fond recollections of the 2002, Sporting Chance Charity that my hero, Tony Adams, held at the Royal Lancaster Hotel. This gave me the opportunity to hold the FA Cup and the Premiership Shield won by Arsenal in the same season. We also performed for the Tottenham Hotspur players' party, Chelsea, Portsmouth, Leicester City, Watford and Wolverhampton Wanderers, plus the Football Association awards at Alexander Palace, when we were support band for Paul Carrack.

I was chuffed to perform at the England Rugby Team celebration party, when they returned home after winning the 2003 World Cup in Australia. This was held at the Royal Lancaster Hotel and we were joined on stage by the team as we performed 'Sweet Chariot' led by Martin Johnson. I also was given the opportunity to hold the Webb-Ellis Cup. What a moment! I had dressed Lynsey and Sue in England rugby shirts and white stockings. No wonder we were popular! We took many spin-off gigs from our sporting events, including England and Northampton rugby player Matt Dawson's 30th birthday party and golfer

Lee Westwood's wedding.

In October 2007 we performed at a private Silver Wedding anniversary party for a wealthy London hotel owner. This was at the Natural History Museum, a gloomy place with dreadful acoustics, which should never be open for live events. We have performed there several times. One of the problems is that the museum closes to the public at 6pm. The client then requires the band, event company and caterers to be set by 7pm, an impossible task.

I always said we would play 'anywhere' for good money. So our wealthy client, to my concern, booked that dark, dinosaur-infested venue. It was a very lavish affair and just proves a point; that if you are fabulously rich then you will attract rich, showbiz friends. I had certainly never heard of our Indian client.

It was nice to see Bruce Forsyth, Cilla Black, Cliff Richard and many other celebrities there, the band being introduced by Gloria Hunniford. We had learned a special song written by Don Black and Tony Hatch, both of whom were at the event. I had liaised with Tony Hatch, who lived in Minorca, by telephone and email. As a result of our performance that night, Don Black booked us to play at his grandson's Barmitzvah party, via his scallywag brother, Michael, who I believe charged him commission.

We had taken time to make sure the one-off song, 'Twenty-Five Years' was note perfect. Although sung beautifully by Tony and Gary, the dreadful acoustics in that huge gallery didn't help our overall sound. Especially as the clueless event company had put in a gigantic 50K. EAW. PA system.

The gig would have sounded better with just a single pair of Bose 802s. The sound engineer had his beer-plugs in and operated on just two settings, 'off' and 'loud'. It was much too loud, but it's never the fault of the sound engineer. It's 'That bloody band are too loud.'

We were to be joined on stage by Sir Cliff Richard, for a special rendition of 'Congratulations', the irritating song that every function band must know, plus the lovely song, 'Miss You Nights'. At least we were not required to do 'Lucky Lips.' Cliff has a God-gifted, beautiful voice. I have been a fan since I was a boy and not ashamed to say I have purchased many of his records over the years. Linda and I have been to several of his live concerts. He has a massive fan base and certainly deserves it, with his immense number of chart hits. I was thrilled to be backing him on stage.

He is, however, a conceited man and he showed it when I warmly introduced myself to him before the gig and asked for an autograph for Linda. 'I don't do autographs.' was his haughty reply. I had a menu and pen held under his nose. No one else was present and I said, 'Just this once please, Cliff, it will make her day!' In a *demanding* tone, as I realized I would never get this chance again. 'Oh, very well then. What's her name?' and he signed it, 'For Linda, love Cliff Richard.' I thanked him and he said, 'I'll be joining you on stage later. I trust you know "Congratulations"?' I assured him we did. I then thanked him again and said, 'I've got tickets for your next concert Cliff! I'll be there!' (Meaning, *I will be* getting tickets) He replied, 'Great. See you there!'

At the start of the second half, Cliff joined us on stage and we did 'Congratulations' and 'Miss You Nights', faultlessly. At the end of his spot, Cliff turned and pointed at me and mockingly said, 'This guy says he has got tickets for my next concert and they are not even on sale yet!' I just nodded dumbly in agreement and scratched my head like Stan Laurel. The words of the classic song by Steve Coogan are quite often true, 'Everyone's a bit of cunt sometimes.'

Our reputation as 'The UK's greatest party band' got as far as Oman.

Diary. Oman
Tuesday 7 October 2008 – Friday 10 October 2008.
On the gig;
Jamie Hardwick.
Terry Wilson
Dave Price
Jon Nicholls
Greg Nicholls
Suzi Jari
Lynsey Shaw
Anthony Moriah
Gary Priestley

The Shah of Oman was requesting top British party band, 'Mixed Feelings' to appear at an outdoor concert on behalf of his car company, to which he had invited 20,000 of his customers. The event at the Marah Land Theme Park, Muscat, was held on Wednesday 8th October 2008.

Also on the bill was soul singer Alexander O'Neal, a small troupe of dancers and a 'Michael Jackson impersonator' from the East End of London. We accordingly turned up at Heathrow airport on Tuesday 7th October 2008. We were going to be away for four days. A brand-new Airbus had been chartered and we were the only passengers. We made a brave attempt to drink the plane dry but the cabin crew outnumbered us. I had planned to crash out in the First-Class cabin, but ended up standing at the back of the plane with Jamie, Greg, Terry, and Dave, guzzling Jewish Cokes.

Our five-star hotel bar stayed open until late and the following day we explored a bit of Muscat before being bussed to the park at 11am, where the stage was still being built. A chattering Arab event crew draped white cotton sheets across wooden supports, to keep the blazing sun off us as we prepared for our sound check at 12 noon. Alexander O' Neil immediately lay down on one of the opulent sofas in the Green Room, a cool tent next to the stage, and fell asleep.

On the PA front, a huge German D&B system and backline equipment, had been hired in by event supplier and friend, Gemma Brown. She was based in Dubai. The main provider of this quality gear is the dependable John Henry, a London-based PA hire firm who we always used, whenever practical, for overseas gigs. Keyboards were always as requested and drums, whether Yamaha, DW or Ludwig, always superb quality. The company never let us down with gear and on some gigs, Dave Price and myself left our guitars at home and simply ordered a Fender Stratocaster and a Fender Jazz, or Precision Bass. These instruments were always top-notch and sometimes of vintage quality.

The only time we came unstuck with the guitar hire policy, was at a gig in Sardinia, when we were playing support to Alfie Boe and his band. The hire company was local and they failed to supply guitars. In fact there were no quality guitars on the island. Fortunately, to the rescue came the friendly musicians of Alfie's band, who lent us their instruments. It was a good job we were not working with the Tony Hadley Band!

As for Oman, we had taken our actual instruments, apart from keyboards and drums and as Jamie remarked, 'It was so hot, that when I set up the Korg stage piano and tried it out, I could not touch the black notes as they were red hot.'

Terry made a similar remark about touching the cymbals and complained that the drum seat, 'was so fucking hot it burned me Chalfonts.' In fact we were all sweating and cursing the merciless sun and the air was blue with good-natured, banter. Our happy singers of Tony, Gary, Lynsey and Suzie, had also joined us on stage, chattering excitedly, like a cage of budgerigars, while Greg was allocating and labelling the mics.

Sure enough, the event came with the inevitable pinstripe-suited and goofy female, who immediately tried to assert her authority. On this occasion, the clip-board carrier was a Kiwi and emerged from stage right. She was skinnier than a vegan's dog. Her New Zealand origin was confirmed when she self-combusted after Gary asked her what part of Australia she was from.

She spoke, 'OK guys, I must ask you to stop swearing! No obscene language please! The Royal Prince is coming to the sound check and bringing his two young sons, so please do not swear in his presence.'

She had hardly spoken, when down the centre aisle of the park, where 20,000 seats had been laid out for the anticipated crowd, swept a big man straight off the set of *Ali Baba and the Forty Thieves*. He was dressed in Arab costume with full flowing, white cotton robes. At his side were two little lads, about seven and nine, who were western clad in shorts, designer T-shirts and Nike trainers.

I also smiled, as the first few seats down the front were huge thrones of deep red velvet, with golden arms. The Royal Prince, or whatever his title was, took the throne closest to the stage. The two little lads sat alongside their Dad, feet swinging and playing with iPads.

We were ready to sound check and I gingerly plugged my Status bass into the hired Trace Elliot rig. I was not sure it would go the distance without breaking down. Dave is treated to a Marshall 500 watt valve top with 4 x12 cab. We have been told by The Kiwi, that the 'Prince likes ABBA.' So I tell the band we will sound check to that. Always keep your client happy. We are sweating profusely and I take a gulp of water and remind everyone, 'No swearing lads!'

Greg is manning the mixing desk 50 metres out front. I give him the thumbs up and he acknowledges. We are about to launch into 'Mamma Mia' when the big figure of Alexander O'Neal, towel around his neck, walks on to the stage. 'Excuse me guys but I am dying in this damn heat.

Can I do my sound check first?' We are in no rush, so I agree and tell the band to stand down. We grab some bottles of water and troop off stage to watch this legendary American singer do his sound check.

Wearing an orange 'prison' jump suit, he steps forward in front of the monitors and shouts out the first song, 'Love So Kind' which Greg launches into. Immediately Alex is waving his arms wildly in the air shouting over the mic, 'Greg! I can't hear a mutha-fucking thing!' and 'Goddam Greg! Give me some more volume in these mutha-fucking monitors!' Greg gives him more sound and he then says, 'Greg! You're gonna need some white fucking gaffa tape on the front of this fucking stage before some fucking arsehole falls off!'

In June 2009, following a wonderful gig at the Elounda Bay Palace Hotel in Crete the previous year and true to her promise, Linda Keller booked the band on a luxury cruise ship for Aviva Insurance. Linda loved our band and our association with her had been fantastic. Based in Norwich, she took us to many lovely places such as Sardinia and Sicily.

Top of the many lucrative gigs we did for her was a wonderful Mediterranean cruise on *The Silver Whisper,* an incredibly lovely yacht, with a capacity for only three hundred people. The whole ship had been chartered by Aviva to provide a week's cruise for their successful insurance brokers and their partners. *The Silver Whisper* being part of the Silver Seas fleet of smaller high-end cruise ships.

What a fabulous treat for them and for us. They were the best gigs any band could wish for. I could think of nothing better. I had never been cruising before and was not interested in the giant 'monsters of the seas' with three thousand people on board. Not my personal idea of a holiday. We also did a fantastic Baltic cruise on *The Silver Whisper* for Linda and Aviva.

During the week aboard ship we were allocated our own cabins and treated like royalty. All alcohol was free and unlimited. It was top dollar with quality brands of malt whiskies like 'The Macallan' and 'Lagavulin', hand poured in giant measures. The food was better than The Ritz. We lay on the deck all day and were served cold beer. I was in heaven and phoned a jealous Linda, who told me it was raining in Hemel Hempstead and so I promised her I would take her on *The Silver Whisper.* Mixed Feelings had better not fuck this up.

Mixed Feelings would provide entertainment most nights, in the form of a piano player in the bar, an 'Irish night' with Kevin Hall on the piano accordion, a film quiz, a Chas n' Dave type sing-a-long, with Terry singing 'Viva Espana' in four different languages, a Michael Bublé evening with Gary Priestley, a *Jersey Boys* show. Versatility was the name of the game.

When we arrived in Nice, we were joined on board ship by the singer Will Young, who brought a prattling entourage of half a dozen or more 'hangers on'. One sturdy lass in comfortable shoes said she was his 'manager'.

During the afternoon, the ship was practically deserted as all the clients had been bussed to a local vineyard, so Will Young took advantage to do his sound check in readiness for the big show that night, where he was to be the surprise cabaret. He was accompanied by a piano player and guitarist and did a monotonously long medley of his hit, 'Leave Right Now'. I was sitting on the edge of the swimming pool and took a quick photograph of him with my little Sony camera and was promptly admonished by a squawking manager. 'No photographs!'

'Who is he?' I casually asked. 'Will Young!' The manager and entourage shrieked in unison. 'Never heard of him.' I flippantly say, pouring a cold beer to howls of outrage.

Indeed, when he appeared on stage that night in his sailor hat at the Gala Dinner Dance, many of the disappointed crowd said, 'Never heard of him!' He did a 20 min set for which he received a lame applause and a mere eighty grand.

Mixed Feelings went on stage immediately after the cabaret and gave the crowd what they really wanted - a good party – and the brilliant Tony Moriah stole the show. He was simply outstanding and it was certainly his greatest performance with the band. He had the crowd in the palm of his hand, but little did I know that it would be his very last overseas gig with us. He had been great company, joining us on deck every day in the Mediterranean sunshine. He never drank water and never a cold beer. He only drank fruit juice. Little did any of us know how seriously ill he was. It was then he first complained of 'backache'.

It was Thursday 17th September 2009 at the Intercontinental Hotel at Hyde Park Corner. I was concerned that Tony had visibly lost weight. His beautiful pink stage suit was now too big for him. He was continually holding his back during the performance and struggling to sing and dance. At half-time I went to the dressing room to see him laying on the carpet, flat on his back. He was in great pain and declined a drink of any sort. Encouraged by the girls he struggled to his feet and expressed his wish to get on stage and finish the show, of which the last song was 'End Of The Road' by Boyz II Men. It was ironic that it was the 'end of the road' for Tony and it would be the last song he would ever sing.

In the dressing room after the gig, Tony was again laying on his back on the floor and in great pain. Greg offered to take him to hospital. Tony said he had his car here so would go himself. He went straight to Kings College Hospital casualty unit and was immediately admitted.

A few days later, Tony called to tell me he was in intensive care and apologized for not being able to appear at the next gig at the Grosvenor House. Tony said he had never known such a terrible pain in his back. He told me he was so dehydrated that his liver had shrunk and he was in line for a transplant. His actual words to me were, 'I am so sorry to let you down on Tuesday mate. When I get out of here, I am going to drink beer all day like you guys.'

A few days later, on Sunday 28th September 2009, I was ironically, on board *The Silver Whisper* in St Tropez harbour. I had promised Linda a cruise on this beautiful little ship after the wonderful time I had enjoyed with the band on the Aviva cruise just two months previously. I got a phone call from Joe Caddy, part time percussionist with Mixed Feelings. He said, 'Tony died this morning.'

Tony Moriah had performed on over eight hundred gigs with Mixed Feelings. I will never forget his delight at travelling to Europe and the Middle East with the band. He was the possessor of the smoothest and warmest voice ever to grace our stage. We all loved him and regarded him as our brother. I could not hold back the tears when I phoned the band to break the news. It was ironic that he should die from liver failure when he didn't drink.

Five days later, the band, with heavy hearts, was booked to appear at the AXA Insurance Party, held in Bristol at the Commonwealth Museum 'passenger shed'. Over six hundred people attended and the eight-piece band was booked. I never took another male singer, but made it up to eight by taking sax-player Jez Guest. It was right that there was only Gary Priestley, Suzi Jari and Lynsey Shaw out front. The last team of singers and friends Tony had performed with. I told Greg to set up four microphones for the three singers. Tony's mic was placed in his usual position on stage. He was with us.

TIME TO SAY GOODBYE. (EPILOGUE)

There are three musical instruments in our house at Wootton Drive, Hemel Hempstead. A Taylor acoustic guitar and an old EKO Jumbo 12-string which I bought from Blanks Music Store in the Kilburn High Road over 50 years ago. It still sounds great.

Then there is the lovely Fender Precision bass, which I bought in Denmark Street in 1997. I still pick up the guitars occasionally. My bass guitar 'collection', including my beloved Fender Jazz bass, was sold in 2015 but I am keeping that Maple Precision bass in case one of my descendants should take an interest. The guitars stand in my basement office, once our rehearsal and audition room and from where I once ran the band. I see that bass every day and it reminds me of the great times I had as a bandleader and bass player in a fabulous band. It's been a wonderful journey and I have taken advantage of 'The Lockdown' to finish this book, for which I had started the notes, many years ago.

Since the passing of Tony Moriah, the band had managed to maintain its popularity and was incredibly busy; working hard, going on further cruises, supporting top acts at Rock Festivals and enjoying performing at more exotic overseas venues. I had established an excellent vocal team, sometimes adding an extra girl singer and for a period in 2012, at a client's request, the band finished its always colourful show with the operatic song 'Time To Say Goodbye', which under Dave Price's brilliant arrangement and direction brought out the best in the voices of Suzi Jari, Lindsey Cleary, Chris Madin and Gary Priestley. Although not everyone's 'cup of tea' we continued with the song for several months. There were few bands on the circuit with singers that could handle that powerful song and would doubtless say, 'We wouldn't want to' but it left the audience singing it as they left. As Leslie Rose OBE of the Make A Wish Foundation commented, 'Only Mixed Feelings could do justice to "Time To Say Goodbye." '

It was time for me to say goodbye also. I finally decided to 'hang up my boots' on New Year's Eve 2015. Ironically, it was at the Metropolitan Police Sports Club Bushey, that hallowed venue of magic memories, where it really all began for Mixed Feelings. That night at the end of the gig, Terry came out with the usual tripe and more. He told me to, 'stick the band up my arse as him and Elaine were splitting up and he was fucking off to the south coast. He had had enough' He also added that, 'Furthermore he was *never* coming back to Hemel Hempstead as it's a fucking shithole.'

December had been another busy month and both a weary Terry and myself had been making mistakes and dropping notes on stage, culminating in him falling asleep on the kit at the Grosvenor House Hotel in the middle of the show. It might have been something to do with drinking the raffle prizes.

On that same New Year's Eve, I had also finally handed over the management of the band to my son, Greg. So Terry's bluff was finally called and Greg accepted his resignation and mine without qualms. Jamie also quit the band at the same time and was superseded on keyboards by his brother Andy.

Five years later and Terry is still living in Hemel Hempstead and still with Elaine. We are still good mates and I regularly see him in The Steam Coach pub and the laughter doesn't stop. He has recently announced on the social media, that he has given up drumming. I doubt it. We talk about the old times and the thirty years he was in the band. He always reminds me 'It was the best band I ever played in and certainly the best time of my life. The wonderful places we went to. What memories.' Some of his memories are best forgotten.

Every month, I meet my old Deanbeats mates, Nick and Tates for a few beers. Tates now lives in Hemel Hempstead. Nick still keeps his 'guitar hand' in by gigging with a Northampton pub band and we occasionally jam together in Arras France, when at the Moderne Hotel with the 'Hampstead Pals.'

In 2010, 'The Deanbeats' played a reunion gig at Deanshanger Memorial Hall in aid of the local Willen Hospice, where Mum had died in 2000. The same 'village kids' who followed the band in 1964, all turned up. It was a joyous reunion but the years were showing on our faces.

Mixed Feelings still survives where most other bands have faded away and is still the most exciting and entertaining party band on the function and corporate circuit. As I write these words, the band like all the others, has been devoid of gigs since March 2020, due to the coronavirus pandemic. Things are looking bleak for the world's entertainment industry and all band musicians, entertainers and performers are sadly out of work. It will all come again but not of the same intensity of 1964-2015.

As the Fanhams Hall roadie and old friend Dusty Miller, long retired from the Metropolitan Police and now running a pub in County Durham, commented to me by text only recently,

> Makes you appreciate the 'old normal', this 'new normal' doesn't it? I used to think we had the best of it and now it seems that we've had the best of times in our lifetime. I wish somebody had told me I was having the best time of my life while I was having it!

Life has certainly been good to me. I am thankful for the great memories and lucky to be part of the music 'scene' for so long. Although, in my opinion, there is a dearth of good songs around in today's world. 'Living In The Past' was a great Jethro Tull song and my generation was lucky to live it. We certainly had the very best of music and I am still 'living in the past' when I listen to the 'old songs' on my Bose system at home. My worn-out ears still pick out the bass guitar lines and I have an arse-kicking, REL Bass bin hidden behind the sofa. I turn the volume up to 10 then back it off to 6. This saves Linda having to do it.

The young musicians and singers in the modern Mixed Feelings are superb. Since the days of the revolutionary and sexy Helen York and Sue Acteson, the band has always recruited gorgeous girl singers. That, coupled with a good male voice and our 'mixed' music programme, have always been our main selling points.

Helen wrote to me in 2020,

How can I sum up my 10 years singing with Mixed Feelings in a few words?

Utter Joy from start to finish! I laughed, cried, ate, drank, sang and danced all around the world with a great bunch of musicians but more importantly, a cracking set of people!! I learnt so much about the business from Jon and the team and took all my experiences with me when I moved on to the next chapter in my career. I will never forget my time in the band. Some of the happiest and funniest of my 30 years in the business! Thank you, Jon for seeing something in me and taking me on that day after my audition, all those years ago.

As Suzi Jari, now a leading guest entertainer for Cunard, commented in October 2020,

I loved being a lead singer for Mixed Feelings, the UK's leading Show band. We were such a busy band and I gave every performance my all. Sung my heart out! I got to see the world thanks to you and the band was my absolute world for many years. Jon was like a second Dad to me and Greg you were always amazing, smiley and a great engineer. I will be forever grateful for the super work you gave me and thank you for the amazing memories.

How I'd love to do it all again...

More recently the band were the choice of Bradley Walsh to perform at his son Barney's 21st Birthday party. Over a few 'Jewish Cokes' we reminisced about the old club and cabaret days and the fun we had. With a tear in his eye he said to me, 'I miss those hungry years.'

The Mixed Feelings that I loved and created lives on but the *mayhem* has gone. As Greg remarked,

There will never be another time like the nineties, when the band were so busy. We had real fun and they were crazy days. I was so proud to be part of all that. It's all changed now. *It's far too sensible.* Musicians are not like that anymore.

'Thank God' I hear you say..

ACKNOWLEDGEMENTS

Writing a book like this relies heavily on memory. I have been assisted however by referring to the diaries, both manual and digital which I have kept since running a band from 1963 until 2014. I have also been considerably assisted and encouraged by the friends and musicians I knew and worked with on my musical journey. Many have given up their time to meet me in the pub and help me in the reminiscences written here. It has all been a lot of fun and I am just sorry that space does not permit me to include tales of our Cretan adventure, The Ford Open Prison gig and the Twickenham Trumpet kicker of Gleneagles. It would all make a good television script.

Top of the 'thank you list' must go of course to the ever-patient Linda, who has put up with my regular absence for over 50 years, due to bands, beer, books and battlefields. She has always been unstinting in her advice (whether I heeded it or not) and as Vaughan Rance said 'She was the glue that held it all together.' Many thanks are also due to my old friend Jon Buoy, who read the first manuscript and gave me much encouragement. Plus, Susan Lomas herself a singer, schoolteacher and my proof reader, who corrected my rusty English. She is also married to a bass player and consequently *understands*.

Finally, I must also offer a special word of thanks to Elaine Wilson also a singer in a band herself, who encouraged me not to be shy when writing about her husband.

The Musicians, Singers, Roadies and associates of Mixed Feelings

Linda Nicholls, Greg Nicholls, Ralph Lewin, Steve Bateman, David Gibbon, Pete Allen, Keith Young, Ken James, Dave Price, Jamie Hardwick, Terry Wilson, Vaughan Rance, Matt Winch, Jez Guest,

Richard Henninghem, Lee Reboul, Jonathan Bremner, Chris Madin, Suzy Jari, Sue Acteson, Helen York, Lynsey Shaw, Lynsey Cleary, Tara Macdonald, Anna Macdonald, Debbie Harris, Kevin Hall, John Maul, Geoff Gammon, Dave West, Jim Rodford, Dave 'Ryka' Howard, Mike Jones, Greg Nicholls Jnr, Alison Cohen, Johnny Amobi, Nick Foister, Anthony Moriah, Dave Peers, Nick Payn, Matt Holland, Tom Walker, John Shults, Barry Elliott, Lianne Elliot, Gary James, Dave Savill, Bruce McConnach, Alan Marshall, Martin Constable, Martin Carew, Martin Fairbrother, Bob Wise, Pete West, Gary Priestley, Debbie Lee, Nick Batt, Mike Mason, Ellen Sluetjes, Damien Flood, Phil Spinelli, Ralph Millington, Andy Hardwick, Lyn Birbeck, Marina Berry Dealey, Lorena Dale, Mark Rideout, Clint Williams, Gerry Howe, Stuart Milner, Ian Manser, Bob Wise, Michael 'Dusty' Miller, Paul Singleton, Mark Nicholls, Matt Stevens, Joe Caddy, Lester Osbourne, Dave Edwards, Steve Coogan, Rocky Delling, Don Rodgers, Nicola Brightman, Mick Mullane, Kathy Edge, Barry Robinson, Ian 'Sparky' Harrison, Gerry Bamfield, Tom Walker, Ken Palmer, John Shults, Jeremy Moore, Matt Horner, Tom Brennan, John McNamee, Pete Callard, Darren Ashford, Glen Mack, Steve Turner, Chris Malkinson, Lee Parkinson, Ben Ofoedu, John Beedle, Sara Raybould, Griff Johnson, Toby Goodman, Ben Richards, Shenton Dixon, Beverley Stone, Lucy McKinnon, Darryl King, Sid Gould, Lizzi Pattinson, Derek Tough, Alex Bhinder, Hannah Slack, Raenette Singleton, Lewis Batt, Nick Batt, Mick Curtis, Doug Mackenzie, Richard Graham, Rick Jackson, Dan Rosen, Steve Hughes.

The Bookers, Bandleaders, Toastmasters, Caterers and Friends

Joanne Tremayne, Pete Richardson, Paul Baxter, Diane Rowley, Bob Kember, Henry Harrison, Alan Taylor, Michael Black, Julie Rodgers, Howard T'loosty, Mike Malley, William Wren, Doug Olney, Tony Averne, Pete Langford, Dave Bedford, Mike Jordan, Vanessa Jordan, Reg Parson Andy Miller, Roland Keech Bradley Walsh, Jim Davidson, Bobby Davro, Tom O' Connor, Jimmy Tarbuck, Howard Robbins, Victor Shack, Robert Shack, John Rose, Keith Gold, Bryn Williams OBE, David Collins, Leslie Rose MBE, Johnny Laycock, Mick Jones, Louise Cecil, Vanessa Feltz, Bob Jackson, John 'Dick' West, Fred Freeman, Geoffrey Hull, Ivy Hull, Bill Glindon, Graham Mann, John Kerton, Johnny Howard, Tony Adams, Lee Westwood, Martin Keown, Ash Adams, Dick Charman, Brett Hulme, Justin Peacock, Russ

Brewster, Steve Cook, Wally Cox, Rodney Smithson, Mike Felix, Tony Hadley, Dave Whale, Mike Lee Taylor, Lew Lewis, Gary Anderson, Steve Warwick, Maureen Sharpstone, Barry Sharpstone,   Henry Margolis, Marian Murray, Tommy Murray, Helen Goide, Richard Goide, Norwell Roberts QPM, Alwyn Jones, Keith Barwell, Sir Alex Ferguson, Brian Greenan, Colin Wilkinson, Ann Booth, Terry Hyams, Keith Colman, Julie Bedford, Ronny Mann, Dave Nash, Harry Hatch, Christine Akehurst, Gordon Pollock, Melvyn Zeff, Stan Taylor, Jack Purvis, Kenny Baker OBE, Jimmy Jones, Gary Wilmot, Taff Rees, Ray Cooper, Kevin Cutts, Gerry Smithers, Graham Logue, Jim McNally, Danny Gates, Don Maxwell, Norman Phillips, Lianne Phillips, Gordon Poole, Brian Rowan, Simon Skinner, Kate Carlisle, Dave Winslett, Don Fox, Mike Slocombe, Nigel Smith, Russ Abbott, John Oliver, Mike Clynes, Ian Richards, Mick Holmes, Val Walter, Alan Lacey, Zap, Rodney Prout, Rod Crowe, Len Goldapple, Ian Foreman, Elliot Porte, Ivor Spencer, Frank Manning, Robert Persell, Deborah Collins, Simon Green, Neil Hunt, Paul Deacon, Ken Tappenden OBE, John Grieve CBE, Jamie Wallace, Sid Chevin, Dave Chevin, Lynda Carpenter, Dave Breen, Charlie Wilson, Kath Wilson, Rod Crowe, John Williams, Jan Leloch, Mick Ward, Rebecca Ferguson, Alexander Burke, Rick Lomas, Susan Lomas.

The Deanbeats and associates

Stan Matthews, Malcolm Taylor, Nick Gould, Dave Crooks, Alan Leeson, Eric Matthews, Jim 'Spinner' Matthews, Gordon Matthews, Sonia Lee, Linda Singleton, Rev. Paul Hoskins, Helen Falconer, Cyril Nicholls, Dora Nicholls, Malcolm White,   Michael Russell, Mark Nicholls, Brian Hollis, John Goldney, Keith Chapman, Kevin O'Brien, Patrick O'Brien, Aggle Meakins, Les Drinkwater, (Snr) Les Drinkwater (Jnr) George Lee, Jack Gould, Robert 'Bilko' Marshall, Susan Marshall, Barbara Marshall, Ian Brown, Kenny Brown.

Working with

Sir Cliff Richard,   Jim Davidson, Bradley Walsh, Brian May, Kenny Ball, Acker Bilk, Bobby Davro, Jethro, The Searchers, The Merseybeats, The Tremeloes, Boyzone, The Fortunes, Bjorn Again, Go West, Madness, Gloria Hunniford, Boney M, Rose-Royce, Chas n' Dave, Jasper Carrot, Richard Digance, Stan Boardman, Gerry & The Pacemakers, Sir Jimmy Tarbuck, The Black Abbots, The Rockin'

Berries, The Drifters, The London Philharmonic Orchestra, Roger de Courcey, Dennis Beards, Lord Geoffrey Archer, Dave Berry, Mike Berry, Wayne Fontana, The Troggs, Lenny Henry, Tom O'Connor, Susan Maughan, Alexandre Burke, Will Young, Herbie Flowers, Lulu, Brian Ferry, Tony Hadley, Edison Lighthouse, Marty Wilde, Alexander O Neal, Brian Conly, Michael McIntyre, Dara O' Briain, Rhydian Roberts, The Tremeloes, Adge Cutler, Mechanical Horse Trough, Jedward, Jimmy Carr, Katherine Jenkins, Edwin Starr, Alfie Boe, Tony Blackburn, David Hamilton, Kid Jensen, Pete Murray, Bruce Forsyth, Joe Longthorne. Hedgehoppers Anonymous, Katrina and the Waves.

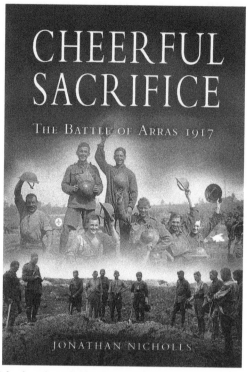

"A highly accomplished and readable documentary and leaves the reader hoping that his first attempt at writing military history will not be his last."
SOLDIER MAGAZINE

"A pleasure to read"
BRITISH ARMY REVIEW

"In all respects a mixture of good scholarship and interesting anecdote"
TANK JOURNAL

"Should you need to remind yourself what sacrifice is all about at 11am on any 11 November then read this book…read it anyway."
ROYAL NAVY CHAPLAINS BOOK REVIEW

"Without doubt an important contribution to the history of the Great War – go out and buy this book – you will certainly not regret it."
MEDAL NEWS

www.pen-and-sword.co.uk
Or
Amazon Books
Kindle or paperback

Lightning Source UK Ltd.
Milton Keynes UK
UKHW010648010721
386461UK00002B/253